Managed Dental Care:

A GUIDE TO DENTAL HMOs

Donald S. Mayes

Managed Dental Care:

A GUIDE TO DENTAL HMOs

International Foundation
of Employee Benefit Plans

The opinions expressed in this book are those of the author. The International Foundation of Employee Benefit Plans disclaims responsibility for views expressed and statements made in books published by the Foundation.

Edited by Mary E. Brennan, CEBS

Copies of this book may be obtained from:

Publications Department
International Foundation of Employee Benefit Plans
18700 West Bluemound Road
P.O. Box 69
Brookfield, Wisconsin 53008-0069
(414) 786-6700

Payment must accompany order.
Call for price information.

Published in 1993 by the International Foundation of Employee Benefit Plans, Inc.

Library of Congress Catalog Card Number: 93-78068
ISBN 0-89154-464-X
Printed in the United States of America

IM-593

Dedication

This book is dedicated to those who wrestle daily with the issues involved in providing quality care at reasonable cost.

Table of Contents

Section III. Performance Evaluation

Section IV. Appendixes

About the Author

Donald S. Mayes, D.D.S., is the principal of Don Mayes & Associates, a dental benefits consulting firm in Hershey, Pennsylvania that specializes in the development and evaluation of dental plans, including: benefit package design, pricing, requests for proposals, proposal evaluation, network development, quality assurance, utilization review and plan audit. The firm works with dental HMOs and PPOs as well as traditional fee-for-service plans.

Prior to forming the firm, Dr. Mayes was in private practice, held positions with two large third party administrators and served as a vice president of Pennsylvania Blue Shield. For the past four years he has evaluated dental capitation plans for the U.S. Department of Labor.

Dr. Mayes, who has served on the Pennsylvania state dental board, writes and speaks frequently about dental benefits. He is a graduate of Gettysburg College and the University of Pennsylvania School of Dental Medicine and is a fellow in both the American College of Medical Quality and the Academy of Dentistry International. He is certified by the American Board of Quality Assurance and Utilization Review Physicians and also serves on its executive committee and board of directors.

Foreword

It is a pleasure to write this foreword to Don Mayes' book. It is a guide for purchasers and consumers of prepaid dental plans, also called *capitation plans* or, as Don refers to them, *dental health maintenance organizations—dental HMOs.* This guide is sorely needed. Since the start of the modern era of third party dental plans in the mid-1950s, what was a relatively simple approach has mushroomed in both size and complexity. Selecting the best plan for a particular group has become a difficult task for an expert consultant, let alone someone not familiar with the peculiarities of dental plans.

Originally, insurance companies and the Blues were not interested in general dental coverage. The feeling was that since everyone was "dentally sick" and there was some certainty of risk for the individual, coverage was not feasible. However, the International Longshoremen's and Warehousemen's Union-Pacific Maritime Association benefit fund decided on a pilot program for children's dentistry. A dual choice involving a staff model group practice paid on a capitation basis for comprehensive care (excluding orthodontics) in each of the two major California port areas and an indemnity program with a maximum benefit of $75 per child for the initial year in all West Coast ports was established. With the urging of this trust fund, the West Coast dental associations were instrumental in establishing the first Delta plans. At about the same time the Los Angeles Hotel and Restaurant Workers, with far less money per person, established a trust fund-controlled dental clinic as the only facility where benefits were available for members.

Since then the number of persons covered has mushroomed to almost 40% of the population, with the prepaid plans covering a significant portion of the total. However, the staff model group practice, owned by either purchasers, consumers or a professional partnership, has become only a small part of the total. Various types of networks, involving intermediaries or administrative agencies, have become the main vehicle for capitation dental benefits (dental HMOs). The participating providers are usually solo or relatively small dental practices. Some of the larger ones have single owners employing many salaried dentists who do not participate in the decision making process.

The original concept developed for the ILWU-PMA and some other programs was that the premium would be sufficient to cover the cost of the estimated dental and hygienist time necessary to service the entire population. Attempts were made to see everyone regularly with a preventive and treatment program to minimize dental diseases and their sequelae. The cost factors included all expenses plus dentist incomes. There were no extra administrative costs since there was no intermediary between the group practices and the purchasers. The necessary data collection and paperwork were part of running the practice and replaced costs of billing patients individually. Such a situation was almost the best of both worlds, since the dentists could plan and provide treatment without regard to the patients' ability to pay, without third party interference, without claim forms and without concern about receiving adequate monies to run that portion of the practice.

Such programs were not cheap, but they were able to provide a better benefit for less cost than the more typical fee-for-service programs that began to function. Most gratifying was the documented improvement in oral health for the eligible populations. Very high use rates were achieved, regardless of the socioeconomic background of those eligible for coverage. It must be noted here that Delta also achieved excellent results for the Longshoremen children's program.

Quality evaluation was achieved by analysis of data generated by the plans and by site visits to review records and operating systems and even clinical examination of samples of patients. It was relatively easy, since a minimum number of locations were involved.

The provider time and cost of that time avoids the need to determine the projected need for specific quantity of various services together with the different fees for those services. If the total allocated time is about right, it matters little what the mix of services turns out to be. Such concerns as expected turnover of eligibles, the change from initial to maintenance care, laboratory costs and the rates can be built into a simple formula. Then actual experience allows projected rates to be adjusted accordingly over succeeding periods of time. Another reason for not using fees is that they contain a large component of "custom" in establishment of their level. Costs of producing the specific services are only part of the picture. Therefore, fees may be below cost for some procedures and way above for others. The use of provider time and cost is more accurate, as well as simpler.

One concern about current developments is that the dental plan market has become bifurcated, much more so than the market for full-service hospital and medical plans. On one hand, there are the traditional fee-for-service plans and their variants. These are usually high priced relative to the benefits. Then there are the capitation plans that usually have much lower premiums and higher benefits. Competition takes place on two different levels. As a result, I believe that many of the capitation premiums are priced too low. When a percentage is taken out for the intermediary, very little is left for the dentist. Being underpaid creates an enormous incentive to reduce access and undertreat, to say nothing about reducing technical quality. At the same time turnover of participating dentists is increased. Following the guidelines and principles in this book will help to avoid this problem. If sufficient funds are not available for a high-benefit plan, then the solution is to increase patient out-of-pocket payments in a manner to minimize constraints on access or to phase in family members as initial backlog needs are taken care of.

Don Mayes has emphasized quality assurance. It is particularly important that a plan has implemented its own internal system. Both the acceptability of the system and its effectiveness must then be validated by an independent expert reviewer for the purchaser. One often neglected quality function is that of dental practice approval prior to acceptance into the plan. When conducted, it usually consists of a review of "structure" but not of the actual process of care. How the practice treats its patients, whether its diagnosis and treatment planning are appropriate and whether its actual treatment is acceptable are critical and should be evaluated ahead of time. It is much more difficult to remove a practice after acceptance than to reject it in advance.

As would be expected to be the case with such a complex subject, Don and I have some disagreements, but they don't affect the value of the material that follows. The differences stem in large part from different experiences and relate primarily to emphasis and priorities. As knowledgeable purchasers know, there is usually more than one exact answer to plan design.

As Don Mayes has indicated, it is impossible to cover all contingencies in a book. Only certain guidelines and parameters can be set forth. However, the knowledge gained from this book permits a plan administrator to ask a potential professional consultant the right questions and to use that person wisely once selected.

Max H. Schoen, D.D.S., Dr.P.H.
Los Angeles
February 1993

Introduction

This book is written for use by purchasers of dental health maintenance organizations (HMOs), more commonly called dental *capitation* and/or *prepaid* dental plans. The author generally will use the term *dental HMO* throughout this book. The book's purpose is to demystify how dental HMOs work: to explain how they differ from other types of dental plans, how to evaluate them, how to get fair value and how to assure that the dental care provided, or not provided, is of an acceptable level of quality. From an actuary's perspective, this book may be considered oversimplified. However, it is not the author's intent to write a text for academicians, or to make the mysteries of actuarial science simplistic, but rather to place in the hands of the "non-actuary" a tool that will assist him or her in effectively evaluating dental capitation plans.

The book is designed to be used as a reference. It is the author's intent that each section stand on its own.

What is a *dental HMO* or *dental capitation plan?* This phrase generally refers to a dental benefits plan that pays the dentist providing the services on a *per capita* basis. Hence the term *capitation.* The dentist provides covered services and in return receives a specific dollar amount on a periodic basis, usually monthly, for each individual or family enrolled in the dental office. The amount the dentist is paid is not directly tied to the frequency or value of services performed. Dental HMOs generally have benefits that are more generous than comparably priced fee-for-service dental plans—in which the dentist is paid a fee for each service provided.

Dental HMOs are a viable option for providing dental benefits. However, they can be fraught with problems. Their history runs the gamut from outright scams to outstanding value. The author has reviewed dozens of plans and has identified plans that are well designed, provide excellent value and offer quality dentistry as well as a high level of satisfaction among the purchasers, patients and the participating dentists.

Other plans evaluated were obviously designed to create an illusion of excellent care and value while, in reality, the plans were little more than sophisticated schemes designed to enrich their creators.

This guide provides the information necessary to identify the major problems encountered in evaluating, selecting, purchasing and monitoring dental capitation plans.

The differences between a good and poor plan may be very subtle. Many times it is difficult to identify these differences. This guide will help in that process by providing, among other things, information necessary to:

1. Better understand various types of dental plans and the differences among them
2. Identify and evaluate the critical components of a dental capitation plan
3. Estimate the value of the services provided in a dental capitation plan
4. Identify "tricks and traps" used by unscrupulous plan administrators
5. Identify the minimum data required to effectively monitor a dental capitation plan
6. Assess plan design, including exclusions and limitations.

It is the author's hope that this guide will enable readers to objectively evaluate dental capitation plans and assist in determining whether a dental HMO is a viable option for their needs. The author has brought together the diverse body of information that is necessary for this process. This guide is designed to be an easy-to-use ready reference and is presented in a format that will facilitate its use.

The term *plan administrator,* as used in this book, refers to insurance companies, third party administrators or any other entity providing dental capitation plans. *Plan administrator* is not used in the ERISA sense as the employer or trust fund. In this book the term *purchaser* is used for the employer or the health and welfare trust fund.

This book is divided into four parts. Section I provides background information on dental plans in general and how they relate to medical plans. Section II describes dental HMOs, their design, problems to look for and how to write an RFP. Section III presents criteria for ongoing evaluation of the dental plan. Section IV consists of appendixes of useful information.

The author welcomes any suggestions, comments and recommendations for improving this book. Please send them to:

Don Mayes, D.D.S., President
Don Mayes & Associates
360 Maple Avenue
Hershey, PA 17033
Phone: (717) 533-1681
Fax: (717) 533-5954

The author would like to pay tribute to those who assisted in the writing of this book.

First and foremost, Patricia J. Ibbs, senior health plan consultant, Corbel & Company, Jacksonville, FL. She has been my long-suffering editor and suggested this book. Without her encouragement and support, this book would not have been written.

I would also like to acknowledge the important contributions of the following who read the prepublication manuscript and made many valuable suggestions: John R. Amsterdam, D.M.D., M.B.A., health care consultant, Radnor, PA; Charlotte Bartzack, Ph.D., director Medicare fraud and abuse, Blue Cross Blue Shield of Michigan, Detroit, MI; Ernest J. Collins, benefits planning and communications manager, Hershey Foods Corporation, Hershey, PA; Robert F. Eckerle, president, RFE Associates, Inc., New Cumberland, PA; Robert B. Edmiston, M.D., health care consultant, Harrisburg, PA; John O. Mayes, D.M.D., general practitioner, Hershey, PA; Wayne Paul, president, Dental Management Corporation, Baltimore, MD; Max H. Schoen, D.D.S., Dr.P.H., the "George Washington" of dental capitation, Los Angeles, CA; and John D. Thorpe, D.D.S., M.P.H., dental director, Blue Cross & Blue Shield of Illinois, Chicago, IL.

Acknowledgments

The author wishes to thank the following for permission to reproduce material originally published under their auspices.

Chapter 2, ''How Dental Is Different Than Medical,'' is an edited version of an article entitled ''Dental Is Different.'' by Donald S. Mayes, that appeared in the September 1990 issue of *Employee Benefits Journal,* published by the International Foundation of Employee Benefit Plans, Inc., P.O. Box 69, Brookfield, WI 53008-0069.

Chapter 3, ''(Costly) Myths About Dental Insurance,'' is an edited version of an article with the same title by Donald S. Mayes that appeared in the December 1991 issue of *Employee Benefits Journal,* published by the International Foundation of Employee Benefit Plans, Inc., P.O. Box 69, Brookfield, WI 53008-0069.

Chapter 4, ''Is It Medical or Dental?'' is an edited version of an article entitled ''Dental Claims Payment: An Open and Shut Case?,'' by Donald S. Mayes, reprinted from *Business and Health,* June 1988, copyright 1988 and published by Medical Economics Publishing at Montvale, NJ 07645-1742. All rights reserved. None of the content of this publication may be reported, stored in retrieval system, or transmitted in any form or by any means (electronic, mechanical, photocopying, recording or otherwise) without the prior written permission of the publisher.

Chapter 6, ''Key Questions to Ask When Evaluating Dental HMOs,'' is an edited version of a report entitled ''Evaluating Capitation Plans, Key Questions Provide Useful Checklist for Employer,'' by Donald S. Mayes, that appeared in *Spencer's Research Reports,* published by Charles D. Spencer & Associates, 222 West Adams Street, Chicago, IL 60606.

Chapter 18, ''One Company's Experience,'' is an edited version of a report entitled

"Cost of Capitated Dental Plan Decreased 4% in 1987-1989 While Indemnity Plan Costs Climbed 27%," by Donald S. Mayes, that appeared in *Spencer's Research Reports,* published by Charles D. Spencer & Associates, 222 West Adams Street, Chicago, IL 60606.

Chapter 19, "The Dentist's Perspective," is an edited version of an article entitled "Is Capitation for You? How to Decide," by John O. Mayes and Donald S. Mayes, that appeared in the December 1987 issue of *Dental Management* and is reprinted with permission of Advanstar Communications, Cleveland, OH.

Appendix B, "Area Adjustment Factors," is from *1993 Dental Cost Guidelines,* by John P. Cookson, FSA, published by Milliman & Robertson, Inc., 259 Radnor-Chester Road, Radnor, PA 19087-5260.

Appendix E, "1990 Code on Dental Procedures and Nomenclature," is from *CDT-1 Current Dental Terminology,* First Edition 1990-1995, published by the American Dental Association, Chicago, IL 60611.

Appendix F, "Glossary of Dental Benefits Terms," is from *CDT-1 Current Dental Terminology,* First Edition 1990-1995, published by the American Dental Association, Chicago, IL 60611.

Appendix G, "Common Dental Terms," is from *CDT-1 Current Dental Terminology,* First Edition 1990-1995, published by the American Dental Association, Chicago, IL 60611.

Appendix J, "National Association of Prepaid Dental Plans Model Act," is used courtesy of the National Association of Prepaid Dental Plans, Indianapolis, IN 46268.

Overview

1

According to the American Dental Association, dental HMOs are the most rapidly growing segment of dental coverage. In 1992 it was estimated that 11% of dental benefits were provided through dental HMOs. This number takes on greater significance when one considers that over 100 million people now have some type of dental benefit coverage. The author believes that dental HMOs will eventually encompass 20-25% of the dental benefits market.

For the uninitiated, dental HMOs, also called *prepaid dental plans* or *dental capitation plans,* utilize a different method of reimbursement to pay dentists than typical fee-for-service reimbursement plans. In a fee-for-service dental plan, the dentist is paid a fee for each service provided. In a dental HMO, the dentist is paid a fixed or *per capita* amount—hence the term *capitation.* This is usually computed on a per family or per person enrolled per month basis, for making specific services available to the enrolled population. Typically, payment is determined by number of enrollees signed up with each dental office, independent of services provided. Therefore, the dentist (dental office) takes on the major risk and—in essence—assumes the role of the insurer, in that he or she is contractually obligated to provide a defined set of benefits to a specific population for a set monthly fee.

Dental capitation is the most common term used for this type of dental care system. However, *capitation* refers to how dentists are reimbursed and not to a delivery system. Therefore, it is the author's opinion that *dental HMO* is the most appropriate designation for any dental care system that pays the dentists on a per capita basis.

A dental HMO may be the ideal vehicle for dental care. Why? Because a dental HMO provider, similar to a medical HMO provider, has no incentive to overtreat but does have a strong incentive to provide preventive services and treat problems before they become more serious and expensive to treat. And in dentistry, preventive services and early treatment have been proven beyond a doubt to be cost effective.

However, one must keep in mind that a dental HMO can be either a valuable addition to a benefits portfolio or a serious mistake.

As occurs with every "new" alternate delivery system, promoters climb out of the woodwork promising great savings and a better delivery system. In truth, some of these people do not have the experience or expertise to successfully design and implement an effective program. They simply copy the idea from the creator and usually do a very poor job of cloning it. It is important to look at the administrator's experience. This book will help in that effort.

The most difficult task facing those who wish to purchase a dental HMO is evaluating the offerings. There is a plethora of choices, all promising to deliver value. The harsh reality is there are a lot of shell games being played.

A dental HMO can be designed so everyone is a winner—the purchaser, the patient and the dentist. This book is intended to assist you in evaluating, purchasing and/or managing a dental HMO. Some of the advantages and disadvantages of dental HMOs are discussed below. Refer to the various sections of this book for more detailed discussions.

Advantages of a *Well-Managed* Dental HMO

1. Quality assurance. Patients are far more likely to receive services of acceptable quality in a well-managed dental HMO than in a fee-for-service dental plan.

In a good dental HMO, the dental offices are carefully evaluated prior to admission into the plan. This is a major benefit to the purchaser and patients that is unlikely to be duplicated in a fee-for-service plan, which generally reimburses any licensed dentist providing covered services.

2. Safer offices. With the increase in the incidence of hepatitis, AIDS and other serious diseases that may be contracted in a dental office, an ongoing review of infection control is taking on greater importance. Therefore, it is critical to know if a dental office is using proper infection control on a regular basis.

Of all dental benefit plans, the dental HMO is the one most likely to assure that a thorough evaluation of infection control has taken place. In most other dental benefit plans, the patient is principally reliant upon the ethics and knowledge of the dentists.

3. Substantial cost savings. A well-designed and well-administered dental HMO will save money over a fee-for-service dental plan with comparable benefits. How much? One should expect a total savings ranging from 15-40%

for the same benefit levels. Among the variables involved are turnover of providers, size of the group, accessibility of care, plan design and quality of plan administration. Also, one must assess the motivation of the plan administrators and the dentists contracted to provide the services.

4. *No incentives for overreporting or misreporting.* *Misreporting* refers to a provider's reporting a service not provided or upgrading a procedure code for services rendered in order to receive a higher reimbursement—for example, classifying cleaning teeth as root planing, a much more difficult and time-consuming procedure. Misreporting can be a significant cost factor in a fee-for-service dental plan. One study revealed that over 30% of dentists will misreport services for their financial gain if no one is monitoring what they are doing. In a dental HMO, usually the reimbursement to the dentist is unrelated to the services provided, so misreporting profits no one. There are times the dentist and/or administrator is reimbursed based upon a "relative value" of the services provided. In that case, there may be an incentive to overstate the number and/or value of services provided, i.e., *overvalue* them.

5. *Incentives changed from treatment to prevention.* Dental plans basically cover the treatment of only two diseases: tooth decay and periodontal (gum) disease. Both of these are largely preventable and may be treated inexpensively if they are diagnosed early and regular preventive measures are implemented at the dental office and at home.

The dentist in a dental HMO will save money for himself or herself and, consequently, the plan over the long run, by seeing the patient early and providing treatment before a condition becomes serious. For example, a small cavity may be filled for $40. However, if the cavity is not treated early and the tooth abscesses, the value of the services needed could be as much as $850—$350 for a root canal treatment and $500 for a crown. It is far less expensive to keep teeth and gums healthy than it is to permit cavities and gum disease to become more serious and expensive to treat.

6. *No incentive for overtreatment.* It is customary in a well-managed dental HMO to see a dramatic rise in the percentage of diagnostic and preventive services and a steep drop in more expensive services. This is not due to undertreatment but to the elimination of overtreatment.

It is the opinion of the author that as many as 30% of crowns—the most expensive component of a dental plan—are not necessary. The frequency of crowns and other unnecessary and expensive services should drop dramatically in a dental HMO.

7. *Better management.* This is a bonus that the purchaser receives at no cost. Only about 15-20% of dentists are good-to-excellent business people. During the selection process, a well-managed dental HMO evaluates not only the quality of a dental office but also the business ability reflected in its management. The fact that 80% of dental offices are not well managed results in higher program costs in fee-for-service plans.

Disadvantages of a Dental HMO

1. It is difficult to evaluate and select a quality dental HMO. Plans offered to buyers vary from excellent to fraudulent.

A purchaser should select a consultant who has extensive experience in dental HMO analysis to review the soundness of the plan from a quality and value perspective. Most major benefits consulting firms do not have this expertise, although they may profess they do. This book will help the reader to avoid major pitfalls in the evaluation and selection process.

2. There will be fewer dental offices delivering services or offices may not be available in some locations. In order for a dental HMO to work, it is necessary to provide a sufficient volume of patients to a dental office in order for it to be actuarially sound and worthwhile for the dentists to participate. If those eligible to participate are widely dispersed geographically, the necessary volume of patients may not be available. This may be a hardship for some offices and also make it difficult for participants to find a convenient dental office.

Sometimes offering too few offices is a deliberate move on the part of the plan operator to reduce utilization. The farther away people live from a dental office, the less likely they are to take advantage of the program. The purchaser must be aware of the distribution of employees as well as the distribution of the dental offices in order to subvert this scheme.

3. Treatment may be discouraged. The fewer the services provided and the fewer the covered individuals using the plan, the more money an unscrupulous dentist can make. The incentive may be to undertreat or not to treat patients. There are many subtle ways to discourage patients from obtaining needed treatment. Among them are:

- Having few and/or inconvenient offices or office hours
- Having a long waiting time for appointments
- Providing only one or two services per visit.

These and other such "barriers" to care will discourage patients and may send them elsewhere to procure dental care at their own expense.

4. Poor quality care may be provided. Examples of poor quality are cheap plastic crowns rather than porcelain with metal, cheap plastic partial dentures rather than those with metal or the use of inferior filling material. Poor quality of care may also occur when "hired guns" (dentists hired for low wages and/or given very high production quotas) must produce more than is consistent with quality dentistry.

Poor quality care also occurs when outdated or poorly maintained equipment is used. For example, an old X-ray machine may result in overexposure to radiation and/or unreadable X-rays. An office also may not employ proper cleanliness and infection controls and thus expose patients to infectious diseases. Unlike most medical practices, where checks and balances are an integral part of patient care, approximately 69% of dentists practice alone. There are only eight clinical specialties in dentistry, compared to dozens in medicine. Few dentists have someone looking over their shoulder.

5. *There is a greater chance of a purchaser not receiving "value" for his or her money.* In a fee-for-service program, it is easy to determine the cost of dental services and the retention for administration and profit. Most reports are standard and usually spell out in detail what portion of the premium went to the dentist and what portion to administration and profit. This is not always so easy in an HMO. Evaluation procedures and reporting methods are not standardized for determining value; consequently, many times the reports are misleading and overstated.

6. *Utilization reports may not be accurate.* Utilization reports that are a byproduct of processing claims in a fee-for-service program can be a problem in dental HMO plans, because most payments to dentists do not require a claim to be submitted to receive payment. Therefore, there is no financial incentive for dentists to submit data on an "encounter" (i.e., claim) form indicating what services were provided. In addition, many plans do not have the capability to report detailed utilization.

2

How Dental Is Different Than Medical

The cost of health care now exceeds 12% of Gross Domestic Product. A consequence of the spiraling cost of health care is a variety of cost-management strategies.

Typically, however, corporate attention has been paid to medical cost management. Dental benefits all too frequently have been an afterthought.

Yet, costly mistakes can be avoided in dental plan reimbursements if benefit planners would realize that "dental is different." These differences must be taken into consideration when revising or restructuring cost-effective dental benefit plans (see Figure 2-1).

Following are the major ways that dental is different.

1. Dental insurance is not insurance *in the classic sense. Most health insurance has a high-loss severity with low frequency. For example, while most people are not hospitalized in any given year, those who are hospitalized incur high costs.*

Dental disease is exactly the opposite: There is a high frequency—the overwhelming majority of the population has some dental disease and low loss severity—most dental disease can be treated at a much lower cost than medical illness or injuries.

Significance: Plan design must differ. Instead of controlling utilization as in a medical plan, a dental plan controls procedures by paying for the low-cost preventive and restorative services, and excluding or limiting high-cost experimental and cosmetic services.

Figure 2-1

HOW MEDICAL AND DENTAL PRACTICE DIFFER

	Medical	**Dental**
Diseases treated	Myriad	Mainly two
Diagnostic complexity	Great	Small
Diagnostic cost	High	Low
Preventive cost/effectiveness	Unknown	Low/high
Institutional based treatment	High	Low
Nature of diseases	Acute/chronic	Chronic
Life threatening	Not uncommon	Rare
Good/better/best treatment	Rare	Common
Audit trail	Varies	Very good

HOW MEDICAL AND DENTAL INSURANCE DIFFER

	Medical	**Dental**
Insures low cost/high frequency	Rare	Standard
Insures high cost/low frequency	Yes	No

2. Dentistry is a cottage profession, and there are fewer specialists in dentistry than in medicine.

According to the American Dental Association, in 1990 about 69% of the nation's dentists were working in a solo practice. In other words, most dentists practice in relative isolation from their colleagues.

Unlike physicians, most dentists are not subject to the constant peer review that occurs in the structured environment of institutional settings, such as hospitals. Consequently, dentistry has far fewer checks and balances than medicine, and less interaction with peers reduces the opportunity for an ongoing educational experience. Moreover, dentists are still fighting what physicians accepted years ago: someone looking over their shoulders checking their diagnoses, the necessity of treatments and the quality of treatments. Therefore, dentistry usually does not have the resultant positive outcomes that peer review brings about.

The American Dental Association recognizes only eight dental specialties. The American Medical Association recognizes 23. In addition, medicine has numerous subspecialties; for example, there are nine recognized subspecialties of internal medicine alone. The American Dental Association recognizes no subspecialties.

In medicine, pathologists look at tissue, radiologists read X-rays, cardiologists review cardiograms, and so forth. Except for the most difficult procedures, the dentist serves as his or her own specialists, taking and reading X-rays, working on adults and children alike, and performing oral surgery as well as filling teeth. This is a double-edged sword. Fewer levels of specialization in dentistry tend to keep fees lower, but the lack of specialization may result in a high incidence of substandard care.

Significance: The aforementioned deficiencies must be addressed. This is best accomplished by using an administrator who provides effective claims processing and review—and has a system and data to back it up. Desired components include:

- A dental system that is plan-specific, captures tooth numbers and surfaces, checks for duplicate submissions and automates plan limitations and exclusions not requiring professional review
- Sophisticated screening parameters that suspend claims for further investigation and claims adjudicators and a review dentist who are knowledgeable about plan design and understand plan limitations and exclusions
- Effective prepayment and postpayment review, with reports documenting results; utilization reports indicating services that may be unnecessary, too expensive or excluded by the plan design; and reports that include profiles on providers that are, or may be, abusing the system
- A professional review system that includes letters to dentists alerting them that they have unusual utilization profiles and a mechanism for followup action, including office audits.

3. There may be good, better and best methods of treatment.

Dentistry frequently has a good, better and best method of treating the same condition. All of the treatments may be professionally acceptable and all will have different costs. The attitude is wrong that the sole criterion for the *best* treatment is that it be the most expensive.

Significance: Dental programs should be designed to pay for procedures that will do the job without involving unnecessary expenditures. For example, if a silver amalgam satisfactorily fills a tooth, the plan should pay for the cost of a silver amalgam, not for a much more expensive gold inlay or crown. If the patient decides to have a gold filling, he or she then pays the difference in cost between silver and gold. This method of reimbursement is detailed in an alternate treatment clause in the plan document and summary plan description (see Chapter 9).

Medical services rarely have a good, better or best option. For this reason, medical plans rarely have an alternative treatment clause. If some dental services are to be covered under a medical plan, the plan has to be written to accommodate the good, better and best choices.

4. Many dental services may be repeated and, if not performed well, may be corrected.

In medicine, when an appendix is removed, it cannot be reattached to the body if it is found to be a healthy appendix that should not have been removed. Many medical-surgical mistakes or poor procedures, once done, are irreversible.

In dentistry, many services are reversible. For example, dentures, bridges, fillings, crowns and root canals may be redone if they are not satisfactory. The plan, however, should not have to pay for the corrective work; the dentist should absorb the cost.

Significance: Frequency limitations are a must for dental plans. Pretreatment review should notice the date prior work was performed to ensure that bridges and crowns have lasted at least five years. If not, the previous dentist and not the plan is responsible for the current treatment.

5. Dental treatment is perceived as postponable, elective and, except in rare instances, is not life threatening.

Many medical problems must be taken care of as soon as possible because of the threat to patients' lives if medical care is not received or is postponed. Postponing a visit to the dentist is common, and most people feel that they can elect when and if they will be treated.

However, it is better to fill a cavity for $50 than to let a tooth continue to decay to the point where it needs a root canal and crown for $800 or a fixed bridge costing $1,200 because the tooth cannot be saved.

Significance: Many people postpone treatment, which results in accumulated neglect. Treatment then becomes more expensive than if the patient were treated early. Because delay in treatment costs a dental plan money, plan design should encourage regular appointments with the dentist.

Deductibles and/or high copayments erect barriers to care. Therefore, they should not be applied to diagnostic and preventive services. These services usually have 100% coverage with no deductible but with frequency limitations.

6. Dental treatment applies primarily to two diseases—tooth decay and periodontal (gum) disease. In medicine, there is a myriad of different disease entities and variations.

Often medical diagnosis is difficult, costly and time-consuming. This is the exception in dentistry because diagnosis and treatment are far more standardized and less varied than in medicine.

Significance: Coding is simpler than in medicine, and relative value scale (RVS) modifiers are seldom needed. Professional review is easier and simpler. For review purposes, looking at dental X-rays is almost as effective as a visual examination of the mouth.

Reimbursement for cognitive services or repeated tests should be severely limited.

7. Tooth decay and gum disease are insidious, are not reversible, usually progress slowly, have cumulative effects, are not subject to self-treatment, and are controllable and can be prevented.

Large cavities and extensive gum disease can develop with few symptoms and little or no pain. A tooth with a serious cavity or loose teeth from gum disease do not occur overnight. It may take months and even years for these two diseases to become serious. And many times, when symptoms are noticed, a very serious dental condition already exists that may be expensive to treat.

Except in rare instances, tooth decay does not reverse or repair itself. If left untreated, cavities become larger, and their numbers increase. Gum disease, if not treated, becomes more serious. Dental problems accumulate and become progressively worse.

And, although self-treatment is not a good option, prevention is. Prevention depends largely on the individual. In dentistry, prevention works, is cost effective and should be encouraged by plan design.

Significance: In dentistry, prevention works. Checkups and early treatments are cost effective because costs increase when treatment is delayed.

8. Dental treatment (or lack of treatment) leaves an audit trail.

Crowns, fillings, root canals, bridges, dentures and many other services, all have a physical presence—or absence. An oral examination or review of dental X-rays not only shows the presence or absence of services but also will assist in determination of the quality of the services provided. There is an 80% correlation between doing an oral examination and looking at dental X-rays. For this reason, requiring the submission of X-rays with certain dental claims can be a very cost-effective method for quality assurance and utilization review.

Significance: Generally, 15% of the dentists cause 80% of the aforementioned problems. Consequently, targeted review of this 15% permits cost-effective auditing.

Dental claims are relatively easy to review, resulting in a very positive cost/benefit ratio. Usually $5 or more is saved for each $1 spent on review.

Summary

Dentistry and medicine have significant differences that are important and must be taken into consideration when designing or administering dental care benefit plans.

A dental plan should not be designed as if it were a medical plan and should not cover medical services. A medical plan should not cover dental services.

Dental is indeed *different* and, if these differences are ignored, costly mistakes can be made.

3

(Costly) Myths About Dental Insurance

There is a myth that the cost of dental insurance is low and carefully monitored to keep it that way. The reality is that dental plans cost more than they should and this cost is increasing dramatically each year. In years 1982 through 1992, the costs of dental services have increased at a faster pace than all items composing the Consumer Price Index (CPI). For four out of the nine years since 1982, dental services have increased more than the medical care component of the CPI.

Yet during 20 years of designing, administering and auditing dental plans, the author has seen only a handful of purchasers take a serious interest in the design and cost of dental plans.

Why? Dental insurance is usually less than 11% of the total cost of health care plans. Cost overruns in dental are viewed more as a dripping faucet than a serious leak. However, as any homeowner knows, the cost of a dripping faucet becomes substantial over time.

If you would like to make your dental benefits program more cost efficient, consider the seven costly myths regarding dental plans.

Myth Number One: Your plan is well designed.

Reality: This is doubtful. Poor plan design is the greatest single cause of unnecessary expenditures. Most dental plans are based upon old, outdated concepts promulgated during the early days of dental insurance. Little has been done to take advantage of the costly experience gained over the past 30 years.

For example, a dental plan's annual maximum payment is a low $500 to $1,000 for the very sound reason that over 90% of people have annual dental expenditures of less than $500. This plan design discourages high-cost optional services because of high out-of-pocket expense to the patient. An increased maximum benefits a few people inordinately while costing money that could be spent more equitably elsewhere. Yet, plans continue to "improve" benefits by increasing the maximum, thereby benefiting few, encouraging more costly services, causing inflationary charge increases and costing the plan more money.

Also, many plans include archaic ideas like . . .

Myth Number Two: The best method for paying dental benefits is based on usual, customary and reasonable (UCR) charges.

Reality: UCR is a system based upon charges made by providers (dentists). It can be characterized as "what you charge is what you get" or "if you want more, charge more." UCR has outlived its usefulness. When there is virtually no limit on what will be paid, there is no limit on what will be charged. It is very common for a dentist to have two sets of fees: one for uninsured patients and another for insured patients. In auditing dental offices, I have found that over 40% of dentists reviewed charge higher rates to insured patients than to private noninsured patients.

Myth Number Three: Pay for crowns at $500 each, with a low patient copayment. It will save money for the plan because a crown will last a lifetime.

Reality: Crowns that are not properly made do not last a lifetime, and far too many crowns are not necessary or are improperly done—30% by the author's estimate. Improperly made crowns cause, among other problems, gum disease and tooth decay, dentist-induced diseases that need to be treated at an additional cost to the plan.

High reimbursements for crowns result in too much of the plan's money going to too few of the enrollees. It is not uncommon to see over 30% of a dental plan's expense be for crowns for 6% of the people enrolled in the plan. A plan should not reimburse more than 50% of the cost of crowns. This will help eliminate overtreatment and stop so much of the plan money from going to a select few.

Remember that not only crowns at $500, but also properly done fillings at $50, can last a lifetime. Plan design should not encourage the $500 reimbursement over the $50 choice. A plan should encourage patients to select the least expensive professionally acceptable treatment.

Myth Number Four: A dental plan is merely a medical plan with dental terminology substituted.

Reality: There are significant differences between the practice of medicine and dentistry and, when these differences are not taken into consideration in writing benefits programs, the oversights can be very costly ones.

Compared to physicians, dentists practice in relative isolation. According to the American Dental Association, 69% of dentists are solo practitioners. Eighty percent of dentists are general practitioners, compared to 40% of physicians who practice primary care; dentistry has only eight recognized specialties, while medicine recognizes 23 and has numerous subspecialties. Consequently, dentistry has less accountability, peer review, peer pressure and fewer checks and balances than medicine. No one is looking over the dentist's shoulder. Therefore, the plan should include office audits; oversight mechanisms, such as pretreatment and posttreatment review; alternate treatment options; and carefully selected limitations and exclusions.

Dentists diagnose and treat mainly two diseases: tooth decay and gum (periodontal) disease. Physicians, on the other hand, encounter a myriad of diagnostic riddles. One could say dentistry is treatment oriented and medicine diagnosis oriented. Therefore, unlike a medical plan, a dental plan should not pay for batteries of tests, X-rays or exploratory treatments generally reimbursed under medical plans.

Myth Number Five: Dental benefits are paid for only under the dental plan.

Reality: Increasingly, dental services are being paid, as medical expenses, under medical plans. Because of this, millions of dollars are unknowingly being misspent because of poor plan design.

The reason why reimbursement is sought under a medical plan rather than a dental plan is threefold: There are higher reimbursement levels; certain procedures are not limited under the medical plan; and there are higher annual maximums.

Medical plans have higher reimbursement levels for expensive procedures. Typically, a dental plan will pay 50% for major procedures, and a medical plan will pay 80%.

The limitations and exclusions in dental plans generally eliminate reimbursement for expensive optional services, like crowning all the teeth at a cost of $30,000. Plus, pretreatment review can many times catch cosmetic procedures and refuse the claim before treatment. Medical plans will pay for these procedures, if the claims are "properly worded."

The annual maximum in a dental plan is usually $500 to $1,000, while annual maximums in a medical plan are usually only for mental/nervous, chiropractic, substance abuse and the like. All other expenses are applied toward a lifetime maximum of $1 million or more.

There are now courses on how to get dental claims paid under medical plans. It is common to see a $15,000 dental claim, usually for cosmetic procedures, being submitted as medical under a medical plan. Such a large claim would stand out among the other dental claims and be recognized by an experienced dental examiner as a noncovered procedure. Even if the claim was paid, the plan maximum would assure that far less would be paid under a dental plan.

However, $15,000 is not an extraordinarily high medical bill and, because there are so many more reimbursable procedures under a medical plan than under a dental plan, the claim has a much better chance to slip through the adjudication mechanism. Without a properly written medical plan and effective professional review, the entire $15,000 may be paid, this for a procedure that is not intended to be covered by either the dental or medical plan. It happens every day.

Myth Number Six: Because the amount saved is so small, the money spent on oversight is a wash.

Reality: Effective claims review will save at least $5 for every $1 spent. Dentists are aware of which companies have effective claims review. Consequently, those who abuse the system modify their reporting accordingly. And even if large cost savings are not apparent, the sentinel effect is at work, i.e., when the dentist knows someone is checking on what's reported, it is less likely that misreporting will occur. Reports should compare current and previous utilization patterns.

Myth Number Seven: You are getting good advice about your dental plan.

Reality: Probably not. There is precious little knowledge or expertise in dental benefits among some of the largest purveyors of advice on benefit plans. The reality is that dental plan design and administration is usually delegated to a lower level of corporate responsibility. It is not uncommon for a consultant to copy from another's plan documents with little understanding of the significance or impact of doing so.

The reason is obvious: Clients have not insisted upon any professional plan design or oversight of dental plans—so they have not received any.

What to Do

There are some basic actions a purchaser of dental benefits can take that will save money with little or no negative impact on employee relations.

1. Have your plan document reviewed to see if it can be improved. Payment at more than 50% for crowns, treatment of gum disease, impacted teeth and other major services is poor plan design and should be rewritten. Expensive optional or experimental services, such as fixed bridges, should not be covered at all. There are far less expensive, but adequate, methods for providing comparable services. Exclusions and limitations must be tightly written. Maximums should not be too high.

2. If you have a plan that has UCR as its payment methodology, change it to a fixed fee schedule. And be careful not to set the schedule too high. A high fee schedule is even **more** inflationary than a UCR plan.

3. Ask your administrator for a report on what is being saved by professional review. This, at a minimum, should be 10% of total plan costs.

4. Have your medical plan audited by an experienced outside dental auditor. Determine what medical services are being paid to dentists for dental services. Ask

the medical plan carrier what safeguards are or will be in place to prevent paying dental claims as medical. Ask for substantiating data.

5. Explore alternative delivery dental systems as a means of providing dental benefits. By so doing you may receive broader coverage for less money.

6. Have your dental plan audited by an experienced independent dental auditor. Be sure quality review is a part of this audit. For this reason, make sure your auditor is a dentist and certified by the American Board of Quality Assurance and Utilization Review Physicians.

7. If your dental guru espouses the myths above as facts, seek counsel elsewhere.

8. Be sure to brush and floss daily.

4 Is It Medical or Dental?

Medical plans cover medical services; dental plans cover dental services. At least that is what most people think. However, benefit plan purchasers may be surprised to discover this may not be true.

Many times services that are clearly dental and should be paid under the dental program are being paid under medical programs. Medical plan reimbursements generally are much higher than dental plan reimbursements. In addition, many cost-management features included in dental plans for dental services are missing in most medical plans. Dental services reported as medical are usually among the most expensive dental procedures and include:

- Bridges
- Crowns
- Dentures
- Diagnostic procedures
- Gold inlays
- Implants
- Orthodontics
- Surgical orthodontics
- Temporomandibular joint (TMJ) therapy
- Treatment of gum disease.

The dental procedures unknowingly paid under medical plans are the very procedures that generally are not reimbursable under a dental plan or have significant payment limitations because they are optional, cosmetic or very expensive.

The movement to obtain payment for dental services under medical plans exists—and is growing. And, intentionally or not, misrepresented dental services are being paid as medical services. Payment of dental services in medical plans deserves a thorough review by the benefits manager.

What Are the Problems?

Dental has not been well defined for insurance purposes, and quite possibly *dental* may be undefinable for insurance purposes. Although those designing medical and dental plans may see clearly in their own minds what *dental* is, when it comes to reducing that perception to contract language, clarity frequently eludes the writer.

Disease is disease; treatment is treatment; bone is bone; and soft tissue is soft tissue. Teeth and gums are tissue and part of the body. Consequently, medical terminology may be used to describe dental conditions and procedures. Adding to the confusion is the fact that over 200 oral surgical procedures can be classified as either medical or dental.

However, the problem is not one of simple overlapping of vocabulary or of procedures that are in a gray area of both medicine and dentistry. What is happening in claim reporting is the following.

1. *Dental diagnoses* may be reported using medical terminology. Gum infections, tooth decay, bad bites and other dental conditions that occur in and around the mouth may be described in medical terms. For example, tooth decay and gum disease are reported as "infections." Other examples include:

- Periodontal (gum) disease reported as osteitis
- Malocclusion (bad bite) reported as maxillo-mandibular dysfunction or developmental anomaly
- A ridge that will not hold a denture reported as mandibular or maxillary atrophy
- Temporomandibular joint (TMJ) problems reported as orthopedic disharmony.

2. *Dental treatment* may be reported using medical terminology. Treatment of tooth decay, gum disease, missing teeth and bad bites are clearly seen as dental services by most people. These treatments, however, may be described using medical terminology. So, drilling a tooth, because it involves cutting tissue, may be called *surgery*. Filling a tooth may be called *plastic repair* or *closure of a wound*. Replacing an arm or leg is *prosthetics;* therefore, replacing teeth may also be called *prosthetics*.

An extreme example of using medical terminology for dental treatments is the following description for filling teeth:

> Excision and debridement of multiple infected benign lesions of the maxilla and mandible, with plastic reconstruction and secondary closure.

Some other actual examples from claim forms are:

- Orthodontic braces reported as an orthopedic appliance or a closed reduction

- Surgical orthodontics (orthognathic surgery) reported as an osteotomy
- Scaling of teeth reported as debridement and/or osseous surgery
- Crowns, inlays and dentures reported as orthopedic appliances
- Implants and bone grafts to help dentures fit better reported as services to prevent pathological fractures.

3. As mentioned, over 200 oral surgical procedures listed as *medical* benefits in a standard medical plan may also be listed as *dental* benefits in a dental plan. Examples are fractures, cysts, tumors—malignant and benign—and treatments for infections.

4. Many procedures performed for medical purposes may also be performed for dental purposes. Some examples are removal of cyst and benign tumors; treatment of infected teeth; bony growths and fractures of the jaw; an obturator for treatment of a cleft palate; and insertion of a prosthesis to replace a portion of a jaw removed in the treatment of cancer.

General anesthesia and IV sedation may also be used for either medical or dental purposes.

5. Dental disease may be related to a medical problem. An abscessed tooth infection may spread to the upper face or brain or, if the infection is in a lower tooth, into the neck. Infected gums can cause serious heart problems in people with a history of rheumatic heart disease.

How Did This Happen?

A combination of factors has created a fertile environment for dental services to be paid as medical.

1. Dental costs tend to be overlooked. Hospital costs and physician fees have high visibility. They are big ticket items. They are, as they should be, in the spotlight. However, not only can dental services paid under a medical plan have high cost, but they also may have a very high incidence and be performed repeatedly.

2. Paying dental as medical is not perceived as a problem. Although dental care may appear to be low in cost compared to medical, it may not be as inexpensive as perceived. Overlooked is the incidence of dental problems. Dental disease is almost universal. In a dental plan, utilization is high, but payment for the very expensive services is controlled by exclusions, limitations, high patient copayments and plan maximums. Medical plans are not designed to control expensive dental services. They are designed to pay for medically necessary utilization—spreading the risk between the well and the sick makes a medical plan economically feasible.

3. Medical plan designers and administrators lack dental knowledge. Many hours and dollars are spent having medical experts design medical benefits plans and their cost management from a medical perspective. As an afterthought, and almost always with a lack of understanding, an exclusion or limitation is inserted for *dental.*

Additionally, when it comes to excluding dental services, many medical plans are poorly administered. No formal review process is in place to identify and question *dental* claims, quantify the extent of the problem or take steps to correct the problem.

4. *Dental limitations and exclusions in medical plans are almost always poorly conceived and poorly written.* The often-used exclusion or limitation, "for dental services" or "if performed by a dentist," is not precise. In addition, many states prohibit denying payment for a service based upon whether the doctor is a physician or a dentist. Consequently, these limitations and exclusions do not work.

There is another problem with poor plan language. Several lawsuits have resulted in judgments directing medical plans to pay for dental services such as crowns, inlays or orthodontics that were thought to be excluded by plan language referring to "mouth conditions" or "dental services." The courts found this kind of plan language "ambiguous" and, when plan language is ambiguous, the judgment is always for the covered beneficiary. An insurance contract is not considered to be a contract between equals, and the plan has the burden of clear, easily understandable language.

5. *Dentists are subject to little review.* Although dental claims review is available for dental programs, such review is virtually nonexistent for dental claims submitted as medical expenses under medical plans. Dentists are rarely questioned on claims they submit, and they are not reviewed by people familiar with dental reporting. Intraprofessional peer review is not an integral part of the dental delivery system. There are numerous levels and types of review in medicine. Yet medical reviewers who find themselves adjudicating claims with which they are not familiar have a tendency to approve and pay the claims because their background is medical and not dental.

6. *There are higher levels of payment under medical plans than under dental plans.* Medical plans have lower patient copayments and higher maximum allowances than dental plans. Dental plans usually have a 50% copayment for expensive services, such as orthodontics, crowns and bridges. Dental plans also usually have a $500 to $1,500 annual maximum. Orthodontics usually has a lifetime maximum of $500 to $1,000. If these expenses are paid under a medical plan, reimbursement will be 80% or 100% if the out-of-pocket maximum has been reached, and the annual plan maximum may be as high as $1 million.

As a consequence, both dentists and patients have a financial incentive to seek payment for expensive dental services under medical plans.

7. *There are no frequency limitations in medical plans.* In dental plans, expensive services often have frequency limitations for reimbursement. For example, payment for dentures, crowns and bridges is limited to once every five years. No such limitation is applied to these and other dental services if reported and paid as medical services in a medical plan.

8. *There are no "alternate treatment" clauses in medical plans.* Unlike in medicine, in dentistry there is usually more than one method for treating a given

condition. For example, an abscessed tooth may be extracted and not replaced for $35; a root canal procedure and crown may cost $600; or if the tooth is extracted and replaced with a permanent bridge, the cost may run $1,200. All these may be professionally acceptable treatments. As a consequence, most dental plans are written to limit the risk by reimbursing for the "least expensive but adequate" treatment or by excluding expensive services. Very few medical plans have these limitations.

9. *Claims reporting is getting more sophisticated.* There is a growing awareness among dentists that dental procedures will be paid as medical if reported in a "sophisticated" manner. Formal courses for dentists have been given on "sophisticated claims submission" to take advantage of these "windows of opportunity."

10. *Some dentists need the higher reimbursement allowed under the medical plans.* There is a national oversupply of dentists. This has furthered the trend of medical claim payments to dentists, particularly when a dental practice is on the edge of unprofitability. Some have found it profitable to specialize in "medical" problems such as TMJ conditions, orthognathic surgery and replacing silver fillings with gold because of "allergic" conditions.

What to Do

All of the above information is of little value unless it is used to address the problem. This milieu of interrelated and conflicting information does present a challenge; however, the following items will assist those responsible for assessing medical plans and claims review.

1. The title *doctor* is used without a degree. Any medical claim submitted by a dentist is suspect. It is not unusual for a dentist to use only the title *doctor,* without using D.D.S. or D.M.D. This may be innocent, or it may be done to avoid being identified as a dentist. It is rare to see an M.D. use only the title of *doctor.*

2. Oral surgery claims present the greatest challenge, since some of the procedures should be paid as medical.

Other than surgery for malignancies, fractures and cleft palate, almost all other surgery to the jaws *that changes their relationship* is surgical orthodontics and/or cosmetic and should either be paid as a dental claim or excluded. The reason is that the primary purpose of these procedures is to reorient the relationship of the upper and lower jaws (teeth) and to improve function (chewing) and appearance (cosmetic). This is dentistry—by license and by definition.

3. It must be kept in mind that there are also other ways to improve function (the bite) besides oral surgery. There are nonsurgical procedures such as dentures, fixed bridges, crowns, fillings, occlusal equilibration (grinding the teeth) and orthodontics.

Consequently, and regardless of the method, all procedures—surgical or nonsurgical—used to improve the bite are dental.

4. The treatment of TMJ conditions is an area of concern. Other than surgery, services related to TMJ conditions are the most rapidly growing area of

abuse. Treatment may consist of many different types of dental services reported as medical, i.e., crowns, orthodontics, surgical orthodontics, splints, equilibration, dentures and gold fillings.

All dental procedures that affect the way the teeth meet (the bite), change the relationship of the temporomandibular joint and may be considered treatment of TMJ. Some dentists will change a diagnosis in order to obtain reimbursement if TMJ conditions are excluded from the plan. For example, if the procedure is orthognathic surgery and services related to TMJ are excluded, the dentist may report the diagnosis as "developmental anomaly" or "loss of function." If, however, TMJ is a covered benefit, the diagnosis will be TMJ, but the same procedure will be performed.

5. Compile a list of suspect diagnoses and services. A good example is *oral orthopedics.* This term is used frequently when attempting to obtain payment for dental service under medical plans. Organized dentistry does not recognize *oral orthopedics* as either a specialty or a category of service. Neither should benefit plans. It appears to have been invented to "fool the claims processors."

Several other examples of inappropriate claims are given in this chapter, and a competent dental reviewer who is familiar with medical terminology used for dental claims can increase the list tenfold.

Recommendations

Purchasers of medical and dental plans should take the following steps:

- Review the medical and major medical plans, particularly looking at the exclusions and limitations that apply to dentistry, services related to dentistry and TMJ procedures. Do not merely deny by procedure.
- Clarify oral surgery and TMJ in both the medical and dental plans.
- Demand tighter claims review with appropriate reports from the claims administrator. Ask for the guidelines used in reviewing claims.
- Do not cover dental services in a medical plan.
- Do not cover medical services in a dental plan.

Summary

Due to a lack of understanding, concern and effective medical claims review, millions of medical plan dollars are being spent for dental services. Most of these services are expensive and not covered under dental plans for sound underwriting reasons.

The problem is compounded by poor contract language and failure to understand that medical plans are improper vehicles to pay for dental services.

5

Dental Plans—A Review

BY JOHN O. MAYES, D.M.D.

TYPES OF DENTAL PLANS

Although this book addresses dental HMOs, this chapter provides a brief overview of the different types of dental plans available in the marketplace and the pros and cons of each.

There is a plethora of different types of dental plans available as vehicles for providing dental benefits. There is no "best" type of dental plan. The type of dental plan selected should be based upon a group's specific needs.

There are two broad categories of plans. In the first category are dental HMOs and individual practice association (IPA) plans, where the dentists generally assume the financial risk. In the second category, fee-for-service plans, the dentist usually is not at risk. Fee-for-service plans, in addition to the traditional indemnity plans, include the preferred provider organization (PPO), the discounted fee PPO and direct reimbursement.

There are many variations and combinations of plans, as well as different meanings and interpretations applied to the terms used to describe the various types of plans. The following reflects the common understanding of the various types of dental plans operating today. (See Figure 5-1.)

DENTAL HMOs

These may also be called *dental capitation plans* or *prepaid dental plans.*

Figure 5-1

MAJOR TYPES OF DENTAL PLANS AND THEIR CHARACTERISTICS

Type of Plan	Fee for Service	Preferred Provider Organization	Dental HMO
How Dentists Are Paid	**UCR/R&C or Table of Allowances**	**UCR/R&C or Fee Schedule**	**Capitation**
Potential for managing	Least	Fair to good	Best
Financial incentives for prevention	Low	Low	High
Financial incentives to overtreat	High	High	Low
Quality assurance	Low	Varies	Very good
Cost/benefit potential	Least	Moderate to good	Excellent
Utilization controls	Least	Moderate	Best
Dr. contract	No	Yes	Yes
Fraud/abuse potential	High	Moderate	Low
Management of fee increases			
Fee schedule	Good	Good	NA
UCR/R&C	Poor	Fair	NA
Capitation	NA	NA	Excellent
Patient access	Excellent	Varies	Limited
Patient satisfaction	Poor/good "On their own"	Good/excellent Charges known Paid-in-full benefits Patient recourse	Good/excellent Charges known Paid-in-full benefits Patient recourse

Description: The most common name for this type of plan is *capitation,* which derives from the payment method. The dentists are paid on a *per capita* basis at a fixed, usually monthly, rate for each individual or family. The dentist is paid irrespective of the number or types of services provided or the number of beneficiaries seen. The term *prepaid* may be inappropriate. *Prepaid* has been and still is being used to describe most dental benefit plans. Historically, the term *prepaid* is intended to distinguish dental benefits that are not *insured* in the classic sense from *insured* benefits. (See discussion in Chapter 2.)

Of all dental plans, dental HMOs have the potential for being either the "best" or "worst" choice for providing dental benefits.

The dentists are individually at risk in dental HMOs. If the value of services exceeds payments, it is the dentist's loss. If payment exceeds value, the dentist gains financially. As a consequence, there are two principal ways for a dentist to make money in dental HMOs: Make sure beneficiaries are provided the services necessary to bring them to a state of good dental health or do as little as possible. (See Chapters 1 and 2 for a more in-depth discussion.)

Pros: HMOs have the potential for being the most cost-effective, preventive-oriented and quality-assured dental plans available. Intrinsic to dental HMOs are incentives for dentists not to overtreat, overuse expensive services or misreport, and to provide preventive services and necessary treatment to as many covered individuals as possible. Preventive services are cost effective. It is far less costly to keep people in a state of good dental health than it is to repair neglect.

Cons: Dental HMOs also have the potential for being the most abused dental plans available in the sense of not receiving value. In poorly managed plans and plans designed to mislead the purchaser, an illusion of care can be created when in reality little (or only emergency/episodic) care is provided. There are incentives for the unethical administrator or dentist to discourage visits, provide as few services as possible and discourage beneficiaries from visiting the dentist. Beneficiaries generally have fewer offices to choose from and, consequently, access may be a problem.

A poorly managed dental HMO will have virtually no monitoring of the care that is provided and little or misleading data available for review, so that the purchaser may be unable to accurately assess the value and the quality of the care being provided.

Individual Practice Association (IPA)

Description: An IPA is in essence a hybrid dental HMO, a delivery system that combines the risk sharing of an HMO with fee-for-service reimbursement. IPAs may be owned and operated by the participating dentists who sign a contract agreeing to certain conditions, including quality assurance, utilization review and risk sharing. The dentists are collectively at risk, as opposed to dental HMOs where they are individually at risk. The dentist is paid on a fee-for-service basis and is at risk if payout exceeds premiums. If this occurs, either fees may be reduced or the dentist may not be paid for treatment beyond a certain amount. IPAs have been organized by local dental societies in response to successful dental HMOs or the threat of one. This type of dental plan is not widespread but, with sophisticated management, shows promise.

Pros: IPAs combine the incentives of fee for service (the dentist receives payment only when a service is rendered) with aspects of dental HMOs. In an IPA if a dentist overtreats participants, he or she may receive a reduced payment or may not be paid. An IPA will usually cause the dentist to carefully consider the services he or she is providing. "Am I overtreating?" "Will I get paid if I do this?" More important, each dentist knows someone is looking over his or her shoulder. IPAs are generally more effective than traditional fee-for-service dental plans because of utilization review activities and strong peer pressure to "play it straight."

IPAs generally provide a wider choice of dental offices than dental HMOs because an invitation to participate is usually extended to all dentists in an area. When properly structured and managed, IPAs combine some of the best features of dental HMOs and fee-for-service plans.

Cons: IPAs are not readily available and require ongoing, sophisticated, hands-on management by an experienced administrator. IPAs are best suited to large groups of beneficiaries in a defined area.

Fee-for-Service Dental Plans

Fee-for-service dental plans pay the dentist on a service-by-service basis and usually are administered by commercial or nonprofit corporations. Some of these plans have a provider agreement between the administrator and the dentist limiting the amount a participating dentist may collect for a service. Many plans do not. Some plans may include utilization review and quality assurance; many do not. Under these plans the dentist is not usually at risk for utilization.

Several specialized plans have been developed that compete more directly with capitation: the preferred provider organization (PPO), the discounted fee PPO and direct reimbursement.

Preferred Provider Organization (PPO)

Description: A PPO is a network of dentists who have signed a contract to accept a specific level of payment for providing covered services. The dentists are not at risk. They are paid on a fee-for-service basis under a fee schedule (a fixed fee PPO) or discounted R&C. Customarily, a list of covered services is provided for the beneficiary showing what services are covered, what the plan will pay and what the beneficiary must pay, if anything. Many times the agreement with the dentists also contains clauses to assure the dentist will agree to certain utilization and quality assurance controls. There is usually less quality assurance and utilization review than in dental HMOs. The beneficiary may go to any dentist but has no assurance the nonparticipating dentist will accept the plan allowance as payment in full. Some plans also pay a lesser amount if the beneficiary uses a dentist who is not participating.

Pros: The dentist signs a contract generally agreeing to accept a specific fee or allowance as payment in full and to submit to certain utilization and quality assurance protocols. The beneficiary and the administrator have recourse to address problems that may arise because of this arrangement. Although quality assurance is usually not as extensive as in well-managed dental HMOs, it is generally far better than plans that do not have the dentist under contract.

The purchaser can usually obtain services at a substantial discount, well below the dentist's usual charge. This type of plan helps fill a dentist's empty chair time and serves as a source of referrals. For the dentist just starting practice, it can be a real practice booster if enough beneficiaries are enrolled in his or her office.

Cons: Unlike dental HMOs, there is an incentive for the dentist to overtreat. If nothing is done, the dentist receives no payment. As mentioned, quality assurance is rarely as thorough as in dental HMOs. And, if the review process is not thorough, dentists who are not busy because they are not "good" dentists may sign up with this type of program. Some dentists may make up in volume what they lose by way of giving a discount.

If fee allowances are too low, there may be too few dentists to serve the population's needs.

Discounted Fee PPO (Dental Referral Plan)

Description: This variation of a PPO may best be described as a marketing strategy for dentists who are seeking new patients. The dentists agree to provide certain services at no charge and other services at an agreed-upon, usually discounted, fee. The patient is responsible for payment of all fees. There is no reimbursement to either the dentist or the beneficiary of the plan by the administrator. The dentists agree to accept a table of allowances as payment in full and sign an agreement to that effect. Customarily, examinations, X-rays and, occasionally, teeth cleanings are provided once a year at no cost. The "marketer" sells the program and keeps the "premium" to cover costs and profits. The dentist usually pays nothing to participate and is listed as a participating dentist in a booklet provided to purchasers of the program.

Pros: Discounted fee PPOs are low-cost dental benefit plans for the purchaser. The purchaser is in essence offering a network of dentists who agree to charge a set, usually discounted, fee for services to those enrolled in the plan. This is one of the few types of dental benefit plans that can be "purchased" by individuals. One of the major advantages of this type of plan is that the beneficiary receives a brochure listing covered services and the fees the dentist will accept as payment in full.

Cons: Of all types of plans offered, this and the direct reimbursement plan have virtually no quality assurance or utilization review because they eliminate any review of the care dentists provide. There are no claim forms and no data collection, and no one reviews the services provided. If the beneficiaries have problems other than with fees, they are on their own. Hence, there are no safeguards against poor quality or mistreatment. Also, the panel of dentists may be small, and there may be no assurance that participating dentists will not drop out of the plan. If that happens, it is possible to have a dental plan with no convenient dentist. Dentists' participation usually depends upon the level of payment—if the fee allowances are what the dentists consider sufficient, dentists may participate; if they consider the allowances too low, dentists will probably not participate. A dentist may decide to participate and then, when the practice grows, decide to drop out of the plan.

Direct Reimbursement

Description: Direct reimbursement is a dental plan in which the beneficiary pays the dental bill and submits the receipt to the employer for reimbursement. There are no claim forms, no utilization review, no quality assurance nor any limitations on what the dentist provides or charges. This type of plan is also referred to as the *bill payer* dental plan. It just pays all, or a portion of, the dental bill with no restrictions, except that there is usually a limitation on the dollar amount that will be paid. This type of dental plan has been heavily promoted by the American Dental Association.

Pros: This and the discounted fee PPO are the simplest type of dental plan offered. Direct reimbursement is particularly attractive to small companies or businesses that wish to offer some type of dental plan but are too small to be able to purchase a plan from a carrier because of antiselection. Direct reimbursement may also be a good choice if cafeteria type benefits are offered.

Cons: The purchaser must usually administer the plan. There are no restrictions on what is covered or what the dentist charges. The only restriction is the amount the plan will pay, and this is usually controlled with low annual maximums and relatively high copayments; for example, copayments of 50% for all dental expenses up to an annual maximum of $500 per person. The plan establishes no priorities for treatment. For example, there is no priority of preventive services over purely cosmetic services; both would be reimbursed at the same level. Utilization review and quality assurance are virtually nonexistent. Dentists can charge what they want because there are no restrictions on payment. This could be called the *dentist's plan* because it strongly favors the dentist. Direct reimbursement places no restrictions on dentists' practices or fees and assists them in collecting their fees. The patient must pay the dentist in order to obtain a receipt to be reimbursed by the employer—hence the term *bill payer* dental plan.

Dental Plan Delivery

Dental capitation and the other specialized plans discussed can be designed with different delivery models. These include the staff model, the network and the closed panel.

Staff Model

This is a dental plan with one or more dental offices that uses salaried (staff) dentists. This model has been used successfully with capitation plans. It may be a closed panel operated by the entity providing services for its own beneficiaries or as a contracted dental office(s) providing services to one or more purchasers. This model has the potential for having the highest degree of quality assurance and the lowest cost because it is generally well managed. If it is owned and operated by the entity receiving the services, there is even more control. However, the degree of success depends upon the quality of the management, and substantial experience and expertise is required in managing large dental offices.

Network

This is a dental plan that uses multiple dental offices in various locations. It is the most common method of delivering dental benefits in a dental HMO. The offices may be limited to a specific geographic area or spread over many states. The administrator usually contracts with private dental offices that are principally fee-for-service dental practices. The purchaser must keep in mind that to establish and maintain a widespread network of dental offices is costly. An acceptable and well-managed dental HMO plan using a large network of dentists may have administrative cost of up to 30%, although it is the author's opinion that anything over 20% must be evaluated very carefully. Evaluating the cost effectiveness of dental HMOs must always be a major consideration.

Closed Panel

This may also be known as an *exclusive provider organization (EPO)*. Beneficiaries usually have a limited choice of offices and must go to one of the offices in the plan or they receive no benefits. A closed panel or an EPO is often used in either a dental HMO or PPO plan. The subscribers must use only the dentists in the network. If services are rendered by a nonnetwork dentist, the participant usually receives no benefit. Beneficiaries' choice of dentists or access to offices may be problems with this delivery model.

Methods of Reimbursing Dentists Under Various Plans

Capitation

Description: A dental HMO pays the dentists providing the services on a "per capita" basis. The dentist provides covered services and in return receives a specific dollar amount on a periodic basis, usually monthly, for each individual or family enrolled in the dental office. The amount the dentist is paid is not directly tied to the frequency or value of services performed by the dentist. Payment usually begins on the day the plan becomes effective, and the dentist is paid for each participant enrolled at the office.

Pros: Usually this is the most cost-effective, preventive-oriented dental program available. (See previous discussion above under dental HMOs.)

Cons: Capitation has the potential for being the most abused and is not readily available nationwide.

Capitation Variations

Payment on Contact

Description: This is not an uncommon "scam" used in conjunction with dental HMOs and is to be avoided at all costs. The plan operator is paid a premium to cover each enrolled individual but does not reimburse the dentist the capitation payment until the beneficiary calls the dentist for an appointment. This practice significantly increases the risk placed upon the dentist. It does not enable the dentist to spread the cost among the users and nonusers. An essential component of insurance is that nonusers' premiums help pay for those who need services. The only way for dentists to make money in this type of plan is to do as little as possible because it is virtually impossible to take care of the dental needs of a group with this type of an arrangement without losing money.

Pros: There are none except for the financial advantage to the administrator of the dental plan.

Cons: This type of plan is nothing more than a scam to give the appearance of providing a dental plan when in reality it is skimming the money needed to assure the plan's success.

Copayments, Deductibles and Maximums

Most dental HMOs have some patient payments affiliated with some services. Deductibles are not desirable and are an unacceptable barrier if applied to diagnostic and preventive services. Copayments may be applied to major dental services. If this is the case, the amount the participant is to pay should be listed in a fee schedule and not be listed as a percent of UCR or R&C. Maximums rarely come into play but, if they do, the same comments on copayments are applicable.

Fee for Service

Description: Fee for service is historically the most common form of payment for dental services. The dentist is paid a fee for each service provided. The plan may be private, noninsured, insured, self-insured, PPO, IPA, EPO or direct reimbursement. Dentists generally prefer fee-for-service dental reimbursements that have no restrictions. They prefer to be reimbursed their "usual" fee. Dentists generally do not care for dental plans that reimburse less than their "usual" fee or that do not allow them to collect the difference between what a plan pays and their fee.

Pros: Fee for service is simple to understand. A service is performed, and a fee is paid. Dentists must report services to the administrator and, as a consequence, utilization data are available to monitor dentists and plan performance.

Cons: There is incentive for dentists to increase charges, overtreat, misreport, upgrade what was done and/or encourage the most expensive treatment.

Fee-for-Service Variations

Usual, Customary and Reasonable (UCR),
Also Called Reasonable and Customary (R&C)

Description: Reimbursement is based upon the dentist's usual charge, unless the charge exceeds certain parameters. For example, the plan will pay the dentist fee unless the fee exceeds 90% of the charges for that service in a given geographic area, usually a three-digit ZIP code area. Some administrators pay up to only the 50th percentile or median charge, i.e., up to what 50% of the charges are in a given geographic area. In this case, 50% of dentists' charges for specific services would be greater than the allowed amount for the service.

In usual, customary and reasonable (UCR), *usual* refers to the charge a dentist usually makes to private noninsured patients. *Customary* refers to fees charged by dentists, for the same service, in the same geographic region with similar training and experience. *Reasonable* refers to an additional payment over and above the dentist's usual charge if unusual circumstances are present and it is *reasonable* to allow more than the dentist's usual charge.

In reasonable and customary (R&C), *reasonable* refers to the dentist's usual charge, and *customary* refers to the fees of dentists in the same geographic region with similar training and experience.

Pros: If the maximum payment level is at the 90th percentile, this is the reimbursement method preferred by most dentists. If payment is less than the dentists' usual charge, they may not care for it.

Cons: From a cost-management perspective, this is the least desirable method of reimbursement. It is inherently inflationary and encourages dentists to increase their fees to keep the level of payment high. Because there is a lag in updating the data by insurance companies, many dentists "play games" by increasing their charges in anticipation of having them reduced.

There is also a tendency for some dentists to increase their fees, over and above what they charge their noninsured patients, when they are covered by a dental plan using the UCR payment methodology.

Table of Allowances

Description: Reimbursement is based upon a *schedule of allowances* or *indemnity schedule.* A list of covered dental services is usually provided to the beneficiaries detailing a specific dollar amount that will be reimbursed for each covered service. The amount listed in the schedule is usually less than the dentist fee, and the dentist may charge the difference between the *allowance* and his or her fee because the dentist has not agreed to accept the amounts listed in the table of allowances as payment in full.

Pros: A table of allowances tends to stabilize costs. There is no automatic, uncontrolled escalation in dental fees as may occur with UCR/R&C-based reimbursement. Usually the fees do not have to be adjusted every year. It is not uncommon to update a fee schedule only once every three years.

Dentists have less incentive to report increased fees when reimbursement is based upon a table of allowances.

The patient knows what is covered and what the plan will pay.

Another advantage is that if a plan has fiscal constraints, the allowances, i.e., costs, can be raised selectively. For example, the allowance for diagnostic and preventive services can be increased (high-frequency, low-cost services) and the payment level for expensive major services (crowns, dentures, root canals—low-frequency, high-cost services) can remain at the current level of reimbursement.

Cons: The participant may not know how much the dentist will charge and will have to pay over and above the amount listed in the table of allowances. The dentist may charge whatever he or she wishes, and the participant will probably have to pay the difference between the allowance and the dentist fee.

Fee Schedule

Description: A *fee schedule* refers to a list of fees the dentist has agreed to accept as payment in full for the services listed in the schedule. It may also be described as a "fixed fee PPO" because the dentist has agreed to accept a listed fee as payment in full.

Pros: In addition to the pros listed under *table of allowances,* fee schedules have some significant advantages. They are a better choice than a table of allowances principally because the dentist agrees to accept the fees listed in the schedule as payment in full. The patient knows exactly what is covered, what the plan will pay and what he or she will have to pay the dentist, if anything.

Cons: If the level of payment is too low, dentists will not accept the payment as payment in full. This is particularly important in plans such as PPOs that depend upon participating dentists to provide care. Dentists have less incentive to report increased fees when reimbursement is based upon a table of allowances.

Salary

Description: Dentists are employed and paid a salary, usually by a group practice, government agency, corporation, welfare trust fund or another dentist. The dentist can be employed full or part time. It is the author's observation that part-time dentists can be a valuable addition to dental group practices.

Pros: There is currently an oversupply of dentists in most areas of the country, and many dentists can be employed part time at a considerable savings. Many are recent graduates, and employment provides them with experience and an income while establishing their own private practices.

There are excellent dentists who prefer to work for someone and not be involved in the problems of administering a practice. They prefer to devote their energies and attention to treating patients. Such dentists can be a valuable asset.

Cons: If the dentists are full time, then it is important that good management principles are applied so they do not end up "just putting in time." Some dentists who are very slow and/or could not make a go of it in private practice seek salaried positions. They may be "poor producers."

Also, many dentists who have had problems with their licenses, for one reason or another, seek salaried positions. A dentist with professional problems may move from one state to another to avoid the problems associated with professional or personal conduct.

Dental HMO Choice and Enrollment

If only one dental plan is available for a beneficiary, enrollment is straightforward. If there is more than one plan, then choice is part of the plan design, and the following terms are commonly used.

Dual Choice: Beneficiaries may select between two types of plans, usually a dental HMO and another dental plan, generally a fee-for-service plan. Beneficiaries have the option to enroll in either plan commonly on an annual, or semi-annual, basis. Point of service may be an exception. (See below.)

Triple Choice: Beneficiaries have three options—usually a dental HMO, an unrestricted fee-for-service plan and a PPO.

Point of Service: Point-of-service plans are rarely stand-alone plans. There is customarily a fee-for-service option for participants in a dental HMO who may elect out of the dental HMO. The reimbursement to the participant is generally based on a low table of allowances with sharply reduced benefits compared to the dental HMO and other fee-for-service dental plans. Participants who elect out of the HMO usually cannot return to it for at least one year.

There are a number of options for enrolling in dental HMOs. The differences can have a significant impact on the plans' experience, the enrollees and on the dentists.

Opt In or Positive Choice

Description: Two or more plans are offered, and the participants usually have the option of selecting either a dental HMO or a fee-for-service plan. They may have a dual or triple choice as described previously. However, if the participants wish to enroll in the dental HMO, they must make a choice to do so. Otherwise the participants are enrolled in the alternative plan. This election usually permits the selection of a dental office also. This option usually occurs annually.

Pros: This is the preferred method of enrollment for dental HMOs. It injects competition into the marketplace. The participating dentists wish to retain their participants, particularly if they have brought them to a state of good dental health. When dentists know the participants can opt out of their office on an annual basis, they tend to be more caring and solicitous.

Cons: None.

Opt Out or Choice by Inaction

Description: This is also known as *primary offering*. Two or more plans are offered, and the participants are enrolled in the dental HMO unless they "opt out," i.e., they choose not to be enrolled. This type of enrollment should have a significant impact on reducing the premium of the dental HMO because anywhere from 20% to 70%, or higher, of those enrolled in the plan will not use it on an annual basis. Those who do not select a dental office (if the choice is offered) are usually assigned to an office. It is important to be assured payment on contact is not the method used to reimburse the dentists providing the services in the plan.

Pros: Opt-out enrollment provides a dental office for those individuals without a dentist.

Cons: Opt-out enrollment is not inherently bad; it is just that it has been widely abused. So many scams have been built around this type of enrollment that it has a bad reputation. If it is used, it is essential that effective quality and utilization monitoring be in place.

Assigned or No Choice

Description: Usually the only plan offered is a closed panel dental HMO. The participants are enrolled in a dental HMO and have no other option unless they go to a dentist of their own choice and pay for their dental care out of their own pocket.

The participants may or may not be assigned to a dental office.

Pros: If the plan is a quality closed panel dental plan, this type of arrangement may provide a high level of quality care at a significant savings for the purchaser. Administration is easier when all participants are assigned to one plan.

Cons: Participant satisfaction and access may be a problem if there are too few offices. Dentists know the participants have no, or few, choices and may be callous toward the participants. Many of these plans have a clinic atmosphere.

6

Key Questions to Ask When Evaluating Dental HMOs

A number of excellent dental HMOs are currently being marketed that provide more benefits, assure quality treatment and achieve greater user satisfaction than comparably priced fee-for-service dental plans. On the other hand, millions of dollars are being spent to develop and implement dental HMOs with too little thought or knowledge as to what constitutes a sound plan.

It is not unusual to see dentists and nondentist entrepreneurs with little experience, knowledge and even less business background involved in developing dental HMOs.

In addition to the customary tools used in evaluating a dental plan, described in Chapters 7, 8, 9 and 14 through 17, there are specific questions a purchaser should ask about a dental HMO. To aid purchasers considering dental HMOs, following are some key questions to ask when evaluating a plan.

Q: Should a dental HMO be considered?

The answer is yes, a dental HMO should be considered when looking at dental plans. To be acceptable, the plan should address the purchaser's needs, be structurally and financially sound, assure quality, manage costs and foster user satisfaction. Dental HMOs can address many of the problematic issues in health care cost including the following.

Better control of costs. According to the Consumer Price Index (CPI), dental services increased at a faster pace than the "all items" component of the CPI every year for the last ten years. An additional consideration is that some dentists will increase their fees if a patient has fee-for-service dental insurance. One series of office reviews found that 40% of dentists had increased their fees for patients who had a fee-for-service dental plan. There is little incentive for dentists to moderate charging practices when they are paid only when they provide a service. A well-structured and -managed dental HMO, on the other hand, will cost less to purchase for the same level of benefits, and the costs will not increase as rapidly as in a fee-for-service dental plan.

Less provider abuse. Another study in a fee-for-service dental plan revealed that over 30% of the dentists reviewed had misreported services they provided for their financial gain. The more services performed or the more services reported, the more the dentist is paid. There are few checks and balances or penalties for misreporting in any fee-for-service dental plan. In a well-managed dental HMO the financial incentives to misreport are minimized.

Improved quality of care. A dental HMO may be the ideal health maintenance organization (HMO). Unlike medical insurance that covers hundreds of diseases, almost 90% of dental insurance dollars are paid to treat the results of only two diseases: tooth decay and periodontal (gum) disease. A well-designed dental HMO changes the dentist's incentive from the treatment of, to the prevention of, these two controllable diseases.

Preventive treatments in dentistry have proven to be very cost effective. Also, audits can be less costly, more thorough and more effective under a dental HMO than in a fee-for-service plan, since there are fewer offices to review, each treating a greater number of patients.

Increased competition. Dental HMOs increase competition in the dental marketplace. Dentists who do not participate in these plans will usually become more cost conscious, considerate and solicitous in their own practices to prevent the loss of patients to a dental HMO office.

Q: Which is better, a closed panel or open panel plan?

It is the author's opinion that a closed panel plan, i.e., one in which an employee must go to one or several capitated offices to receive benefits, is not a good plan design. Although the premiums are usually (or should be) quite low in closed panel dental HMOs, this is not necessarily because they are good dental plans; it is more likely because many people will not use the plan for various reasons. The open panel arrangement, in which patients can elect between a dental HMO and fee for service, is a far better option. Free choice provides checks and balances in the system. The marketplace becomes much more competitive.

Q: How are dental offices selected?

The selection of dental offices is one of the most critical aspects of dental HMOs. It is essential that relevant objective criteria be used for the selection and that an in-depth evaluation of the dental office occur prior to selection to participate.

Those evaluating and selecting the offices must be knowledgeable in analyzing two key aspects of the dental office to assure that it will be a successful participant in a dental HMO plan. These are the two key aspects.

Management expertise. Dental office management expertise is essential for involvement in dental HMOs. It is the author's opinion that only 15-20% of dentists are excellent business managers. If a dentist is a mediocre manager in a fee-for-service dental plan, he or she is likely to be a disaster in managing a dental HMO plan.

Dedication to quality. This is the second critical element of a good dental HMO office. Participating dentists must provide quality dental care. Quality can only be determined through a preselection office audit.

The dentist to avoid is the good businessman who is a poor dentist. Dentists who are good business managers and also dedicated to quality dentistry are the cornerstone to the success of a dental HMO.

Appropriate office evaluations and objective analysis by experienced auditors will identify those best suited to participate in dental HMOs.

Q: Are quality audits conducted by qualified independent dentists?

Clearly, there is just as much room for abuse in dental HMOs as in fee-for-service dental plans. Therefore, it is essential that any dental HMO include an independent outside quality audit conducted on a periodic basis, by a qualified dentist. Frequency of audits is determined by the findings.

Although many HMOs tout quality assurance, the reality is that few plans use objective standards and criteria or an independent auditor. Most quality assurance audits are performed by dentists employed or retained by the company selling the plan. These individuals may have little to gain by conducting a critical audit. If they are employed by the plan, they should be in a position to be objective and not be subjected to pressures to find unacceptable offices acceptable.

Q: What is the minimum number of enrollees and dental offices?

It is better to have too few offices than too many. Too many dental offices or too few enrollees per office can cause severe antiselection for the dentists and result in the failure of the plan. For example, a dental office that has enrolled five patients at $5 a month, two of whom require $2,000 worth of periodontal services, obviously suffers a severe financial loss. The office has little chance of recouping losses under these circumstances. It is essential that enough lives be enrolled and that an appropriate number of offices be selected so that each dental office has a sufficient enrollee population to make the plan actuarially sound.

More important than the number of offices is their geographic location in relation to enrollees and the offices' ability to see those enrolled on a timely basis. If dental offices are few and not conveniently located, the purchaser may be better off providing other dental plan options than attempting to provide a dental HMO plan in a manner that is bound for failure.

Q: What dental experience does the administrator need?

It is the author's observation that far too many administrators attempt to manage a dental HMO plan as if it were a fee-for-service plan. This can be a costly mistake, for the elements of its success lie in a good relationship between the dentists and the administrator. Success in a fee-for-service plan depends substantially on its claims operations. In dental HMOs, success depends upon the administrator's maintaining good relations with the dental offices.

Dental HMOs demand far more expertise in dental practice and practice economics than other types of dental plans. It is essential to have an administrator who understands all aspects of a dental practice, not only to identify appropriate dental offices for the network, but also to help offices with management problems that may arise.

The administrator must have a dentist experienced in dental HMOs, quality assurance, dental insurance and dental office management to effectively interface with the dental offices. Nondentists may certainly be used for administrative matters, but it is the author's experience that dentists should be used to interface with the dentists at the dental offices.

Q: Should the administrator provide all the services to the plan or should some be subcontracted?

In selecting a dental HMO plan, it is important to review the interrelationship of the various dental options offered. Subcontracting the administration of a dental HMO or professional claims review or the preferred provider network or other aspects to separate entities can result in loose ends, lack of accountability or rigidity.

It is very helpful if the administrator has the capability to administer and provide all necessary services in-house. This ensures a smooth transition for participants electing in or out of various dental plans. Having one administrator usually results in greater flexibility for enrollees. For example, participants should be able to move easily from a PPO into a dental HMO or vice versa. This also provides accountability for the overall benefits administration. Economics of scale made possible by this in-house approach should also result in lower administrative fees.

Q: What percent of program dollars should be spent for dental services, administration and profit?

Percent of dollars to the dentists providing the services. A key question is, "What percent of dollars is going to the dentists providing the services?" Some HMOs are designed so that dentists receive as little as 50% of the dollars paid into the plan. This is not enough to provide appropriate dental care. The incentive can then become to withhold needed treatment. Less-than-ideal dental offices are more likely to be found in this type of plan. Unless extenuating circumstances are present, 70% is the minimum percentage of plan dollars the dentists should receive; 85% is very good; 90% is excellent.

Percent of dollars for administration and profit. When costs for administration and profit exceed 20%, they may be out of line and should be carefully reviewed. Over 25% for administration and profit must be justified. In addition, the purchaser should not pay any cost due to poor management. Between 10% and 15% for administration and profit is usually an indication of a well-managed plan. Under 10% merits careful review, as this is probably too low for a viable plan. However, when administrative costs approach or exceed 30% of premium, it may be to the purchaser's advantage to consider another type of managed care plan, such as a preferred provider organization.

However, there are exceptions. For example, if a plan has its participants spread out in many different locations and the administrator must set up and manage offices at many different geographic locations, administrative costs of up to 30% may be justified. Another consideration: Some fee-for-service dental plans have premiums that are 30-40% higher than a comparably structured dental HMO. Consequently, the fee-for-service dental plan will have more administrative dollars from a 20% administrative factor than a lower premium dental HMO. Assuming that the dental HMO is a well-managed plan, the dental HMO premium decreases and the benefits increase; the dental HMO has additional costs associated for network development and maintenance and for performing effective quality assurance in each dental office.

Any dental HMO that does not clearly identify the percent of dollars going to the dentists for dental services should be carefully evaluated.

If the plan is a closed panel, i.e., the participants must use only one or two dental offices, and the office(s) is principally dedicated to a specific group, there should be no allowance for administrative cost because there is virtually no cost to the office over and above the normal operating cost of operating a dental office.

Administrative costs require careful analysis. This book and your consultant will be able to assist you in that process.

Q: What should a dental HMO plan save?

Typically, a well-structured and -administered dual choice dental HMO will save a minimum of 15-30% over a fee-for-service dental plan with the same benefits. If the dental HMO is a closed panel plan with few offices, savings can approach 50%.

Q: What dental services are provided, and what is the dollar value?

In a dental HMO, it is essential to know the dollar value of the services provided. This may be expressed in terms of the offices' usual fees as they relate to the capitation payments or, in a closed panel, on a time-unit basis described elsewhere in this book.

When a plan has been operating for at least a year, the purchaser should look also at the mix of services that have been provided. There may be wide variations depending upon a group's previous experience, demographics, copayments and deductibles.

One critical area to monitor is the frequency of teeth extractions. A high incidence of extractions can be an indication of a poor plan. The experienced dental auditor will be of great value in evaluating the relevancy of the data.

Q: Is the dentist at risk for care by a dental specialist?

The dentist should be at risk, at least partially, for all dental services except orthodontics. Orthodontics, due to its lifetime maximum, has little impact on total plan cost but can have a negative impact on the dental office through adverse selection. For other services by a dental specialist, such as oral surgery or endodontics, the primary dentist should at least share in the risk. If not, some of the principal incentives created by a dental HMO, such as management of costs and prevention of overtreatment, are compromised.

Some HMOs pay for care by dental specialists on a fee-for-service basis. Payment is usually on a reduced fee schedule basis. If this method is used, it must be closely monitored to assure overtreatment by the specialist does not become a problem. If the services are not properly priced, it is to the primary dentist's advantage to refer patients to a specialist for services he or she could provide because it reduces the services the primary dentist has to provide the patient.

In a dental office, time is money. If referral to a specialist frees an hour of time for the primary dentist to treat someone else, he or she will generate additional income.

If the primary dentists are at risk, they will not mistreat or overtreat when properly selected and monitored, and they will refer patients to a specialist only when appropriate. Also, the primary dentist when at risk is likely to negotiate a better fee arrangement from the specialist than the administrator could.

Q: When does the dental office start receiving payment?

As in any insurance plan, the premium money represents the costs for a few people who will use the plan spread out over the entire group—those who will use the plan and those who will not. Therefore, once this risk is assumed, it is important that the money be in hand to pay for services rendered, even if these services are rendered to only a small portion of the group.

It is fiscally and actuarially essential that the dental offices begin receiving payments the date the plan starts or an individual enrolls. It is the practice in a few plans not to start paying the dental office for services until the enrollee appears at the dental office. The dentist starts supplying services to patients while he or she is receiving capitation payments for those specific people only. The capitation payments are usually not sufficient to cover the costs of treatment. In the meantime, the money being paid for the rest of the group is collected by the plan operator.

Although this chapter has attempted to provide a purchaser of dental HMOs with key questions, ways to "beat the system" are ever-changing and it is wise to be alert for new wrinkles by unscrupulous vendors.

7 Benefit Design

Suggested Dental Benefit Designs for Dental HMOs

Figure 7-1 shows three suggested benefit and payment models for dental HMOs. However, there is a vast array of acceptable combinations and options, including low-cost plans limited to providing diagnostic and preventive services. Plan benefits should reflect the particular needs of the covered group, providing, of course, that critical components of the plan are not violated. The three models are intended to be used as references when designing and/or evaluating benefits in a dental HMO.

The suggested benefit and payment options outlined in Figure 7-1 are levels I, II and III. Exhibit 7-A shows a comprehensive list of services suggested for each of the models, using the American Dental Association's Code on Dental Procedures and Nomenclature.

It is important to keep in mind when reviewing the models and the lengthy list of procedures that 56 dental procedures will represent approximately 93% of the value of the plan in a fairly valued dental plan.

As discussed in Chapter 1, dental HMOs have an entirely different set of incentives and disincentives for dentists than fee-for-service dental plans. The model plans have taken these differences into consideration.

A note of caution. The model plans for dental HMOs

Figure 7-1

DENTAL HMO OPTIONS

SUGGESTED MODELS
(Based upon usual, customary and reasonable charges)*

	Level I	**Level II**	**Level III**
Deductible	None	None	None
Maximum benefits (annual—per individual)	$500-$1,000	$500-$1,000	$1,000-$5,000
Basic Services	**Patient Pays**	**Patient Pays**	**Patient Pays**
Diagnostic	0%	0%	0%
Preventive	0	0	0
Minor restorative	0	0	0
Perio—nonsurgical	50	30	20
Oral surgery—minor	0	0	0
Emergency services	0	0	0
Major Services			
Deductible (annual—per individual)	None to $25	None	None
Crown, inlay and onlay	Not covered	50%	20%
Endodontics	50%	50	20
Prosthetic services	Not covered	50	20
Periodontal—surgical	Not covered	50	20
Orthodontic services	Not covered	50	50
Oral surgery—major	50%	50	50
Lifetime maximum under age 18	NA	$600	$1,000

See following exhibits for detailed list of services covered under each category.
*Dollar amounts may be substituted for percentages by applying the percentage to a fee schedule.

should not be used in the design of fee-for-service dental plans. If they are, it could be a costly mistake.

There are several key points in designing any dental plan. First of all, maintaining good oral hygiene is the most critical element of good dental health. If the patient does not maintain good oral hygiene, the best and/or most expensive dentistry will fail.

Money alone cannot buy good dental health. Of the 8,760 hours in a year, the patient spends very few in the dental office. The dentist cannot maintain a clean mouth for the patient. Within hours of teeth cleaning, patients' good oral health can begin to deteriorate if they do not continue to clean their teeth well. Plaque forms on the teeth. Bacteria multiply and start to infect and damage the teeth and gums. After a short period of time, plaque is almost impossible to remove with a toothbrush. Then, silently and often painlessly, dental disease continues with its costly deterioration of dental health.

The success of dental treatment requires a partnership between the patient and the dentist. If either fails to do his or her part, the result may be expensive—and painful. An example is gum treatments that can cost from several hundred dollars to thousands of dollars. If the patient fails to maintain good oral hygiene, the treatment may have to be repeated—at an additional expense. If the patient shares in the cost of the treatment, especially expensive treatment, the author believes that he or she will have a greater interest in assuring the success of the treatment. For this reason, the model plans are designed to have patients share in the cost of expensive treatment. Cost sharing provides incentives for patients to protect their investments.

Although the need for expensive major services is not always due to patient neglect, the success of these services invariably depends upon the patient's maintaining good oral hygiene after the services are provided.

Therefore:

Rule #1. Incentives should be developed to encourage patients to maintain good oral hygiene, and they should share in the cost of expensive major services and/or services needed because of poor oral hygiene.

"Psychological barriers" can interfere with going to the dentist; in addition, plan designs can erect barriers that discourage regular checkups and needed care. Regular visits to the dentist save money and result in better dental health. Consequently, barriers to basic services—i.e., diagnostic, preventive and minor restorative (tooth-colored and silver fillings)—should be eliminated or drastically reduced.

Although only financial barriers to care are addressed in this section, others that must be kept in mind are geographic and dentist-induced barriers (see Chapter 11).

A study conducted by the Rand Corporation[1] concluded, "Reducing the level of cost sharing increases the demand for dental services." The study found that the demand for services increased 46% when the patients' portion of the cost was reduced from 95% to no out-of-pocket expense. Obviously, cost can be a significant barrier to care. This is reflected in the suggested model plans. There are no financial barriers to basic services.

Geographic barriers are simply a physical access issue. If the offices are not convenient, fewer patients will use them for their dental care.

Among dentist-induced barriers are long waiting times for appointments, long waiting times at the office, few services provided per visit and many other subtle barriers that discourage patients from receiving needed care.

Therefore:

Rule #2. Basic services must be available at little or no cost to the patient. Dental offices must be convenient and there can be no "dentist-induced" barriers.

Extensive and expensive dental treatment, performed to save teeth in very bad condition and with a questionable future, is often referred to as "heroic" dentistry. An example is teeth that have lost almost all of their support—they are loose. A method of treating this condition is to place crowns on all the teeth in order to "splint" them together. This treatment costs as much as $30,000—and will probably fail in a short period of time if the patient does not maintain good oral hygiene. Then, other treatment must be performed at an additional cost. Unless benefit dollars are unlimited, it is best not to cover payment for this type of heroic dentistry. Usually this type of treatment is a plan exclusion.

Keep in mind:

Rule #3. A dental plan cannot afford to pay for everything.

Dental HMO Models

The recommended dental HMO models contain two classifications of services: basic and major services.

Recommended Basic Services

Basic services are the essential component of a dental plan. They are the least costly and the most critical to good oral health. This is where the purchaser gets "a big bang for the buck." These are services almost everyone needs or can use. Because of the low cost and high benefit ratio, there should be no financial barriers to their use. Generally, the more a dental group uses these low-cost procedures, the less it will need high-cost procedures.

The only exception to no patient payment in basic services is periodontal scaling and root planing. The reason for this is that, if a patient does not maintain good oral hygiene, the need for these services can be frequent and the cost significant. This is the one basic service that should have a patient copayment.

Recommended basic services include:

- Diagnostic services consisting of examinations, X-rays and other services as listed in Exhibit 7-A
- Preventive services consisting of prophylaxis (cleaning of teeth), fluoride treatments, nutritional counseling, oral hygiene instruction, sealants (plastic material painted on the tops of newly erupted back teeth to prevent decay from starting) and space maintainers (maintain a space for a permanent tooth when the first tooth is lost prematurely)
- Restorative services consisting of fillings of silver amalgam and tooth-colored resin
- Endodontic services consisting of pulp capping, i.e., placing a treatment in a deep cavity when it is near or involves the tooth's pulp (nerve)

- Nonsurgical periodontal services consisting of scaling and root planing (scraping calculus from the root surface, above and below the gum)
- Oral surgery services consisting of extraction of nonimpacted teeth, removal of small cysts and tumors, preparation of the mouth for dentures, and several other surgical services as listed in Exhibit 7-A
- Adjunctive services consisting of emergency treatment and treatments that are otherwise unclassified services. This is the miscellaneous catch-all for services that do not fit into other categories.

Recommended Major Services

Major services differ from basic services in several ways. They are generally far more expensive, are more likely to fail and, in some cases, may not be necessary to maintaining good oral health. They are the most expensive services and, from a plan coverage perspective, they are not as necessary for good dental health. Unlike basic services, they have a high cost and low benefit ratio. In other words, fewer people will need the services, but the services may represent a significant portion of the cost of a plan.

Major services include:

- Restorative services consisting of crowns (caps) and gold inlays. These services are expensive. It is not uncommon to have crowns, including those in fixed bridges, to account for over 30% of premium dollars while being provided for only 3% of the eligibles. It is the author's opinion that in fee-for-service dental plans, this is the most overused procedure. Many times a filling will permanently correct the problem without the need of an expensive crown.
- Endodontic services consisting of root canals. Although not all root canals are needed because of patient neglect, many are. If the teeth are filled before tooth decay reaches the nerve, there is usually no need for root canal treatment. There are exceptions, of course, such as trauma. A blow to a tooth may cause the nerve to die and root canal treatment will be needed. Because of the expense, it is important for the patient to share in the cost of the procedure.
- Surgical periodontal services consisting of bone and gum surgery. There are few dental services that are as expensive and, at the same time, can fail as quickly, as periodontal treatments. This is one area that absolutely requires the patient to maintain good oral hygiene if the treatment is to be successful. It is the author's opinion, and experience, that when patients share in the cost of dental treatment they have a greater interest in doing their part to assure its success by maintaining good oral hygiene.
- Removable prosthodontic services consisting of removable full and partial dentures. Removable dentures are almost always a far less costly method of replacing missing teeth. A copayment is required because of the cost, although this is not nearly as costly as fixed prosthodontics (see below).

Usually when a patient has teeth missing, it is best to replace them; however, that may not always be the case, particularly if only one or two teeth are missing in the back part of the mouth. Removable dentures are many times referred to as a "less expensive but professionally acceptable" alternative for replacing teeth.

- Fixed prosthodontic services consisting of a permanent or fixed bridge. Fixed bridges are usually composed of crowns (caps) with the replacements (pontics) for the missing teeth attached to the crowns. They usually are far more expensive than removable dentures. It is rare that missing teeth cannot be replaced by a less costly removable denture. Certainly fixed bridges are very comfortable to wear; however, because they are expensive, they are usually considered as an optional treatment to the less expensive removable denture. Patients should pay all cost over and above the cost of replacing the teeth with a less expensive removable denture unless a fixed bridge is the only professionally acceptable treatment. For example, if only one tooth is missing, a removable denture is rarely an acceptable option.
- Orthodontic services consisting of services to reposition the teeth. Orthodontic services are considered to be primarily cosmetic by many. In addition, like periodontics, the success of orthodontic treatment depends largely upon patient cooperation. If the patient does not wear the appliances, having them adjusted when necessary, the treatment may fail. This is compounded by the fact that teeth continue to move on their own, throughout a person's lifetime. And it is not uncommon for retreatment to be necessary. A lifetime maximum benefit for orthodontic treatment in addition to a copayment is essential.

See Exhibit 7-B for a list of major services.

Discussion

Basic and major services appear to send conflicting messages to patients. The plan will remove as many as possible of the financial and geographic barriers that can prevent patients from receiving basic dental services and will encourage their use. For major services, the patients should be required to participate in the cost for the reasons cited above. However, the patients will get the message that if they visit the dentist regularly and maintain good oral hygiene, they will not only have good dental health, but they will also save money.

Unnecessary treatment, particularly very expensive treatment, is rarely a problem in dental HMOs. However, sometimes patients believe they are covered for everything. When this happens, it is necessary to explain that "everything" is not covered. It is important that the patient understands that plans generally do not cover all possible care but cover only "necessary" and "appropriate" dental care. (See Exhibit 7-C.)

Endnote

1. W. G. Manning Jr. et al., "The Demand for Dental Care: Evidence From a Randomized Trial in Health Insurance," *Journal of the American Dental Association* 110 (June 1985).

Exhibit 7-A

Dental HMO—Basic Services

These services ***are considered essential and*** should be provided at no, ***or minimal***, cost to the patient.

Diagnostic

00110 Initial oral examination
00120 Periodic oral examination
00210 Intraoral—complete series (including bitewings)
00220 Intraoral—periapical—first film
00230 Intraoral—periapical—each additional film
00240 Intraoral—occlusal film
00270 Bitewings—single film
00272 Bitewings—two films
00274 Bitewings—four films
00330 Panoramic film
00460 Pulp vitality tests
00470 Diagnostic casts

Preventive

Dental prophylaxis (cleaning teeth)
01110 Prophylaxis—adult
01120 Prophylaxis—child
Topical fluoride treatment
01201 Topical application of fluoride (including prophylaxis)—child
01203 Topical application of fluoride (excluding prophylaxis)—child
01204 Topical application of fluoride (excluding prophylaxis)—adult
01205 Topical application of fluoride (including prophylaxis)—adult
Other preventive services
01310 Nutritional counseling for the control of dental disease
01330 Oral hygiene instruction
01351 Sealant—per tooth
Space maintenance (passive appliances)
01510 Space maintainer—fixed—unilateral
01515 Space maintainer—fixed—bilateral
01520 Space maintainer—removable—unilateral
01525 Space maintainer—removable—bilateral
01550 Recementation of space maintainer

Restorative (basic fillings)

Amalgam restorations (including polishing)
02110 Amalgam—one surface, primary

02120 Amalgam—two surfaces, primary
02130 Amalgam—three surfaces, primary
02131 Amalgam—four or more surfaces, primary
02140 Amalgam—one surface, permanent
02150 Amalgam—two surfaces, permanent
02160 Amalgam—three surfaces, permanent
02161 Amalgam—four or more surfaces, permanent

Resin restorations

02330 Resin—one surface, anterior
02331 Resin—two surfaces, anterior
02332 Resin—three surfaces, anterior
02335 Resin—four or more surfaces or involving incisal angle (anterior)
02336 Composite resin crown—anterior—primary
02380 Resin—one surface, posterior—primary
02381 Resin—two surfaces, posterior—primary
02382 Resin—three or more surfaces, posterior—primary
02385 Resin—one surface, posterior—permanent
02386 Resin—two surfaces, posterior—permanent
02387 Resin—three or more surfaces, posterior—permanent

Other restorative services

02910 Recement inlay
02920 Recement crown
02930 Prefabricated stainless steel crown—primary (first) tooth
02940 Sedative filling
02951 Pin retention—per tooth, in addition to restoration
02970 Temporary crown (fractured tooth)

Endodontics

Pulp capping

03110 Pulp cap—direct (excluding final restoration)
03120 Pulp cap—indirect (excluding final restoration)

Pulpotomy

03220 Therapeutic pulpotomy (excluding final restoration)

Periodontal services

04341* Periodontal scaling and root planing—per quadrant

Oral surgery

Extractions

07110 Single tooth
07120 Each additional tooth
07130 Root removal—exposed roots

Surgical extractions—includes local anesthesia and routine postoperative care

07210 Surgical removal of erupted tooth requiring elevation of mucoperiosteal flap and removal of bone and/or section of tooth

Other surgical procedures

07270 Tooth reimplantation and/or stabilization of accidentally evulsed or displaced tooth and/or alveolus

Alveoplasty—surgical preparation of ridge for dentures
07310 Alveoloplasty in conjunction with extractions—per quadrant
07320 Alveoloplasty not in conjunction with extractions—per quadrant
Removal of tumors, cysts and neoplasms
07430 Excision of benign tumor—lesion diameter up to 1.25 cm
07450 Removal of odontogenic cyst or tumor—lesion diameter up to 1.25 cm
Excision of bone tissue
07470 Removal of exostosis-maxilla or mandible
Surgical incision
07510 Incision and drainage of abscess—intraoral soft tissue
Treatment of fracture—simple
07670 Alveolus—stabilization of teeth, open reduction splinting
Repair of traumatic wounds

Adjunctive general services

Unclassified treatment
09110 Palliative (emergency) treatment of dental pain—minor procedures
Miscellaneous services
09910 Application of desensitizing medicaments

*A copayment is recommended on periodontal scaling and root planing—because if the patient maintains good oral hygiene the need for this service may be reduced significantly.

Exhibit 7-B

Dental HMO—Major Services in Addition to Basic Services

The following services ***should have a reasonably significant patient copayment***.

Services that may not be covered because they are considered cosmetic, alternate treatment or a component of another procedure are noted.

Restorative

Inlay restorations

02510	Inlay—metallic—one surface	Alternate treatment
02520	Inlay—metallic—two surfaces	Alternate treatment
02530	Inlay—metallic—three surfaces	Alternate treatment
02540	Onlay—metallic—per tooth (in addition to inlay)	Alternate treatment
02610	Inlay—porcelain/ceramic—one surface	Cosmetic/alternate treatment
02620	Inlay—porcelain/ceramic—two surfaces	Cosmetic/alternate treatment
02630	Inlay—porcelain/ceramic—three surfaces	Cosmetic/alternate treatment
02640	Onlay—porcelain/ceramic—per tooth (in addtion to inlay)	Cosmetic/alternate treatment
02650	Inlay—composite/resin—one surface (lab processed)	Cosmetic/alternate treatment
02651	Inlay—composite/resin—two surfaces (lab processed)	Cosmetic/alternate treatment
02652	Inlay—composite/resin—three surfaces (lab processed)	Cosmetic/alternate treatment

Crowns—single restoration only

02710	Crown—resin (laboratory)	Component of another procedure
02720	Crown—resin with high noble metal	Cosmetic/alternate treatment
02721	Crown—resin with predominantly base metal	Cosmetic/alternate treatment
02722	Crown—resin with noble metal	Cosmetic/alternate treatment
02740	Crown—porcelain/ceramic substrate	Cosmetic/alternate treatment
02750	Crown—porcelain fused to high noble metal	Cosmetic/alternate treatment
02751	Crown—porcelain fused to predominantly base metal	Cosmetic/alternate treatment
02752	Crown—porcelain fused to noble metal	Cosmetic/alternate treatment

02790	Crown—full cast high noble metal	Alternate treatment
02791	Crown—full cast predominantly base metal	Alternate treatment
02792	Crown—full cast noble metal	Alternate treatment
02810	Crown—¾ cast metallic	
Other restorative services		
02950	Core buildup, including any pins	Alternate treatment
02952	Cast post and core in addition to crown	Alternate treatment
02954	Prefabricated post and core in addition to crown	Alternate treatment
02980	Crown repair, by report	

Endodontics

Root canal therapy (including treatment plan, clinical procedures, and followup care)

03310	Anterior (excluding final restoration)	
03320	Bicuspid (excluding final restoration)	
03330	Molar (excluding final restoration)	
Periapical services		
03410	Apicoectomy/periradicular surgery—anterior	
03421	Apicoectomy/periradicular surgery—bicuspid (first root)	
03425	Apicoectomy/periradicular surgery—molar (first root)	
03426	Apicoectomy/periradicular surgery (each additional root)	
03430	Retrograde filling—per root	
03450	Root amputation—per root	
03470	Intentional replantation (including necessary splinting)	
Other endodontic procedures		
03960	Bleaching of discolored tooth	Cosmetic

Periodontics

Surgical services (including usual postoperative services)

04210	Gingivectomy or gingivoplasty—per quadrant	
04211	Gingivectomy or gingivoplasty—per tooth	
04220	Gingival curettage, surgical, per quadrant, by report	
04240	Gingival flap procedure, including root planing—per quadrant	
04249	Crown lengthening—hard and soft tissue, by report	
04250	Mucogingival surgery—per quadrant	
04260	Osseous surgery (including flap entry and closure)—per quadrant	
04261	Bone replacement graft—single site (including flap entry and closure)	
04262	Bone replacement graft—multiple sites (including flap entry and closure)	
04268	Guided tissue regeneration (includes the surgery and reentry)	
04270	Pedicle soft tissue graft procedure	
04271	Free soft tissue graft procedure (including donor site)	
Adjunctive periodontal services		
04320	Provisional splinting—intracoronal	

Prosthodontics (removable)

Complete dentures (including routine postdelivery care)

05110	Complete upper	
05120	Complete lower	

05130 Immediate upper
05140 Immediate lower

Partial dentures (including routine postdelivery care)

05211 Upper partial—resin base (including any conventional clasps, rests and teeth)
05212 Lower partial—resin base (including any conventional clasps, rests and teeth)
05213 Upper partial—cast metal base with resin saddles (including any conventional clasps, rests and teeth)
05214 Lower partial—cast metal base with resin saddles (including any conventional clasps, rests and teeth)
05281 Removable unilateral partial denture—one piece cast metal (including clasps and pontics)

Adjustments to removable prostheses

05410 Adjust complete denture—upper
05411 Adjust complete denture—lower
05421 Adjust partial denture—upper
05422 Adjust partial denture—lower

Repairs to complete dentures

05510 Repair broken complete denture base
05520 Replace missing or broken teeth—complete denture (each tooth)

Repairs to partial dentures

05610 Repair resin saddle or base
05620 Repair cast framework
05630 Repair or replace broken clasp
05640 Replace broken teeth—per tooth
05650 Add tooth to existing partial denture
05660 Add clasp to existing partial denture

Denture rebase procedures

05710 Rebase complete upper denture
05711 Rebase complete lower denture
05720 Rebase upper partial denture
05721 Rebase lower partial denture

Denture reline procedures

05730 Reline complete upper denture (chairside)
05731 Reline complete lower denture (chairside)
05740 Reline upper partial denture (chairside)
05741 Reline lower partial denture (chairside)
05750 Reline complete upper denture (laboratory)
05751 Reline complete lower denture (laboratory)
05760 Reline upper partial denture (laboratory)
05761 Reline lower partial denture (laboratory)

Prosthodontics, fixed (each abutment and each pontic constitute a unit in a bridge)

Bridge pontics

06210	Pontic—cast high noble metal	Alternate treatment
06211	Pontic—cast predominantly base metal	Alternate treatment
06212	Pontic—cast noble metal	Alternate treatment
06240	Pontic—porcelain fused to high noble metal	Alternate treatment

06241	Pontic—porcelain fused to predominantly base metal	Alternate treatment
06242	Pontic—porcelain fused to noble metal	Alternate treatment
06250	Pontic—resin with high noble metal	Alternate treatment
06251	Pontic—resin with predominantly base metal	Alternate treatment
06252	Pontic—resin with noble metal	Alternate treatment
Retainers		
06520	Inlay—metallic—two surfaces	Alternate treatment
06530	Inlay—metallic—three or more surfaces	Alternate treatment
06540	Onlay—metallic—per tooth (in addition to inlay)	Alternate treatment
06545	Retainer—cast metal for acid etched fixed prosthesis	Alternate treatment
Bridge retainers—crowns		
06720	Crown—resin with high noble metal	Alternate treatment
06721	Crown—resin with predominantly base metal	Alternate treatment
06722	Crown—resin with noble metal	Alternate treatment
06750	Crown—porcelain fused to high noble metal	Alternate treatment
06751	Crown—porcelain fused to predominantly base metal	Alternate treatment
06752	Crown—porcelain fused to noble metal	Alternate treatment
06780	Crown—¾ cast high noble metal	Alternate treatment
06790	Crown—full cast high noble metal	Alternate treatment
06791	Crown—full cast predominantly base metal	Alternate treatment
06792	Crown—full cast noble metal	Alternate treatment
Other fixed prosthetic services		
06930	Recement bridge	
06940	Stress breaker	Alternate treatment
06970	Cast post and core in addition to bridge retainer	Alternate treatment
06971	Cast post as part of bridge retainer	Alternate treatment
06972	Prefab post and core (in addition to bridge retainer)	Alternate treatment
06973	Core buildup for retainer, including any pins	Alternate treatment
06975	Coping—metal	Alternate treatment
06980	Bridge repair, by report	

Oral surgery

Other surgical procedures

07290 Surgical repositioning of teeth

Surgical extractions—includes local anesthesia and routine postoperative care

07220 Removal of impacted tooth—soft tissue

07230 Removal of impacted tooth—partially bony

07240 Removal of impacted tooth—completely bony

07241 Removal of impacted tooth—completely bony, with unusual surgical complications

07250 Surgical removal of residual tooth roots (cutting procedure)

07281 Surgical exposure of impacted or unerupted tooth to aid eruption

Vestibuloplasty

07340 Vestibuloplasty—ridge extension (secondary epithelialization)

07350 Vestibuloplasty—ridge extension (including soft tissue grafts, muscle reattachments, revision of soft tissue attachment, and management of hypertrophied and hyperplastic tissue)

Other repair procedures

07960 Frenulectomy (frenectomy or frenotomy)—separate procedure
07970 Excision of hyperplastic tissue—per arch
07971 Excision of pericoronal gingiva

Orthodontics

Minor treatment for tooth guidance

08110 Removable appliance therapy
08120 Fixed appliance therapy

Minor treatment to control harmful habits

08210 Removable appliance therapy
08220 Fixed appliance therapy

Interceptive orthodontic treatment

08360 Removable appliance therapy
08370 Fixed appliance therapy

Comprehensive orthodontic treatment—transitional dentition

08460 Class I malocclusion
08470 Class II malocclusion
08480 Class III malocclusion

Comprehensive orthodontic treatment—permanent dentition

08560 Class I malocclusion
08570 Class II malocclusion
08580 Class III malocclusion

Other orthodontic devices

08650 Treatment for the atypical or extended skeletal case
08750 Posttreatment stabilization
08999 Unspecified orthodontic procedure, by report

Adjunctive general services

Anesthesia

09220 General anesthesia—first 30 minutes
09221 General anesthesia—each additional 15 minutes
09230 Analgesia
09240 Intravenous sedation

Miscellaneous services

09910 Application of desensitizing medicaments
09930 Treatment of complication (postsurgical)—unusual circumstances, by report
09940 Occlusal guards, by report
09941 Fabrication of athletic mouthguards
09950 Occlusion analysis—mounted case
09951 Occlusal adjustment—limited
09952 Occlusal adjustment—complete

Exhibit 7-C

The following services ***are generally not a benefit for the reasons stated.***

Restorative

Gold foil restorations		
02410	Gold foil—one surface	Alternate treatment
02420	Gold foil—two surfaces	Alternate treatment
02430	Gold foil—three surfaces	Alternate treatment
Other restorative services		
02931	Prefabricated stainless steel crown—permanent tooth	Component of another procedure
02932	Prefabricated resin crown	Component of another procedure
02960	Labial veneer (laminate)—chairside	Cosmetic
02961	Labial veneer (resin laminate)—laboratory	Cosmetic
02962	Labial veneer (porcelain laminate)—laboratory	Cosmetic
03460	Endodontic endosseous implant	Expensive/alternate treatment
Adjunctive periodontal services		
04321	Provisional splinting—extracoronal	Expensive/temporary service
Other removable prosthetic services		
05810	Interim complete denture (upper)	Component of another procedure
05811	Interim complete denture (lower)	Component of another procedure
05820	Interim partial denture (upper)	Component of another procedure
05821	Interim partial denture (lower)	Component of another procedure
05860	Overdenture—complete, by report	Expensive/alternate treatment
05861	Overdenture—partial, by report	Expensive/alternate treatment
05862	Precision attachment, by report	Expensive/alternate treatment

Implant Services

06030	Endosseous implant (in the bone)	Expensive/alternate treatment
06040	Subperiosteal implant	Expensive/alternate treatment
06050	Transosseous implant	Expensive/alternate treatment
06055	Implant connecting bar	Expensive/alternate treatment
06080	Implant maintenance procedures, including: removal of prosthesis, cleansing of prosthesis and abutments, reinsertion of prosthesis	Expensive/alternate treatment
06090	Repair implant, by report	Expensive/alternate treatment
06100	Implant removal, by report	Expensive/alternate treatment
06199	Unspecified implant procedure, by report	Expensive/alternate treatment

Adjunctive general services

Anesthesia

09210	Local anesthesia not in conjunction with operative or surgical procedures	Component of another procedure
09211	Regional block anesthesia	Component of another procedure
09212	Trigeminal division block anesthesia	Component of another procedure
09215	Local anesthesia	Component of another procedure
Miscellaneous services		
09930	Treatment of complication (postsurgical)—unusual circumstances, by report	Component of another procedure

Mix of Services

8

It is recommended that the plan administrator be requested to provide a simple quarterly and annual report listing the mix of services provided by category of services and the percentage of total services represented by each category.

This quarterly report, combined with a report showing the number of discrete individuals using the program, will enable the purchaser to monitor the overall performance of the dental plan on a regular basis. The report should use the categories of services outlined in this chapter. (See Figure 8-1.) This list may then be compared to the *generally expected range* shown in Figure 8-2.[1]

Several words of caution: There is no substitute for an audit of both the dental offices and the utilization reports. One cannot totally rely on this simplified report because it is too easy to "massage" the data to reflect good results. An annual audit is absolutely essential to assure the integrity and quality of the plan.

When using categories of services for plan analysis, individual services are not broken out or analyzed. For example, in the diagnostic category under *expected range of utilization,* the percentage could be within the range listed; however, closer scrutiny may reveal most of the examinations were emergency examinations, usually an indication of a poor plan. So, when comparing the plan's experience with the expected range of utilization in Figure 8-3, it is important to keep in mind the limitations of this type of comparison.

Also, this comparative method does not take into con-

Figure 8-1

Category	Principally Includes
Diagnostic	Examinations, X-rays and various tests
Preventive	Teeth cleanings, fluoride treatments, space maintainers, sealants and education
Basic restorative	Basic fillings of silver (amalgam), tooth-colored fillings (resin), temporary crowns (caps), temporary fillings and cementing crowns and inlays
Crowns and inlays	Crowns (caps) and gold fillings
Endodontics	Root canals, treating tooth nerve
Periodontics	Scaling and root planing, osseous surgery, treating diseases of the gums
Prosthodontics, removable	Replacements for all or a few missing teeth with dentures that are removable by the patient
Prosthodontics, fixed	Replacement of missing teeth with "permanent" bridges (fixed dentures), usually consisting of crowns with missing teeth attached
Oral surgery	In dental plans primarily removing teeth, simple and surgical extractions, impacted teeth and cysts
Orthodontics	Straightening teeth and/or correcting a "bad bite"
Adjunctive general services	Miscellaneous services, emergency treatment, general anesthesia and consultations

sideration the percent of participants using the plan. If only 15% of the participants are using the plan, it is a poor plan even though that 15% may be receiving good care. At a minimum, one should expect at least 50% of participants to use the plan at least one time during a year.

Another problem may be misrepresenting which services were provided. This has not been an infrequent occurrence and has been well documented by, among others, the Pennsylvania Crime Commission[2] in its investigation into dental HMO plans. Although this report is somewhat dated, it is the author's experienced opinion that the practice has not disappeared.

Finally this comparison does not take into consideration many factors such as turnover of participants, age, occupation, length of time participants have been covered by a dental plan and many other variables.

However, the comparison should be valid for an "average group" that has had dental benefit coverage for at least two years.

When monitoring a dental HMO using the expected range of utilization, it is important to understand what is included in the various categories. Figure 8-1 contains the list of recommended categories of services to be used for monitoring a dental plan and a brief explanation of what is included in each category.

Figure 8-2 contains the list of categories of services and the expected range of utilization. *Expected range of utilization* as used here refers to the frequency,

Figure 8-2

Category	Expected Range of Utilization
Diagnostic	35-43%
Preventive	20-28
Basic restorative (fillings)	12-20
Crowns and inlays	2-3
Endodontics	1-2
Periodontics	3-5
Prosthodontics, removable	1-2
Prosthodontics, fixed	1-2
Oral surgery	3-5
Orthodontics	3-6
Adjunctive general services	1-3

expressed as a percentage, that a category of services was performed compared to all services performed.

What to watch out for:

Diagnostic: Unless the covered group just obtained dental benefits for the first time, diagnostic services should not drop below 35%. When a group has coverage for the first time, there is usually an increase in the frequency of fillings, root canals, dentures and other services until the group reaches maintenance, i.e., most of the dental conditions have been corrected. This usually takes one to two years and, as a consequence, the diagnostic services as a percent of all services should increase over time. Once the group is on maintenance, the percentage of treatments decreases and the percentage of diagnostic services will increase. There should be relatively fewer fillings, extractions, root canals, etc., in comparison to the frequency of examinations, X-rays and other tests to check patients' dental health, which should remain relatively constant in terms of frequency.

It is also important to keep in mind that a group with a high turnover is not likely to reach the same level of maintenance as a group with a low turnover. In a group with a high turnover, the mix of services may look more like the first year's experience of a group that has coverage for the first time and the incidence of fillings, root canals, dentures and other services may not decrease over time.

Preventive: The above discussion applies also to preventive services.

Basic restorative—fillings: A group that has coverage for the first time may have over 20% of services in this category. If the level of fillings remains over 20%, it is important to check to see if patients are being seen or treated appropriately. It could signify they are not being treated appropriately. It could also signify that they have a very high rate of decay or the group has a high turnover. If fillings drop below 11% of the total, it may signify that basic needs are not being met and an audit of the dental offices would be in order.

Crowns and inlays: The number of crowns and inlays should decrease significantly in a dental HMO compared to a fee-for-service plan. It is not uncommon to see crowns and fixed prosthodontics (crowns and bridges) represent over 30% of the total dollar equivalent value of services in a fee-for-service dental plan. The significant decrease does not necessarily indicate poor or undertreatment; it usually indicates the elimination of overtreatment. In most cases, a filling is just as adequate, and may be better, than an unnecessary and expensive crown.

Endodontics: In a mature group, endodontics should not exceed 4% of the total services. If it does, it could indicate the patients are not being treated on a timely basis, i.e., the cavities are not being filled and the teeth are becoming abscessed, which necessitates a root canal.

Periodontics: This should remain relatively steady between 3% and 5% of total services, unless the covered group tends to be in the older age category. In that case, a higher incidence than 5% may be appropriate. Over 5% may also indicate an attempt to increase the value of services by classifying teeth cleanings as more costly *scaling and root planings.*

Prosthodontics, removable (dentures): The percentage should remain between 1% and 3% of total services for a mature group. If coverage is new, the percentage may be over 3%. However, it will drop below 3% once the covered group reaches a state of good dental health.

Prosthodontics, fixed (fixed/permanent bridges): This is a method of replacing teeth that uses expensive crowns instead of removable dentures. The same experience discussed under crowns, above, applies to fixed bridges.

Oral surgery: If the percentage goes over 5% of total services, it may indicate the teeth are being extracted instead of being treated or filled.

Orthodontics: Because orthodontics usually involves a large patient copayment and a lifetime maximum plan liability, the percentage rarely exceeds 6%. If this category appears high, look for minor orthodontic services, such as space maintainers, being reported as major, more expensive services in order to increase the apparent value of the services.

Miscellaneous: Any time this category exceeds 4%, it is important to determine the reason. Many times broken appointments, local anesthesia (Novocain) and items that are generally recognized as a component of another service are given a value in order to increase the apparent value of the services provided.

Endnotes

1. The author's classification varies slightly from that of the American Dental Association's (ADA) category of service in that it "breaks out" crowns and inlays. Normally crowns and inlays are classified under the restorative category of service. They are listed as a separate category here because, although the percentage may be small, the impact on cost or value may be very significant. Several ADA categories, maxillofacial prosthetics and implant services, are not used because these services are rarely a benefit in any type of dental plan.
2. Pennsylvania Crime Commission, *Health Care Fraud: A Rising Threat,* December 1981.

Figure 8-3

EXPECTED RANGES OF UTILIZATION (AS A PERCENT OF SERVICES)
IN A COMPREHENSIVE AND MATURE DENTAL HMO

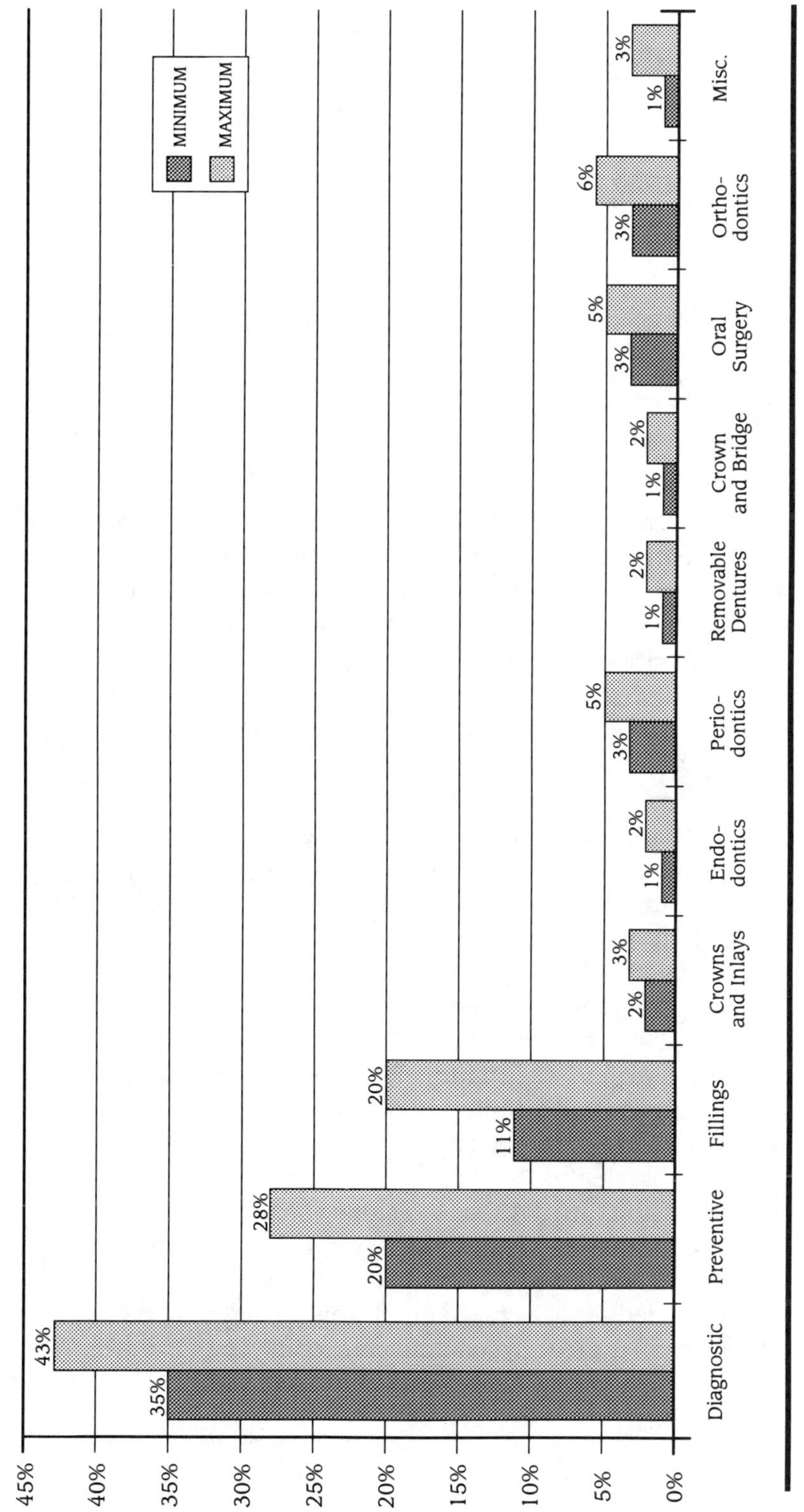

9

Exclusions and Limitations

And now for the small print.

Exclusions and limitations are essential to assure the fiscal integrity of a dental plan and convey (hopefully!) to dentists and covered individuals the limitations of coverage—what will not be covered under the plan.

Exclusions and limitations also should serve to establish priorities for care, prevent abuse and assure cost effectiveness of the plan and should not be restrictive to the point of being a barrier to receiving necessary covered services.

In a fee-for-service dental plan, the exclusions address services that should not be covered. The limitations are a list of services that may be appropriate but may be subject to overtreatment or may be very costly. These exclusions and limitations protect the plan.

In dental HMO plans the dentist is not as likely to overtreat a patient. As a consequence, there is no need for as many, or as restrictive, exclusions and limitations as in a fee-for-service dental plan. As a matter of fact, in dental HMO plans many exclusions and limitations are written to protect the dentist from unwarranted risk; the dentist is the major risk taker in most dental HMO plans.

Exclusions are written to exclude specific items. They usually address nonstandard risks, services and items not intended to be covered by a dental plan.

Excluded services are generally either very expensive (crowning all the teeth), cosmetic (bleaching teeth to make them lighter), disease caused by patient neglect (failure of gum treatments because the patient did not brush and floss), unnecessary services, experimental treatments, services with a poor prognosis or services typically covered by a medical plan.

Limitations usually apply to frequencies (examinations, teeth cleanings and bitewing X-rays limited to two per year), life expectancy of a service (crowns, bridges and dentures limited to once every five years), age limits for certain types of treatment (limiting fluoride treatments to persons 16 years of age and younger) and limitations on expensive types of services (allowing payment for an "adequate," but less costly service, such as removable denture instead of an expensive fixed bridge).

The limitation on expensive or specialized services when a less expensive service would "adequately" correct the condition causes some consternation among patients. As noted in Chapter 2, dentistry has many "alternate" methods of treatment, some of which may be very expensive while at the same time are not essential for good dental health. Unfortunately, many individuals would like to have every service covered. The reality is few plans can afford to cover everything for everyone. They were never meant to; almost all dental plans were designed to assist in providing needed basic dental care. For example, if everyone in a plan with three missing teeth insisted on—and received—a fixed bridge, the cost could be as high as $3,000 for each individual. If a less costly, but adequate, "alternate" removable denture is provided, the cost would be approximately $500—a difference of $2,500! A plan that does not limit this type of risk will either fail or have extremely high premiums. This is usually addressed by an "alternate method of treatment" limitation. This limitation is so important that it usually is broken out under a separate heading from the other limitations in order to call attention to it before expensive services are received.

Exclusions and limitations listed in this chapter are recommended for incorporation in a dental HMO. Comments have been added where appropriate.

Exclusions and Limitations

The following statement should appear in the plan document and summary plan description:

> Not all dental services are covered by the dental benefits plan. Coverage is limited to only those services listed in the plan document and is subject to the following *exclusions* and *limitations*.

Exclusions

Acts of War

> Services required because of, or in connection with, acts of war, declared or undeclared.

Armed Services

Services or supplies paid for or provided because of services in the armed forces of any government.

Benefits at Termination

Dental services or supplies furnished after the date coverage ends are not a covered benefit, any costs becoming the responsibility of the participant. However, the following are exceptions under "work in progress": completion of dentures, crowns, inlays or bridges when the dentist took the impressions and/or prepared the teeth while the participant was covered; and/or root canal therapy if the dentist opened the tooth while the participant was covered; and these services are completed within 60 days of the end of coverage.

Broken Appointments

The cost of broken appointments is not a benefit and shall be the responsibility of the patient.

Comment: Broken appointments can be very costly to a dental office. If office overhead is $90 an hour, a broken appointment may be a $90 loss for the dentist. Many dentists charge for appointments that are not kept unless at least 24-hour notice was given. Patients are often unaware of the fact that dentistry is a very expensive profession to practice and, with the addition of federally mandated infection controls (OSHA), it is becoming more so.

The plan does not pay for these charges.

Cosmetic Services

Charges for services or supplies that are principally cosmetic in nature, including, but not limited to, bleaching, veneers facings, crowns, charges for personalization or characterization of crowns, bridges and/or dentures.

Comment: "Beauty is in the eye of the beholder." Cosmetic dentistry can be very costly. It is a common exclusion in dental plans simply because there seems to be no limit to individuals who want their teeth whiter, straighter, smaller, larger or whatever they perceive will make them more attractive. Cosmetics is a very significant part of the practice of dentistry. The perceived value of cosmetic enhancement cannot be denied; however, it is too costly to include in most dental plans because patient demand simply may be unlimited.

Dental Necessity (Appropriateness)

Services that are not necessary in the judgment of the attending dentist.

Drugs

Prescription drugs, vitamins or dietary supplements are not a covered benefit.

Duplicate Dentures, Appliances or Devices

Duplicate dentures, prosthetic devices or any other duplicate appliances.

General Anesthesia

General anesthesia is not a covered benefit. If the attending dentist determines general anesthesia is medically necessary in connection with a covered service, reimbursement should be sought from the medical plan.

Comment: Medical necessity will exclude unnecessary general anesthesia. There are virtually no dental procedures covered in this plan that would necessitate general anesthesia. The problem is that many patients want it; therefore, it is best to specifically reference it in the exclusions. However, there are exceptions, handicapped individuals as an example. In this example, general anesthesia should be paid by either the medical plan or the administrator.

Harmful Habits

Training and/or appliance to correct or control harmful habits, including, but not limited to muscle training therapy (myofunctional therapy).

Hospitalizaiton

Hospitalization and services rendered in a hospital are not a covered service. If the attending dentist determines hospitalization is medically necessary in connection with a covered service, reimbursement should be sought from the medical plan.

Comment: Hospitalization is rarely, if ever, necessary for covered dental services. There are exceptions: The severely handicapped individual is one instance where the plan should look for coverage under a medical plan or underwrite the risk itself. Few, if any, dental offices can afford to take the risk.

Implants

Implants, surgical insertion and/or removal of, and any appliances and/or crowns attached to implants.

Comment: An implant is usually an artificial root buried in the jaw bone used to attach an artificial tooth or denture. Implants have improved and may be valuable when indicated. However, they are expensive and are not always successful. A less expensive, but satisfactory, method of replacing teeth is almost always an option, i.e., "alternate treatment."

Lost, Missing or Stolen Dentures and Appliances

Replacement of a lost, missing or stolen prosthetic device or orthodontic appliance.

No-Fault

Services paid for under no-fault laws.

Orthodontics (if a benefit)

Expenses for replacement or repair of an orthodontic appliance.

Other Coverage

Services that are covered by any other plan.

Periodontal Splinting

Periodontal splinting (connecting) teeth by any method including, but not limited to, crowns, fillings, appliances or any other method that splints or connects teeth together.

Comment: Splinting teeth because they are loose can be very expensive. It is generally done because the teeth and/or the tissues supporting the teeth are in very bad condition. As in reconstruction, the treatment may involve crowning all, or most of, the teeth. And, if the participant fails to maintain good oral hygiene, the treatment may fail. See previous discussion in this section.

Reconstruction—Crowning Many Teeth and/or Changing the Bite

Services and/or appliances that alter the vertical dimension—change the way the teeth meet (the bite)—including full mouth rehabilitation (crowning all or almost all the teeth), splinting (connecting) teeth with crowns, fillings, appliances or other methods.

Comment: This is heroic, and very costly, dentistry. Usually the teeth and/or the tissues supporting the teeth are in very bad condition. Treatment may involve crowning all or most of, the teeth. And, if the participant fails to maintain good oral hygiene, the treatment may fail. See previous discussion in this section.

Replacement of Existing Dentures

Replacement of existing dentures that are, or can be made, satisfactory.

Self-Inflicted Injury or Illness

Charges resulting from voluntary self-inflicted injury or illness, whether the patient is sane or insane.

Services by Other Than Primary Dentist

Services rendered, or ordered, by other than the primary, attending dentist, when participant is enrolled under this program. (See out-of-area treatment in limitation section.)

Services Necessary Because Patient Failed to Cooperate

The costs for any services that are necessary because the participant failed to cooperate and/or maintain good oral hygiene are the responsibility of the participant and are not a benefit.

Comment: As discussed previously in this section, unless the patient maintains good oral hygiene, the finest dental care will probably fail. In addition, patient cooperation is essential in wearing appliances and keeping appointments when under treatment. For example, if a root canal treatment is started and the patient fails to return on a timely basis, the tooth may become reinfected and the process will have to be repeated.

Services Performed Before Effective Date

Dental procedures performed before the effective date are the responsibility of the participant.

Services/Supplies That Are Experimental, Nonstandard, Not Recommended or Approved by the Treating Dentist

Services or supplies that are not necessary, according to accepted standards of dental practice, or are not recommended nor approved by a dentist, or are experimental in nature.

Comment: This addresses a whole range of services that the patient may want or request of the dentist that may be unnecessary, unrelated to the problem or harmful to the patient. The treating dentist must make the decision about what constitutes acceptable, needed care, subject, of course, to the professional review that should be a component of the program.

TMJ-Related Services

Diagnostic services and treatment of jaw joint problems by any method. These jaw joint problems include such conditions as temporomandibular joint (TMJ) syndrome and craniomandibular disorders or other conditions of the joint linking the jaw bone and skull and the complex of muscles, nerves and other tissues related to that joint.

Comment: *TMJ* refers to the temporomandibular joint, the joint linking the lower jaw to the upper jaw. Problems with this joint have been reported to be caused by everything from flat feet to poor posture. Treatment ranges from hot compresses to radical surgery of the jaws. While there is no question that serious problems can, and do, occur with the temporomandibular joint, there is also no question that it may be one of the most overtreated entities in dentistry. Until sound scientific studies are more supportive of the wide variations in treatment, it is best to completely exclude any form of treatment of TMJ in dental (and medical) plans.

Transportation

Transportation is not a benefit.

Workers' Compensation

Services that are covered by any workers' compensation laws or employers' liability laws, or services that an employer is required by law to furnish in whole or in part.

Limitations

Age Limitations

Age limitations apply as follows:

Orthodontics (if a benefit): Payments limited to participants under 19 years of age.

Alternate Treatment

If a condition can be corrected or treated by professionally acceptable service at a lower cost, the plan covers only the lower cost service. If a participant chooses a more costly service or treatment, he or she is responsible for the difference in cost.

Alternate treatment may include, but is not limited to, use of gold, crowns, inlays, fixed bridges, dentures and partial dentures.

Gold: If a participant elects gold for fabrication of a filling, crown, denture or appliance instead of a less expensive but adequate material, the participant will be responsible for the difference in cost for using gold.

Crowns and Inlays: If a regular amalgam (silver) or resin (white) filling will adequately restore (fill) a tooth and the participant and the dentist decide on a more costly crown or inlay, the benefit allowed is for the less costly filling. The participant will be responsible for any cost in excess of the least expensive and professionally adequate alternative treatment.

Fixed Bridges: If a removable partial denture will restore the dental arch satisfactorily, only the appropriate amount for such a denture will be allowed toward a fixed bridge that the participant and his dentist may choose to use. The participant will be responsible for any cost in excess of the least expensive and professionally adequate alternate treatment.

Dentures: If, in the provision of dentures, the participant and the dentist decide on personalization of the denture or specialized techniques instead of standard procedures (such as an over denture), the value of the standard service will be applied to the more costly service.

The participant will be responsible for any cost in excess of the least expensive and professionally adequate alternate treatment.

Removable Partial Dentures: If a cast chrome or acrylic partial denture will restore the dental arch satisfactorily, only the appropriate amount for such a denture will be allowed toward a more elaborate or precision appliance that the participant and the dentist may choose to use. The participant will be responsible for any cost in excess of the least expensive and professionally adequate alternate treatment.

Comment: Dentistry can be very expensive. As discussed in Chapter 2, there may be a number of different ways to treat a dental condition, all professionally acceptable, but carrying significantly different costs. This limitation allows the dentist and patient the freedom to choose a more expensive course of treatment while protecting the financial integrity of the plan.

Comment: The list of covered services is quite extensive and covers over 99% of needed dental services. Those not listed are either very expensive, experimental, controversial, generally not considered a dental benefit or are a component of another procedure.

Covered Services

Services are limited to those listed in the plan document. If a service is not listed, it is not a benefit.

Dollar Limitations—Maximum Benefit Allowance

Dollar limitations apply as follows:

Plan Maximum (not including orthodontics): Maximum allowance for dental services by plan is $ _________ per year for each participant.

Orthodontics (if a benefit): Maximum allowance is limited to a lifetime benefit of $ _________.

Oral Surgery

Oral surgery is limited to removal of teeth, preparation of the mouth for dentures and removal of tooth-generated cysts up to 1.25 cm.

Comment: Because of wide variation in the types of surgical services dentists may provide from state to state and hospital to hospital, it is virtually impossible to define *oral surgery* for insurance purposes. There are over 200 oral surgery procedures that may be classified as either *dental* or *medical*. Over 90% of routine oral surgery costs consist of procedures encompassed within this limitation. Fractured jaws, tumors, salivary gland problems and a host of other procedures should be covered and paid under the medical plan. If, for example, a lesion in the mouth must be biopsied to determine if it is cancerous, it should be covered by the medical plan. If a lesion is removed so dentures will fit better, it is then preparation of the mouth for dentures, and it should be covered by the dental plan.

Out-of-Area Emergency

If you are at least 50 miles from home and have a dental emergency, the dental plan will reimburse you up to $50 for necessary emergency services. It is necessary to submit a paid receipt listing the services and the charge(s).

Services Ordered by Primary Dentist

Services and/or treatments are limited to those ordered or prescribed by the primary dentist, subject to the terms and conditions of the dental plan. The *primary dentist* is the dentist or dental office where the participant is enrolled. Services and/or treatments ordered by any other dentist, either prior to coverage, or during coverage by the participant in this plan, are not covered under this dental plan.

Time Limitations

Time limitations apply as follows:

Dentures, Full and Partial: Once in a five-year period
Crowns, Bridges and Inlays: Once in a five-year period.

Services That Should Not Be Excluded or Limited in a Dental HMO

Preventive Services

Sealants, athletic mouth guards, oral hygiene instruction, plaque control program and dietary or other educational programs.

Teeth Missing Prior to Coverage

Replacement of natural teeth extracted or missing prior to effective date of coverage.

Time, Age and/or Frequency Limits

No limits on examinations, teeth cleanings (prophylaxis), fluoride treatments, X-rays, sealants, oral hygiene instructions and other educational programs. These are, however, subject to the "patient failed to cooperate" exclusion.

10

Checklist of Good Plan Design and Management

The following is a list of factors that are suggested as a checklist for assessing dental HMO plan design and management. The more factors that are utilized, the surer the purchaser is of a quality dental plan and ongoing cost management.

Request for Proposal

- Request for proposal (RFP) sent to a minimum of three reputable entities.

Administrator

- Has experience with dental HMOs
- Employees experienced in dental HMOs to communicate with and visit dental offices
- Has satisfied clients.

Enrollment

- Plan is dual choice, i.e., patients have the option of either a dental HMO or a fee-for-service plan.
- Participants must select (positive choice/opt in) dental HMO and are not assigned to the plan.
- Participants have an annual option to change to or from a fee-for-service plan.

Premium and Value

- No more than 56 dental procedures equals 93% of plan value.

- If plan is a closed panel dental plan and dentists are salaried, the premium is substantially less than a fee-for-service plan with comparable benefits.
- If dental services are provided principally by salaried dentists, then valuation of services is by time-unit value method.
- If the purchaser contracts directly with a private dental office(s) for dental care, valuation of services is by time-unit method and no fee should be paid for administration.
- If plan provides dental services principally with private, nonsalaried dentists in multiple offices, valuation of services should not be greater than the equivalent of the Health Insurance Association of America (HIAA) 50th percentile.
- Increases in premiums are less than the increases in the dental component of the Consumer Price Index.
- A minimum of 70% of dollars goes to dentists for providing care.
- Retention (administration and profit) does not exceed 15% without justification.

Reports

Annual reports are provided to purchaser that reflect:

- Number and percent of discrete individuals using the plan
- Services provided by category (number and value—by totals and percent): diagnostic, preventive, basic fillings, crowns and inlays, endodontics, periodontics, removable dentures, fixed bridges, oral surgery and orthodontics
- Individual services provided by type, frequency (number and percent) and value
- Services provided to each individual patient by Social Security number, name, relationship, date, type, frequency, value and copayment or deductible, if any.

Participant satisfaction surveys are conducted.

No unbundling or fragmentation is used to increase the value of services, i.e., placing a value on a service that is considered a component of another service, for example, a separate value for an injection in conjunction with a filling.

ADA procedure codes are used.

Audits

- Dental offices have qualified for participation by passing a quality audit.
- Independent, experienced auditor selected by the purchaser performs an annual audit of administrator's reports on utilization and quality—random or extensive as conditions warrant.
- Administrator conducts ongoing dental office utilization and quality audits.
- Quality assurance system has written criteria and guidelines.

Dental Offices

- ZIP code analysis assures dental offices are convenient to participants: 80% of eligibles are within 20 minutes of a dental office.
- A list of participating dental HMO dentists is available to beneficiaries when the dental plan is offered.
- List of participating dentists includes:
  - Address
  - Phone number
  - Hours
  - Names and number of dentists in each office
  - Dental school attended and date of graduation
  - Dental specialists: name, type of specialist and whether board eligible or certified
  - Number of dental chairs
  - Number and types of staff
  - Emergency care procedures
  - Services likely to be provided at first appointment
- An annual or periodic independent audit to certify dental offices meet accepted standards of dental care and are accurately reporting data
- First visit within four weeks of request
- First visit includes: examination by doctor, X-rays if indicated and teeth cleaning.
- Followup appointments are available within three weeks.
- As many services as possible are performed during a visit.
- No value is assigned for broken appointments.
- Patients are notified of future checkup appointment.
- Emergency coverage is available 24 hours a day, seven days a week.
- Patient complaints are responded to within four working days—record of complaints and resolutions is maintained for review by purchaser.
- Charges for noncovered services are itemized, and patient is informed in writing prior to services being performed.
- Dental offices have agreed by contract to report all services provided, comply with OSHA standards, be audited and to correct any problems.

11 Tricks and Traps

The unwary purchaser of a dental HMO plan may be "tricked" by games played by either the plan administrator and/or the dental office or "trapped" by a contract that is flawed by significant omissions.

As stated in Chapter 1, dental HMOs have a different set of incentives for dentists than fee-for-service plans. As a consequence, purchasers cannot rely on experience gained or use the same auditing procedures as used in fee-for-service plans to monitor dental HMOs. In fee-for-service plans the primary auditing activities by, or on behalf of, the purchaser are directed toward the administrator. In HMO plans the primary emphasis for audit is the dental office, because in dental HMOs the risk shifts dramatically to the dentist.

A purchaser should not accept, or sign, a fee-for-service contract that is rewritten for a dental HMO plan. The contract for providing dental benefits on a capitated basis must be written to reflect the significant difference between the two types of plans. Listed in this chapter are some of the "tricks and traps" the author has observed being used by unethical dental HMO operators and dentists, either to falsely increase the value of services and/or create the mythical impression that they have a "great" dental plan. These issues become extremely important in closed panel dental HMOs, i.e., those in which the patient must use a panel dentist or receive no dental benefits.

It is important to keep in mind that this section does not contain a complete list of tricks and traps. An exhaustive list cannot be developed because the dishonest person's ability to "play games" far exceeds the author's capability to maintain a current list of all possibilities. Therefore, the reader is cautioned to view these only as examples and not as a complete list.

It is also prudent for the purchaser to have the contract with the administrator, and the administrator's contract with the dentists, reviewed by an attorney and a dental consultant.

As explained in Chapter 1, there are two ways for a dentist to make money in a dental HMO—either treat the disease and get patients into a maintenance mode or do as little as possible and discourage patients from seeking and/or receiving care. The dentist is paid the same capitation payment regardless of the number and types of dental services provided. Theoretically, the dentist could see no patients and still receive substantial capitation payments. When a number of the following tricks and traps are combined by the unscrupulous plan operator, the purchaser may overpay significantly for the plan.

TRICKS

Barriers to Care

Barriers to care may be invisible or subtle and still be extremely effective. If the patients do not show up at the dental HMO office, the dentist may gain financially. The author has seen widespread use of the subtle barriers discussed below.

Geographic Accessibility

A dental HMO may tout full coverage, wonderful dental office(s), availability of specialists and attractive facilities. All that is of little value if the facility is not easily accessible to the participants.

The number and location of dental offices is critical. The greater the number of dentists participating and the closer the dental office(s) is to the participants, the greater the utilization. Travel time of over one-half hour will sharply limit utilization. A ZIP code analysis of the participants' locations relative to the dental office(s) is essential.

Appointment Control

Discouraging patients through appointment control is generally done by one, or all, of the following.

Long wait for initial appointment. The maximum waiting time for an initial or checkup appointment should be four weeks. (Emergencies should be seen either within three hours or within 24 hours, depending upon the type of emergency.) When patients call for an appointment, they may have to wait six weeks or more. The author has seen waiting times of up to two and three months, and that is just for the initial appointment.

Long wait between appointments. The maximum time between appointments should be three weeks. After waiting six weeks for an initial appointment, it is not unusual to see the same waiting time occur as for a treatment appointment.

Long wait at the dental office. The term *waiting room* takes on a new meaning. After waiting weeks for an appointment, patients face another subtle invisible barrier when they have to wait long after their appointment time.

Short appointments and/or few services per visit. The author has seen plans that use the following scenario to discourage visits to the dental office:

- First visit—X-rays
- Second visit—teeth cleaned
- Third visit—examination
- Fourth visit—one filling (of many needed) done
- Fifth visit—one more filling done.

With the above obstacles, it is not surprising that participant use of some plans is less than 10%. Few individuals have the luxury of time to waste. Consequently, they may decide it is easier to go to another dentist, even though they may have to pay for the services out of their pockets. This is exactly what the unscrupulous dentist in a closed panel dental HMO plan hopes to achieve: low utilization. The fewer participants seen and the fewer services provided, the higher the profits. The dentist is paid per participant, not per service.

Patient Copayments and Deductibles

Patient cost is a barrier to care. A study conducted by the Rand Corporation[1] demonstrates the dramatic impact reducing the cost barrier can have on the use of a dental plan. In the study, first year use was 69% when no payment was required of the patient. Only 47% used the plan when they were required to pay 95% of the cost. The study found the impact of cost sharing was greater for low-income groups, who had 46% more visits when there was no cost sharing than when they had to pay 95% of the cost.

The impact of deductibles and copayments is obvious. As the patients' financial liability is increased, the likelihood they will use the plan decreases.

This study supports the author's contention that there should be no cost barrier to basic services, i.e., checkups, teeth cleanings, extractions, emergency care, and silver and white filings (see Chapter 7). There should be no deductibles or copayments on these basic services.

Copayments and deductibles. If copayments and/or deductibles are to be used, they should apply to major services only. If the plan needs to have a low premium, it may be acceptable to have a deductible and/or a copayment on basic fillings. If this is necessary, it should be kept as low as possible. However, it is strongly recommended that no deductibles or copayments be placed on diagnostic or preventive services. The key is to encourage the patient to get into the dental office, get a checkup, find out if anything needs to be done and have it corrected before the problem becomes more serious and costly to treat. Once a patient finds out there is a problem, it is more likely he or she will have it treated.

Maximums. In reality an *annual maximum* on benefits in a dental HMO usually has little impact or significance except for dentists providing services in the plan. It offers them some protection by placing a maximum dollar limit on the services they are required to provide. Plan maximums are rarely reached because the dentist has no incentive to overtreat or provide unnecessary or expensive treatment. Orthodontics is an exception. Because it is usually cosmetic and "relapse" may be frequent, it is essential to limit liability, usually with a lifetime maximum.

False Value

Broken Appointments

There are several key points to be made.

The ethical dentist who reserves time exclusively for a patient suffers a loss when the patient does not show up. Broken appointments can cost the dentist from $60 to $90 per hour in fixed costs. If time is reserved exclusively for a patient and the patient does not keep the appointment or notify the dentist, the dentist is entitled to be paid for that empty and lost chair time.

Most dentists understand, and forgive, broken appointments due to an unforeseen emergency, but emergencies are uncommon. The patient who just decides not to show up should bear the burden of paying for the empty chair time.

Secondly, there is no rationale for a plan to recognize broken appointments as a "benefit." Allowing a value for broken appointments is indefensible and a breach of fiduciary responsibility by the purchaser. It sends the wrong message to both the participant and the dentist. Paying for an individual's irresponsibility is, well, irresponsible. Also, in dental HMOs the unethical dentist takes advantage of this "benefit" by overbooking, by scheduling more than one patient in the same time period, similar to the way airlines handle "no shows." The dentist may also accept walk-ins, people who just show up or have an emergency. Unethical dentists do not care if patients break appointments if the plan allows a "value" for the broken appointment. The unethical dentist, by overbooking and not discouraging broken appointments, is paid for the broken appointments while working on other patients. In most plans reviewed by the author, allowing a value for broken appointments becomes nothing more than a bonus for unethical dental offices.

Increasing Value

When the value, or premium, of a dental plan is based upon the number and value of services provided, many times tricks are employed to increase the apparent value of a dental plan. Listed below are some of the most frequent methods used to create an illusion of value.

Upgrading or Upcoding

Upgrading is reporting a more complex, and higher value, procedure than the one actually performed. Reporting these services is not in itself an indication

Figure 11-1

Reported as	May Be Upgraded From
Ten or more periapical X-rays reported separately	Full mouth X-rays
Scaling and root planing	Teeth cleaning
Two surface filling	One surface filling
Three surface filling	One or two surface filling
Four surface filling	One, two or three surface filling
Crown with precious metal (gold)	Crown with little or no gold
Surgical extraction	Simple extraction
Full bone impacted tooth	Soft tissue, partial impacted tooth or surgical extraction
Partial bone impacted tooth	Soft tissue impacted tooth or surgical or simple extraction

that upgrading is occurring. The key is the frequency with which they are reported. Examples are shown in Figure 11-1.

Fragmentation

Fragmentation or *unbundling* refers to adding a separate value to a service that is already a component of that service. The examples in Figure 11-2 show services broken out or reported as two or more values when only one value should be reported.

Using Higher Than HIAA 50th Percentile to Value Services

The best determination of fair value for a dental HMO is to find out what those services could have been purchased for in that specific market. The best source of this information, if it is available, is to be found in the fees accepted by dentists participating in a preferred provider organization (PPO). It is common for networks of dentists to accept fees that are less than the average fee being charged in the community.

It is not uncommon for some plans, particularly closed panels, to value individual services at the 90th percentile, i.e., only 10% of dental services in that area cost more. That is extremely high and nothing more than an effort to inflate the value of the plan.

If fees from a local PPO are not available, the HIAA (Health Insurance Association of America) 50th percentile of dentists charges is a good benchmark to determining value of dental services. The HIAA 50th percentile should be used principally with dental offices that are performing fee-for-service dentistry (see Chapter 17).

Figure 11-2

Reported as	And Performed With
Emergency examination	Root canal, denture adjustment, etc.
Over two examinations per year	Root canal, denture, etc.
Injection (Novocain)	Filling, extraction, etc.
Oral hygiene instruction	Teeth cleaning
Periapical X-ray	Root canal treatment
Bitewing X-rays	Full mouth X-ray
Temporary filling	Inlay or root canal
Protective base (under filling)	Filling
Temporary crown	Permanent crown
Cementing crown	Crown
Indirect pulp cap	Filling
Pulpotomy	Root canal
Denture adjustment	Within six months of receiving denture
Occlusal adjustment	Within six months of receiving denture
Office visit	Any services—just an additional charge unless after hours
Palliative treatment	Any services—usually just an additional charge
Postoperative treatment	Oral or periodontal surgery
Suturing	Oral or periodontal surgery

Unique Codes

In addition to the above, some dentists will report "unique codes" developed to artificially increase value. Examples are: denture try-ins, delivery of dentures, root canal in progress, root canal medication, acid etch, light cure (in addition to filling), impressions and suture removal.

Enrollment

Opt-Out Enrollment

This is a clever way for the plan administrator to make money at the expense of the purchaser, participants and the dentists providing services for the plan. It is frequently seen when participants, supposedly, have the option between two or more dental plans. Patients are enrolled in the dental HMO unless they specifically select another type of plan. Many times as high as one-third of the participants are not aware they are enrolled in the dental HMO until they go to their "regular dentist" and find out they have no benefits. In the meantime the administrator is pocketing the premium for that patient. It is not paid to any dentist for care. This may be combined with the following tactic.

Withholding Payment to Dentists

Payment to the dentists does not start until the patient calls for an appointment. In this ploy, the plan does not begin paying the dentist a capitation fee until the patient calls for an appointment. This places an undue burden upon the dentist in that he or she is being paid a capitation fee only for the users rather than the eligible population. In the meantime the administrator is pocketing the premium for nonusers. The author believes profits and administration in this type of an arrangement can reach as high as 50-70% of premium.

Traps

It is critical when purchasing a dental HMO plan that the purchaser is not "trapped" into a poor plan because of an inadequate contract or not taking the right precautions. After a plan is selected and the contract is signed, the purchaser is in a poor negotiating position to obtain needed changes. If the purchaser does not avoid the traps listed below, the purchaser and the participants may pay dearly for the lack of foresight—the purchaser will suffer financially and the participant may not receive needed care.

Some common traps are listed below.

Less Than Three Bids Solicited

It is essential to put any dental program out for bid. It is so elementary that it would appear unnecessary to mention it. However, the author frequently has seen instances where this has not happened; as a result, the purchaser received poor value, and the participants received a poor plan. No fewer than three viable bids should be solicited.

No Audited Statement of the Dollars Going to Dentists

It is not uncommon to see less than half of the dollars paid to an administrator going to the dentists for providing care. A report containing this information, on an annual basis, is an essential component of the purchaser's contract with the administrator (see Chapter 14).

No Independent Audit of Dental Offices

The administrator should perform preselection and ongoing audits of the dental offices. However, the purchaser should have the right, by contract, to have the dental offices audited by an experienced outside auditor of his or her choice (see Chapter 16 on audits) if there is any concern about the validity of the administrator's audit reports.

The dental office audit consists of several parts. The first is a record audit to verify that what was reported was actually performed. The second part of the audit is to verify that dental care provided is at an acceptable level of care (see Chapter 15).

The old warning against "the fox guarding the chicken coop" is apropos when the purchaser permits the plan administrators to audit their own dentists without having the audits reviewed by an independent consultant. If an independent audit is not done, the process is inherently flawed because of the obvious conflict of interest. The author is amazed at how widespread is the practice of accepting at face value an administrator's dental office audits. All dental office auditing must be reviewed by the purchaser's consultant and, if necessary, an audit should be performed by an independent entity retained and paid for by the purchaser. To do otherwise is foolhardy.

What appears in a presentation or proposal as a dental plan offering quality dental care at a reasonable cost and what is actually being provided may be two different things. Without the contractual capability to have independent audits performed, the purchaser may unknowingly be trapped in a dental HMO plan providing poor value and poor quality care.

Audits for quality of care are essential because the participants cannot evaluate the quality of the services provided. The patient has virtually no ability to judge the quality of care being provided. Time after time the author has observed personable dentists who provide low-quality care but have quite large practices.

No Annual Reporting of the Number of Discrete Individuals Using the Plan

It is common to see reports reflecting the number of visits and the number of times patients visited the dental office in the plan. What is not common, and is essential for monitoring the acceptability of the plan, is the number of *different individuals* who use the plan on an annual basis. Quality of care also encompasses the number of participants using the plan. If 10% receive excellent care and 90% are left out of the plan, it is not an acceptable plan.

No or Inadequate Utilization Data and/or Reports

(See Chapter 14.) No data is worse than false data. With no data there is not only no way to check on its validity, there is just no way to check on anything. Yet, in spite of this obvious major flaw, many dental HMO plans being sold today do not provide any meaningful utilization data. The purchaser must insist, by contractual obligation, that the administrator provide meaningful utilization data.

Falsifying data is as old as recordkeeping. An audit of the utilization data is an essential component of a plan. What is provided and supporting documentation must be a part of every contract.

Little or No Experience in Administering Dental HMO Plans

Few dentists have experience in insurance matters. Few administrators have experience running dental offices. The problems begin when both think the other's job is easy. A dental office or an inexperienced administrator may develop and market a "dental plan" without the experience in both areas required to make a dental HMO work.

An audited financial statement and a review of the administrator's experience are essential. A smart purchaser will call former and current clients before making a commitment and also call the dentists participating in the plan. Otherwise, the purchaser may be left holding the bag.

Automatic Premium Escalation

It is not unusual to see multiyear contracts with annual automatic increases in premium that are not related to the value of the services received. Automatic increases should not be permitted unless they are related to the value of the services received. All reports on the value of services must be audited.

Not Experience Rated

Experience rating refers to determining the value or premium for a particular group based upon that group's own experience; i.e., if the value of services received is greater than the premium paid, the group will pay more. On the other hand, if the value of the services received is less than the premium, the group will get a refund or a reduced premium.

It is important that a purchaser not be trapped into paying a fixed premium without an agreement to adjust premiums based upon experience. An audited annual accounting of the value of services provided, plus an allowance for administration, is an essential component of a contract for the purchasers of dental HMO plans. A rebate may be in order if the utilization is below expectations and the administrator has paid less than 70% of premium to the dentists providing the services. The purchaser must not be trapped into paying an exorbitant premium. However, a good plan may have higher-than-expected utilization for several years and then lower utilization than expected. To allow for this, there should be a carry forward provision.

Fraud

The methods for fraudulently obtaining premiums are limited only by the imagination of the perpetrators. Fraud can be perpetrated at any level, from total fabrication of utilization data to falsification of administrative cost. A few of the fraudulent practices most frequently observed by the author are: falsification of services provided, reporting services not provided, duplicate reporting and games with administrative cost.

Preexisting Condition Exclusion

A preexisting condition exclusion has no place in a dental HMO plan. A contract that contains this exclusion is not acceptable.

Endnote

1. W. G. Manning Jr. et al., "The Demand for Dental Care: Evidence From a Randomized Trial in Health Insurance," *Journal of the American Dental Association* 110 (June 1985).

12

Dental Health Maintenance Organizations

It should be relatively easy to find dental health maintenance organizations (HMOs) in your area. There are an increasing number of dental plans patterned after the HMO model. In fact, the growth rate reported by these plans in 1991—25%—is reminiscent of the explosive growth of the medical HMO market in the 1980s. Growth rates for 1992 were recently reported at 17%, bringing enrollment in these plans to approximately 12 million. Dental HMOs appear to be the most rapidly growing segment of dental benefit plans. Dental HMOs are known by many names. Many original state statutes licensing dental HMOs called them *dental service organizations* or *dental plan organizations.* More recent statutory licensing schemes refer to them as *single service HMOs, prepaid dental plans* or *prepaid limited health service organizations.* In some states dental HMOs are licensed under general insurance company statutes, making them even more difficult to identify. By any name, these plans have a key factor in common. That factor is the replacement of *fee-for-service* reimbursement with *capitation* or payment of the dentist on a per member/per month basis. In the early 1990s the growth in these plans and other single service benefit plans led the National Association of Insurance Commissioners (NAIC) to develop a recommended pattern for operation and regulation of dental and other single service HMOs. The growing dental HMO industry was active in the development of this model act entitled the "Prepaid Limited Health Service Organization Model Act" (see Appendix J).

This model focuses regulation on the financial and basic operational structure of limited health service plans. It establishes basic provisions for financial systems, evidence of coverage and provider networks of dental HMOs. It also requires a complaint system and provides for examination of these companies.

State Agencies

A good source of information on dental HMOs available in a particular state is the state licensing or regulatory authority. The most common licensing/regulatory authority is the Department of Insurance in a particular state. Some states, however, are regulated by the Department of Corporations (California), or the Department of Health (Minnesota), or a combination (the Department of Insurance and the Department of Health in Pennsylvania). If the state requires licensure, or some other approval process, a listing of currently operating dental HMOs should be available from one of these agencies.

Benefit Consultants

Your benefit consultant may be another source of information. Consultants are generally knowledgeable about the plans available in a given area. However, since the structure of this industry is relatively new and different from that of the general insurance industry, consultants' knowledge may be limited. This industry has a plethora of single state or regional companies as opposed to a large number of nationally recognized insurers or administrators. The single state or regional companies often network to service businesses that are seeking coverage over a large number of states.

National Association of Prepaid Dental Plans (NAPDP)

The National Association of Prepaid Dental Plans was formed by the dental HMOs active in the debate over a model act for prepaid dental plans. A criterion for membership in the association is compliance with the financial and operational standards outlined in the model act. The association maintains the most comprehensive listing of operational dental HMOs. Its listing is published here with permission. A more current listing and/or a copy of the model act can be obtained from the association, which can be contacted at the following address:

Evelyn F. Ireland, Executive Director
National Association of Prepaid Dental Plans
One College Park, Suite 620
8910 Purdue Road
Indianapolis, Indiana 46268
(317) 871-7283 FAX (317) 871-7270

All members of NAPDP provide dental capitation (prepaid) benefits through a network of contracted dentists. Many members also offer traditionally insured dental plans, PPO plans and administrative services only (ASO) arrangements along with their capitation plans. Member companies operate in 48 states and have more than 12 million enrollees. Most states require dental HMOs to be licensed, and licensure is a criterion for membership in NAPDP. However, some states do not require licensing.

The information contained in this chapter about company operations has been provided by member companies of NAPDP and individual companies. (See Exhibit 12-A.) It has not been independently verified by NAPDP or the author. Neither the association nor the author is endorsing any listed company or its dental plan.

Exhibit 12-A

Members of the National Association of Prepaid Dental Plans

Advantage Dental Health Plans, Inc.
8000 N. University Drive
Ft. Lauderdale, FL 33321-2118
(305) 724-4188
FAX (305) 724-4230
Sales Contact(s):
Tim Donoho, President
Operations Since: 1984
Service Area(s): Licensing Authority:
Missouri/Kansas/Florida—Division of Insurance
Oklahoma/Illinois/Washington, DC

Alpha Dental Plan of Colorado, Inc.
1873 South Bellaire, #935
Denver, CO 80222
(303) 691-5166
FAX (303) 691-5199
Sales Contact(s):
R. K. McFarland, Executive Vice President of Marketing
Operations Since: 1990
Service Area(s): Licensing Authority:
Colorado—Insurance Commission

American Dental Corporation
14800 Landmark Blvd., #700
Dallas, TX 75240
(214) 661-5848/1-800-441-0380
Sales Contact(s):
Gary B. Downey, Senior Vice President
Operations Since: 1979
Service Area(s): Licensing Authority:
Texas—State Bd. of Insurance

American Dental Providers
523 Louisiana, #450
P.O. Box 34045 (ZIP 72203-34045)
Little Rock, AR 72201-5704
(501) 376-0544
Sales Contact(s):
Dale L. Beeber, Vice President
Operations Since: 1986
Service Area(s): Licensing Authority:
Arkansas—Insurance Department

American Prepaid Professional Services, Inc.
d/b/a American Dental Plan, Inc.
8800 Roswell Road, #295
Atlanta, GA 30350
(404) 998-8936/1-800-633-1262
FAX (404) 998-6871
Sales Contact(s):
Marty Thorsen, Vice President of Marketing
Operations Since: 1978
Service Area(s): Licensing Authority:
Florida Department of Insurance
Georgia—not regulated at present
Ohio Department of Insurance
Alabama—Department of Insurance

Associated Dental Services, Inc.
9052 North Deerbrook Trail
Milwaukee, WI 53223
(414) 357-2040/(800) 544-3330
FAX (414) 354-3177
Sales Contact(s):
Peter W. Van Lare, Vice President, Sales
Operations Since: 1984
Service Area(s): Licensing Authority:
Georgia—not regulated at present
Illinois OCI—agreement with IGIC
Wisconsin OCI—Wisconsin LSHO

Associated Health Plans, Inc.
P.O. Box 32590
Tucson, AZ 85751
(602) 325-0691/1-800-621-5517
4055 So. 700 E.
Salt Lake City, UT 84107
Sales Contact(s):
Timothy J. Moncher, President
Operations Since: 1981

Service Area(s): Licensing Authority:
Arizona—Dept. of Insurance
Utah

California Dental Health Plan
Dental Plan Administrator
P.O. Box 899
Tustin, CA 92681
(714) 731-4751/1-800-622-6388
Sales Contact(s):
James R. Lindsey, President
Operations Since: 1978
Service Area(s): Licensing Authority:
California, Hawaii—Dept. of Corporations
Colorado—Dept. of Insurance

Champion Dental Services, Inc.
940 West Port Plaza, Suite 300
St. Louis, MO 63146
(314) 453-1700
Sales Contact(s):
Barbara McDill, Manager
Operations Since: 1985
Service Area(s): Licensing Authority:
Illinois—Dept. of Insurance
Missouri

CIGNA Dental Health
1525 N.W. 167th Street
Miami, FL 33169
(305) 620-9922
Sales Contact(s):
Gail M. Garcia, Vice President
Operations Since: 1975
Service Area(s): Licensing Authority:
Operational in 34 states—Depts. of Corporations, Insurance, Health or Commerce

CompDent Corporation
3939 Atkinson Drive
Louisville, KY 40218
(520) 456-1800/1-800-456-5500
FAX (502) 456-2772
Sales Contact(s):
James H. Knox, Regional Vice President for KY, IN, OH, WV
Charles E. Brightwell Jr., Regional Vice President for MO, KS, IL
Operations Since: 1977
Service Area(s): Licensing Authority:
Kentucky—Dept. of Insurance
Indiana/Missouri/Kansas/Ohio/West Virginia/Illinois

Consumer Dental Care
Executive Court
1734 Elton Road, Suite 231
Silver Spring, MD 20903
(301) 439-6500
Sales Contact(s):
Steven H. Keller, D.D.S., President

Delta Dental Plan of Michigan
Delta Care Program
Box 30416
Lansing, MI 48909-7916
(517) 349-6000
Sales Contact(s):
C. Richard Seitz, Executive Vice President

DENCAP Dental Plans
7600 Second Avenue
Detroit, MI 48202-2402
(313) 972-1400
FAX (313) 972-4662
Sales Contact(s):
Joseph T. Lentine, President
Operations Since: 1984
Service Area(s): Licensing Authority:
Michigan—Dept. of Insurance

Dentacare United Wisconsin Services, Inc.
401 West Michigan
Milwaukee, WI 53203
(414) 226-5703
Sales Contact(s):
Barbara Wunrow, Director
Operations Since: 1976
Service Area(s): Licensing Authority:
Illinois
Wisconsin LSHO—State of Wisconsin

Denta-Chek of Maryland, Inc.
5565 Sterrett Place
Columbia, MD 21044
(301) 622-3300/1-800-638-1134
Sales Contact(s):
Rhoda Chanin

Operations Since: 1977
Service Area(s): Licensing Authority:
Maryland—Maryland Insurance Division
Affiliates handle Massachusetts, D.C. and Virginia

Dental Benefit Providers, Inc.
7200 Wisconsin Avenue, #800
Bethesda, MD 20814
(301) 654-6900/1-800-445-9090
Sales Contact(s):
Guy Hunt, Vice President
Operations Since: 1984
Service Area(s): Licensing Authority:
IN, DC, MD, GA, IL, IA, info. not available
NC, VA, KS, CA, MA, AL, MI, MO, CO, NY, CT, OH, TX, PR

Dental Care Affiliates, Inc.
4360 Chamblee-Dunwoody Rd., #428
Atlanta, GA 30341
(404) 452-8773
Sales Contact(s):
Charles E. Brody, President
Operations Since: 1991
Service Area(s): Licensing Authority:
Georgia—not regulated at present

Dental Care Network
(Aff. of Blue Cross/Blue Shield)
25925 Telegraph Road
P.O. Box 2225
Southfield, MI 48037
(313) 799-6500
FAX (313) 799-6950
Sales Contact(s):
Barbara Derian, Manager
Operations Since: 1983
Service Area(s): Licensing Authority:
Michigan—Dept. of Insurance, Dept. of Public Health

Dental Care Plus Management Corp.
770 North Halsted St., #308
Chicago, IL 60622
(312) 829-1295/1-800-837-2341
FAX (312) 829-7965
Sales Contact(s):
Richard F. Sawicz
Operations Since: 1985
Service Area(s): Licensing Authority:
Illinois—Dept. of Insurance

Dental Concern, Ltd., The
222 North LaSalle, #2140
Chicago, IL 60601
(312) 201-1260/1-800-253-9745
Sales Contact(s):
Marketing Department
Operations Since: 1987
Service Area(s): Licensing Authority:
Illinois—Dept. of Insurance, Missouri

DENTAL NET
(Blue Cross of California)
21555 Oxnard Street
Woodland Hills, CA 91367
(818) 703-3781
Sales Contact(s):
Lynette King, Business Manager
Operations Since: 1972
Service Area(s): Licensing Authority:
California—Dept. of Corporations

Dental Plan of America
2601 N.W. Expressway, Ste. 201W
Oklahoma City, OK 73112
(405) 840-1613
FAX (405) 848-5703
Sales Contact(s):
John E. DeBee, Vice President Operations
Operations Since: 1983
Service Area(s): Licensing Authority:
Oklahoma—Oklahoma Insurance Commission

DentalPLUS
Pennsylvania Blue Shield
100 Senate Ave., 6th Floor, West Wing
P.O. Box 898836
Camp Hill, PA 17089-8836
(717) 975-7182
Sales Contact(s):
Robert K. Rembisz, Thomas Dzuryachko, Vice Presidents
Operations Since: 1981
Service Area(s): Licensing Authority:
Pennsylvania—Dept. of Insurance

DentiCare, Inc.
14141 Southwest Freeway
Sugarland, TX 77478
(713) 242-1099
FAX (713) 242-1007
Sales Contact(s):
Henry G. New, President
William Gartland, Sr. Vice President
Operations Since: 1979
Service Area(s): Licensing Authority:
Texas—Dept. of Insurance

DentiCare, Inc.
National Health Care Systems of Florida, Inc.
8130 Baymeadows Way West, #200
Jacksonville, FL 32256
(904) 731-1870/1-800-347-1870
FAX (904) 731-5600
Sales Contact(s):
Stan Alekna, President
Don Titcomb, Vice President, Sales
Operations Since: 1975
Service Area(s): Licensing Authority:
Florida—Dept. of Insurance
Kentucky/North Carolina
Tennessee/Georgia/Alabama

DentiCare of California, Inc.
National Health Care Systems, Inc.
#1 Park Plaza, #1250
Irvine, CA 92714
(714) 553-1577/1-800-999-2848
Sales Contact(s):
Valerie A. Clark, Vice President
Operations Since: 1972
Service Area(s): Licensing Authority:
California—Dept. of Corporations

Denticare of North Dakota
513 E. Bismarck Expressway
Box 1974
Bismarck, ND 58504
(701) 223-1822
FAX (701) 222-1413
Sales Contact(s):
Gorman H. King Sr., Director
Operations Since: 1983
Service Area(s): Licensing Authority:
North Dakota—Dept. of Insurance
Minnesota—Secretary of State
Montana—Secretary of State

Denticare of Oklahoma, Inc.
Wembley Center
7112 South Mingo, #108
Tulsa, OK 74133
(918) 254-9055
Sales Contact(s):
Robert E. Acklin, President
Peggy Kahler, Vice President
Operations Since: 1982
Service Area(s): Licensing Authority:
Oklahoma—Department of Insurance
Missouri
Arkansas

Employers Dental Services Arizona Dental Care, Inc.
7202 E. Rosewood, #150
P.O. Box 12010
Tucson, AZ 85732-2010
(602) 722-0808/(800) 722-9772
(602) 266-3424 (Phoenix)
Sales Contact(s):
Scott McCall, President (Phoenix)
Donna Reynolds, Vice President, Sales (Phoenix)
Rebecca Martinez, Vice President, Sales (Tucson)
Operations Since: 1974
Service Area(s): Licensing Authority:
Arizona—Dept. of Insurance

First Commonwealth, Inc.
444 N. Wells, #600
Chicago, IL 60610
(312) 644-1800
FAX (312) 644-1822
Sales Contact(s):
J. Tony Freeman, Corporate Director, Sales
Barbara Maura, National Accounts Coordinator
Operations Since: 1987
Service Area(s): Licensing Authority:
Illinois—Dept. of Insurance
Indiana—Dept. of Insurance

Flagship Health Systems, Inc.
Delta Dental Plan of New Jersey, Inc.
959 Route 46
Parsippany, NJ 07054
(201) 334-6225
Sales Contact(s):
Doug Smyth, Vice President
Operations Since: 1986
Service Area(s): Licensing Authority:
New Jersey—Dept. of Insurance

Golden West Health Plan
888 West Ventura Boulevard, #7
Camarillo, CA 93010
(805) 987-8941/(800) 995-4124
FAX (805) 987-6110
Sales Contact(s):
Troy Becker, President
Jim Fuhrman, Marketing Director
Operations Since: 1974
Service Area(s): Licensing Authority:
California—Dept. of Corporations

Group Health, Inc.
2829 University Avenue, S.E., #642
Minneapolis, MN 55414
(612) 623-8770
FAX (612) 623-8686
Sales Contact(s):
Stephanie Frost, Marketing Manager
Operations Since: 1977
Service Area(s): Licensing Authority:
Minnesota—Health Dept.

HealthDent of California, Inc.
2848 Arden Way, #100
Sacramento, CA 95825
(916) 486-0749
Sales Contact(s):
E. L. Cruchley, D.D.S., President
Operations Since: 1983
Service Area(s): Licensing Authority:
California—Dept. of Corporations

Healthplex, Inc.
Dentcare Delivery Systems, Inc.
International Healthcare Services, Inc.
60 Charles Lindbergh Blvd.
Uniondale, NY 11553
(516) 794-3000/1-800-468-0600
Sales Contact(s):
Dr. Stephen J. Cuchel, Healthplex Chairman
Mario Masciandaro, Vice President, Marketing
Operations Since: 1978
Service Area(s): Licensing Authority:
New York (Dentcare)—Dept. of Insurance, New Jersey (IHS)

HealthStream Corp.
P.O. Box 24508
Chattanooga, TN 37422-4508
(615) 892-5668/1-800-633-3442
Sales Contact(s):
Tina M. Copeland, Vice President
Lynda Hunnicutt, President
Operations Since: 1980
Service Area(s): Licensing Authority:
Tennessee—Dept. of Insurance
Alabama/Mississippi/Louisiana/Georgia/North Carolina/South Carolina
TPA: TX, OH, FL

Humana Inc.
500 West Main Street
Louisville, KY 40201
(502) 580-1409
Sales Contact(s):
Harold C. Leppert Jr., Manager
Operations Since: 1987
Service Area(s): Licensing Authority:
Kentucky, Indiana, Texas—Dept. of Insurance
Florida, Missouri, Kansas, Illinois
AOP: Arizona, Ohio, Colorado

Independent Dental Plans, Inc.
15200 Jefferson, #105
Grosse Pointe Park, MI 48230
(313) 331-8270
Sales Contact(s):
Edward K. Halstead, President
Operations Since: 1988
Service Area(s): Licensing Authority:
Michigan—Dept. of Public Health/Dept. of Insurance

International Dental Plans, Inc.
2500 East Hallandale Beach Blvd.
Hallandale, FL 33009
(305) 947-7916/1-800-741-7711
Sales Contact(s):
Stanley G. Greenstein, President
Lois L. Kutun, Marketing
Operations Since: 1983
Service Area(s): Licensing Authority:
Florida—Dept. of Insurance

JustDental
Annapolis Plan of Dental Health Care, Inc.
6115 Falls Road
Baltimore, MD 21209
(301) 377-2000/1-800-272-8865
Sales Contact(s):
Richard L. Jones, Dir. Marketing and Sales
Operations Since: 1988
Service Area(s): Licensing Authority:
Maryland—Maryland Ins. Div.

Kansas City Dental Care
912 E. 63rd Street
P.O. Box 16137
Kansas City, MO 64112
(816) 523-8388/1-800-234-8388
Sales Contact(s):
John E. Carlin
Operations Since: 1981
Service Area(s): Licensing Authority:
Kansas—Kansas Insurance Commission
Missouri—Missouri Insurance Commission

Medica
Route 7770
P.O. Box 1587
Minneapolis, MN 55440-7001
(612) 936-4968
FAX (612) 936-4966
Sales Contact(s):
Gretchen Eckes, Dir. of Dental Programs
Operations Since: 1974
Service Area(s): Licensing Authority:
Minnesota—Dept. of Health/Wisconsin

MIDA Dental Plans, Inc.
2000 Town Center, #2200
Southfield, MI 48075
(313) 353-6410
Sales Contact(s):
Janet Oleszkowicz, Senior Vice President
Operations Since: 1981
Service Area(s): Licensing Authority:
MI, CA, DE—Bureau Ins. Dept. Public Health—(MI)
OH, MO, KY, AZ—Dept. of Corporations (CA)
IN, MD, PA, VA, KS—Dept. of Insurance
MA, GA, FL, DC, WV

Midwestern Dental Plans, Inc.
5050 Schaefer Road
Dearborn, MI 48126
(313) 582-8150
Sales Contact(s):
John Morgan Jr., Vice President
Operations Since: 1981
Service Area(s): Licensing Authority:
Michigan—Dept. of Insurance/Health

National Dental Health
3111 Camino Del Rio North, #1000
San Diego, CA 92108
(619) 283-8611/1-800-288-9992
Sales Contact(s):
Keith C. Macumber, Vice President, CMO
Operations Since: 1977
Service Area(s): Licensing Authority:
AL, AZ, CA, CO—Dept. of Insurance
FL, ID, IL, IN, KS—Dept. of Corporations
CA, LA, MO, MT, NE, NV, NM, OR, PA, SD, TX, UT, WA, WY

National Prepaid Administrators of Wisconsin, Inc.
747 Reid Street
DePere, WI 54115
(414) 336-2939/1-800-236-2226
Sales Contact(s):
Gary Zaskey, President
Operations Since: 1983
Service Area(s): Licensing Authority:
Wisconsin—Insurance Commissioner

OraCare Dental Health Plans, Inc.
8000 Sagemore Drive, #8302
Marlton, NJ 08053
(609) 983-3838

Sales Contact(s):
Lisa M. Mazzone, President
Operations Since: 1981
Service Area(s): Licensing Authority:
New Jersey—Dept. of Insurance

Oral Health Services of Florida, Inc.
5775 NW Blue Lagoon Drive, #400
Miami, FL 33126
(305) 262-1333/1-800-223-6447
(in Florida only)
Sales Contact(s):
Ralph Cabrera Jr., Dir. of Marketing
Marisela Palacios, Dir. of Prof. Rel.
Operations Since: 1979
Service Area(s): Licensing Authority:
Florida—Dept. of Insurance

Private Medical-Care, Inc.
5122 Katella Avenue, #206
Los Alamitos, CA 90720
(310) 493-6661
FAX (310) 493-1041
Sales Contact(s):
Lee Schneider, Vice President, Marketing
Operations Since: 1969
Service Area(s): Licensing Authority:
Arizona/California—Dept. of Corporations
Colorado/Florida
Georgia/Illinois
Minnesota/Nevada/New Mexico/
Texas/Utah

Professional Dental Plan, Inc.
P.O. Box 44966
Madison, WI 53744-4966
(608) 831-9292
FAX (608) 831-4243
Sales Contact(s):
Tammie L. Smithback, Administrator
Operations Since: 1982
Service Area(s): Licensing Authority:
State of Wisconsin

Prudential Insurance Co.
57 North Livingston Avenue
ROS 2, Stop 402
Roseland, NJ 07068
(201) 716-4095
Sales Contact(s):
William Jackson, Vice President
Operations Since: 1985
Service Area(s): Licensing Authority:
California/Georgia—as appropriate
Texas/New Jersey

Signature Dental Plan
200 North Martingale Rd.
Schaumburg, IL 60173
(708) 605-4951
FAX (708) 605-7304
Sales Contact(s):
Charles Misasi, Director
Maryanne Metz, Asst. Vice President
Operations Since: 1988
Service Area(s): Licensing Authority:
Multistate

SmileSaver Dental Plan
Greater California Dental Plan
7009 Owensmouth, #200
Canoga Park, CA 91303
(818) 348-1500
Sales Contact(s):
Robert S. Sofsky, President
Operations Since: 1981
Service Area(s): Licensing Authority:
California—Dept. of Corporations

UDC Life & Health Insurance Co., Inc.
200 N.W. 66th Street, #925
P.O. Box 54339
Oklahoma City, OK 73154
(405) 848-6351
FAX (405) 842-3214
Sales Contact(s):
Don Germany, President
Charles M. Montgomery, Chairman
and CEO
Donna Aitson, Executive Vice President
Operations Since: 1984
Service Area(s): Licensing Authority:
Oklahoma—Dept. of Insurance

United Dental Care, Inc.
14755 Preston Road, #300
Dallas, TX 75240
(214) 458-7474/1-800-262-5388
FAX (214) 478-7963

Sales Contact(s):
Jeff P. Hollansworth, Vice President of Sales—Texas and Ohio
Craig H. Martin, Director of Sales, Texas
Operations Since: 1986
Service Area(s): Licensing Authority:
Texas—Department of Insurance
Ohio

United HealthCare Dental, Inc.
1445 N. Loop West, Suite 1000
Houston, TX 77008
(713) 861-3231/(800) 232-0990
Sales Contact(s):
William H. Slavin, CEO
Shelley Porter
Operations Since: 1982
Service Area(s): Licensing Authority:
Maryland/DC—DMO
Texas—State Board of Insurance Virginia

U.S. Dental Plan
1702 East Highland Avenue, #110
Phoenix, AZ 85016
(602) 277-7432/(602) 263-0187
FAX 1-800-456-2345
Sales Contact(s):
Dolores A. Kordek, Principal
Christopher A. Jehle, Principal
Nathan C. Kleinberg, CEO
Operations Since: 1980
Service Area(s): Licensing Authority:
Arizona/New Mexico—Dept. of Insurance
Colorado/Nebraska/Utah

Unity Dental Health Services
1219 Main Avenue
Clifton, NJ 07011
(800) 648-0146
FAX (201) 772-3989
(800) 722-0948 (out of state)
Sales Contact(s):
Robert Dubman, D.D.S., President
Operations Since: 1978
Service Area(s): Licensing Authority:
New Jersey—Dept. of Insurance
New York/Pennsylvania

Western Dental Services
300 Plaza Alicante, #810
Garden Grove, CA 92640
(714) 938-1600
FAX (714) 938-1611
Sales Contact(s):
Peggy Mooney, Vice President
Operations Since: 1985
Service Area(s): Licensing Authority:
California—Dept. of Corporations

Wisconsin Dental Service Plan, Inc.
13555 Bishops Court, Ste. 315
Brookfield, WI 53005
(414) 796-1675
FAX (414) 796-2784
Sales Contact(s):
Jeanne Hensel, Executive Director
Operations Since: 1987
Service Area(s): Licensing Authority:
Wisconsin—Commissioner of Insurance

Dental HMOs With Enrollment of Over 300,000

CIGNA Dental Health
1525 N.W. 167th Street
Miami, FL 33169
(305) 620-9922
Sales Contact(s):
Gail M. Garcia, Vice President
Operational in 36 states
Total lives covered by dental HMOs
1,300,000

Dental Benefit Providers, Inc.
7200 Wisconsin Avenue, #800
Bethesda, MD 20814
(301) 654-6900/1-800-445-9090
Sales Contact(s):
Guy Hunt, Vice President
Operational in: information not available
Total lives covered by dental HMOs
1,300,000

Dental Network of America
Two TransAm Plaza Drive
Oakbrook, IL 60181
(708) 691-0233
Sales Contact(s):
Vince DiBenedetto, Vice President Marketing
Operational in 32 states
Total lives covered by dental HMOs
850,000

DentalPLUS
Pennsylvania Blue Shield
100 Senate Ave., 6th Floor, West Wing
P.O. Box 898836
Camp Hill, PA 17089-8836
(717) 975-7182
Sales Contact(s):
Robert K. Rembisz, Vice President Sales
Thomas Dzuryachko, Corporate Vice President, Dental Operations
Operational in Pennsylvania
Total lives covered by dental HMOs
320,000

MIDA Dental Plans, Inc.
2000 Town Center, #2200
Southfield, MI 48075
(313) 353-6410
Sales Contact(s):
Janet Oleszkowicz, Senior Vice President Operations
Operational in 21 states
Total lives covered by dental HMOs
810,000

National Dental Health
3111 Camino Del Rio North, #1000
San Diego, CA 92108
(619) 283-8611/1-800-288-9992
Sales Contact(s):
Keith C. Macumber, Vice President, CMO
Operational in 22 states
Total lives covered by dental HMOs
500,000

PMI Private Medical-Care, Inc.
5122 Katella Avenue, #206
Los Alamitos, CA 90720
(310) 493-6661
FAX (310) 493-1041
Sales Contact(s):
Lee Schneider, Vice President, Marketing
Operational in 11 states
Total lives covered by dental HMOs
750,000

Prudential Insurance Co.
57 North Livingston Avenue
ROS 2, Stop 402
Roseland, NJ 07068
(201) 716-4095
Sales Contact(s):
William Jackson, Vice President
Operational in 46 states
Total lives covered by dental HMOs
1,600,000

Randmark Inc.
1211 Connecticut Ave. NW, Suite 200
Washington, DC 20036
(202) 833-6830
Sales Contact(s):
Annette Rolin-Batson, Director of Marketing
Operational in 21 states
Total lives covered by dental HMOs 325,000

Safeguard Health Enterprises, Inc.
505 North Euclid Street
P.O. Box 3210
Anaheim, CA 92803
(714) 778-1284
Operational in 16 states
Total lives covered by dental HMOs 665,000

(Based upon information available to the author as of 2-1-93.)

Request for Proposal (RFP)

13

Key Elements

It is important to obtain a minimum of three proposals when purchasing a dental HMO plan. Your benefits consultant will be the best source for preparing a request for proposal (RFP) and identifying those entities that should receive it. However, few consulting firms have experience with dental HMO plans and, as a consequence, many RFPs may leave out key elements necessary for an effective RFP for this type of plan. This is understandable since dental HMO plans currently are estimated to be only about 11% of all dental benefit plans.

As an aid in reviewing the contents of an RFP, the following key elements may be used as a checklist to ensure they are included. Some basic "boilerplate" elements that are incorporated in most RFPs are not repeated here.

Company

- History
- Officers/owners and percent ownership by each
- Background information on all officers and key individuals
- Audited financial statement
- Individual with principal accountability for dental HMOs. Experience in dental HMOs
- Dentists employed: names, full or part time, background and experience

Lines of Business

- List lines of business and percent of each expressed as gross revenues.

Clients

- Current clients—other benefit plans
  - Names and addresses
  - Size of covered population
  - Type of plan(s)—describe
  - Length of time as a client
- Current dental HMO clients
  - Names and addresses
  - Size (expressed in lives) of covered population
  - Types of dental HMO plan(s)—describe
  - Contact person and telephone number
  - Length of time as a client
- Name and address of clients lost during last two years
- Contact person and telephone number

Dental Plans Offered

- Types of dental benefit plans offered (see Figure 13-1)
- Types of dental HMO plans offered (see Figure 13-2)

Premiums

- Do you offer a one-, two- or three-year guarantee?

Retention

- Expressed in dollars and percentage of total premium

Benefits

- Can you provide and administer our benefit plan?
- Provide a sample plan document.

Exclusions and Limitations

- Can you incorporate and administer our exclusions and limitations?

Dental Office Information

- Is dental office network currently in place?
- Number of offices
- Location of offices in relation to employees. Provide ZIP code analysis.
- Respond for each office:
  - Location, including ZIP code

Figure 13-1

Type of Plan	% of Total Business	Lives Covered	Premium Dollars	% of Premium to Dentists
Dental HMO				
Fee for service				
PPO				
EPO				
Other				

Figure 13-2

Type of Plan	% of Total Business	Lives Covered	Premium Dollars	% of Premium to Dentists
Closed panel				
Open panel				
Dual choice				
Triple choice				
IPA				
Other				

  - Number of chairs
  - Number of dentists, names, specialty, list of continuing education courses for each dentist during the past three years
  - Office hours? List by day.
  - How are nonoffice hour emergencies handled?
  - Average waiting time for: initial appointment, recall appointment, followup appointment
- If multidentist office, how are dentists paid? Fee for service, capitation, salary, combination or other. Describe.
- Office selection
  - Describe office selection standards/process.
  - Provide sample copy of office evaluation/selection report.

Contract With Dentist(s)

- Does it contain clauses that dentists agree to:
  - Meet quality standards?
  - Abide by peer review, as determined by administrator?
  - Not charge patients over and above amounts agreed upon?

  - Submit data on services provided?
  - Follow patient complaint resolution procedure?
  - Provide sample contract?

How Are General Dentists Reimbursed?

- Capitation?
- Fee for service: UCR, R&C or schedule? Other? Describe.
- When do payments to dentists start? At inception of program? Describe.

Specialty Services

- How, and where, are dental specialty services provided?
- How many dental offices have specialists in the office? List number and types of specialist by location.
- How are dental specialists reimbursed? Describe.
  - Capitation
  - Fee for service: UCR, R&C or schedule
  - Other

Quality Assurance

- Describe in detail including:
  - Standards and review process
  - Frequency.
- Provide sample copy of quality review report.
- Are reports available to client?

Office Selection by Participants

- When and how do participants select dental offices?
- At enrollment?
- What information are they given concerning the dental offices? Describe.

Use by Participants

- What percentage of eligibles use each of the plans you administer? List by group.

Value

- How often are payments to dentists determined? Describe.
- How often are payments to dentists reviewed/changed? Describe.
- How is value of dental services determined? Provide sample report(s).
  - HIAA? What year and percentile are used?
  - Time unit? Describe methodology and source of time and dollar value.
  - Other? Describe procedures and methodologies.

Data Collection

- How are patient and dentist utilization data collected?
- Provide sample report.
- Are electronic data transfer capabilities available?
  - How used? Between dental office and administrator?
  - Eligibility? Maximum, deductible and copayment information? Describe.

Utilization Review and Reports

Utilization reports (see Chapter 14) must include:

- Percentage of population using dental plan—annualized
- Frequency and percentage of total for each individual service; individual procedure value, total value and percentage of total value
- Frequency of individual services for each patient, by visit and total annual
- Frequency and percentage of total for the following categories of service:
  - Diagnostic
  - Preventive
  - Basic fillings (nongold)
  - Single crowns and inlays
  - Endodontics
  - Nonsurgical periodontics—scaling and root planing
  - Surgical periodontics—periodontal surgery, miscellaneous
  - Removable dentures
  - Fixed bridges
  - Oral surgery
  - Adjective general services.
- Individual dentists profiles—by above categories of service.

See suggested format in Chapter 14.

Regulatory

- What state and/or federal agencies regulate your dental HMO plan? Address and phone number
- Does plan conform with state regulatory requirements?
- If state evaluates plan, provide a copy of report.

Patient Complaint Resolution

- Describe procedure.

Patient Surveys

- Provide sample report.
- Frequency

14

Minimum Data Criteria

"Ignorance is bliss—or disaster."

This section outlines the "minimum data" that a purchaser should expect from a dental HMO plan administrator. It also suggests a format for the data.

There is no comfort in not knowing what's going on in your dental HMO plan. If accurate, comprehensive and audited reports were available on all dental HMO plans in operation today, it is the author's opinion that there would be many shocked purchasers and embarrassed plan administrators. The author never ceases to be amazed at how hard-headed business people who count paper clips and track every penny buy dental HMO plans that have either few or no data. On top of that, the data may be invalid and/or incomprehensible. When the credibility of the data is not established, or is absent, there is no possible way of determining the value of a dental HMO plan.

It is the author's opinion that many purchasers do not know what data to ask for or how the reports should be formatted. This section is written especially for these purchasers. If data are required in the report format suggested in this section, the purchaser will have a good grasp of plan performance and value.

There is an important and overriding consideration about any reports on plan performance. The data must be audited. Auditing is not an option; it is a necessity. It is the only way to ascertain the validity of the data in the reports. And the audit must be performed by an independent auditor. It may not be necessary to audit every report, every year, but all reports for the first year should be audited. After the first year the purchaser may use judgment as to the extent of auditing necessary for the particular plan. Auditing must be an ongoing and integral part of the purchaser's responsibility.

It is important to keep in mind that the reports in this section represent only the "minimum reporting standards." They may not contain all necessary information, due to variations in plan design and administration, or specific group peculiarities. Any variations must be taken into consideration when designing and/or requesting reports. However, the sample reports may be used as a basis to determine what other types of reports may be necessary to effectively monitor the dental plan.

The reports and their data should be made available to the purchaser on computer tape and disk(s). This will enable the purchaser or the consultant to perform various analyses easily. This is an individual purchaser's decision. Depending upon the in-house capability of the purchaser or consultant, it may be easier and less costly to request different data sorts, reports and formats from the plan administrator than to create them in-house. However, it is the author's experience that the purchaser and/or consultants have a greater interest than the plan administrators in identifying real and/or potential problems.

Any proposal from a dental HMO plan administrator that does not specifically state the administrator will provide, at a minimum, reports containing the data outlined in this section should be rejected. The reports in this section are essential and basic. There is nothing complicated, difficult or unusual in capturing and reporting these data. All reputable plans are computerized and routinely capture, and report, these basic data. A reputable dental plan administrator will have no problem providing the reports suggested in this section. And, the administrator should have no trouble sorting or formatting the data into an easily understandable report, when requested to do so by the purchaser.

The data must be in a format that is clearly understandable to both the purchaser and the purchaser's consultant, if one is used. There is an old saying in surgery that "to do well what you do, you must see well what you do." There is an analogy in monitoring dental plan performance—"to manage well what you manage, you must see well what you manage." Attempting to manage, or evaluate, a dental plan without the right kind of data, in an easily understandable format, precludes effective monitoring of plan performance.

Reports

Reports to be requested break down into two key types: summary reports and comprehensive reports.

Summary reports are important for ongoing monitoring of plan performance. They must be clear enough to allow anyone with a minimal knowledge of dental plans to understand and interpret their significance. They must measure key elements of plan performance and be clear, concise and frequent enough to enable the purchaser to tell at a glance how the plan is performing. Generally these short reports are provided monthly and annually. They should be one or two pages at most. Favorable and unfavorable trends can usually be identified early through summary reports. If the summary data suggest a problem, then the purchaser or consultant must be able to go to the detail in the comprehensive reports to determine the underlying cause and, if necessary, take corrective action. If the problem appears to be related to the dental offices, then an audit of the dental offices should occur (see Chapter 16).

In addition to summary reports, *comprehensive reports* on plan performance containing far greater detail are essential for an in-depth analysis of plan performance. Comprehensive reports are generally provided on an annual basis. However, if there appears to be a problem, the plan administrator should be able to provide them upon request. Generating these reports is NOT rocket science. Any well-managed plan administrator should be able to produce them within a short period of time.

Summary Reports

Two summary reports are illustrated in this chapter: Summary of Services and Value, and Summary of Participant Utilization.

Summary of Services and Value

The Summary of Services and Value allows the purchaser to monitor the following key elements of plan performance.

Frequency of services. Frequency of services should be expressed in both the number and percentage of total services, by category of service. The reports are issued on a monthly and year-to-date basis. The percentage data permits the monitoring of the mix of services and permits a comparison of the data to data from other sources (see Chapter 8 for high and low values for comparison). If the plan is low on diagnostic and preventive, it may be an indication that the plan is not being used. If it is high in diagnostic and preventive but low in restorative—basic fillings—it may indicate the participants are not receiving necessary care. It could also indicate they are in a state of good dental health. This can then also be checked with the incidence of oral surgery. If the incidence of oral surgery is high, it may be a warning that only emergency care is being provided; i.e., decayed teeth are not being filled, they are being extracted.

Value of services. The value of services is reported in same format as the frequency of services. This enables the purchaser to compare the value of services with the premiums, also included in the same report. (See Exhibit 14-A.)

Summary of Participant Utilization

The Summary of Participant Utilization enables the purchaser to monitor the use of the plan by the participants.

Use of the plan by the participants must be expressed in the number of discrete, or distinct, individuals who have used the plan. As stated earlier, a plan that is wonderful in many aspects but is not, or cannot be, used by the participants is seriously flawed. Low utilization requires a very careful review to determine the reasons. Are the dentists discouraging utilization by erecting barriers to care? Has the plan administrator purposely made the dental offices geographically inaccessible to the participants? Have the participants been informed where the participating dentists are located and how to contact them? Low utilization by the participants requires prompt and effective remedial action. (See Exhibit 14-B.)

Comprehensive Reports

Two comprehensive reports are illustrated in this section: Comprehensive Report on Services and Value, and Detail of Treatment.

Comprehensive Report on Services and Value

The Comprehensive Report on Services and Value enables the purchaser to study the following areas in greater detail.

The frequency and value of each individual service in each category. Because the categories report only summary data, it is possible to be misled if one does not look at the detail supporting the summary data. For example, restorative (basic fillings) may have an acceptable percentage of the total services rendered, but on looking at the detail one may find frequency "pumped up" by the use of many temporary fillings. This is unacceptable dentistry if it is a deliberate effort to circumvent placing more time-consuming, and costly, permanent fillings. This is commonly referred to as "patchwork" dentistry.

Reporting patterns. It is easy to pick up "fragmentation," also known as "a la carting." The dentist adds an additional charge (or *value* in an HMO) for services that are normally a component of another service. Examples are injections with fillings or temporary crowns reported with permanent crowns. See Chapter 11 for a discussion on fragmentation. (See Exhibit 14-C.)

Detail of Treatment

Detail of Treatment enables the purchaser to study in depth how the participants are being treated by the dentists.

A Detail of Treatment report will reveal if patients are required to return unnecessarily. For example, are the examinations, X-rays and teeth cleanings all occurring on one visit? Is the waiting time between appointments appropriate? And are the treatments timely?

It is also possible to add codes for individual offices to monitor individual performance. This report is also valuable to identify "double billing," i.e., giving a value to a procedure more than one time (yes, this occurs). Fragmentation may also be uncovered in this report.

The better dental HMO plan administrators also report the number of the tooth upon which a service was performed. Each tooth has a number from 1 through 32 and, if this number is reported in the Detail of Treatment report, that information permits a very focused audit.

If an office audit is necessary, this report is extremely valuable to verify that the services reported by the dentist were indeed provided. As discussed in Chapter 2, dental treatment leaves an audit trail. Fillings, bridges, dentures, crowns, etc., can be visually verified. (See Exhibit 14-D.)

One area not revealed in the reports in this section, one that is very important, is the level of satisfaction of the participants (see Appendix H for an example of a questionnaire that can be used to evaluate user satisfaction). What on paper appears to be a wonderful plan and provides a wide range of benefits is of little value if the participants are not satisfied. Surveys of participants can be a valuable source of information on a plan's strong and weak points. Many times patient surveys reveal problems that are not evident in the data.

In summary, minimal reporting standards include:

- Auditing the data
- Accurate data
- Providing key data
- Summary data that are clear and concise
- Comprehensive data
- Easily understood format
- Participant surveys
- Data available on computer tape or disk(s).

Exhibit 14-A

Summary of Services and Value (Monthly and Annual)

			No. of Procedures Current Month	% of Procedures Current Month	No. of Procedures Year to Date	% of Procedures Year to Date	Total Value Year to Date	% of Value Year to Date
00100-00999	I.	Diagnostic examinations and X-rays						
01000-01999	II.	Preventive teeth cleaning and fluoride						
02000-02399 & 02900-02999	III.	Restorative—basic fillings						
02500-02899	III.	Restorative—crowns and inlays						
03000-03999	IV.	Endodontics—root canals						
04000-04299	V.	Periodontics—surgical						
04300-04999	V.	Periodontics—nonsurgical						
05000-05899	VI.	Prosthodontics—removable dentures						
06200-06999	IX.	Prosthodontics—fixed dentures						
07000-07999	X.	Oral surgery						
08000-08999	XI.	Orthodontics						
09000-09999	XII.	Adjunctive general services						
		Grand Totals						
		Premium—Year to Date						

Exhibit 14-B

Summary of Participant Utilization
Number of Different Individuals Who Visited the Dentist
(Monthly and Annual)

	Total Eligible	Number Using	Percent Using
Current month	____________	____________	____________
Year to date	____________	____________	____________

Exhibit 14-C

Comprehensive Report on Services and Value (Annual)

Code	Procedure	Number of Procedures	Value of Procedure	Total Value	% of Total Value	% of Total Procedures
00100-00999	**I. DIAGNOSTIC**					
	Clinical oral examinations					
00110	Initial oral examination					
00120	Periodic oral examination					
00130	Emergency oral examination					
	Radiographs					
00210	Intraoral—complete series (including bitewings)					
00220	Intraoral—periapical—first film					
00230	Intraoral—periapical—each additional film					
00240	Intraoral—occlusal film					
00250	Extraoral—first film					
00260	Extraoral—each additional film					
00270	Bitewings—single film					
00272	Bitewings—two films					
00274	Bitewings—four films					
00330	Panoramic film					
00340	Cephalometric film					
	Tests and laboratory examinations					
00415	Bacteriologic studies for determination of pathologic agents					
00425	Caries susceptibility tests					
00460	Pulp vitality tests					
00470	Diagnostic casts					

Code	Procedure	Number of Procedures	Value of Procedure	Total Value	% of Total Value	% of Total Procedures
00471	Diagnostic photographs					
01000-01999	**II. PREVENTIVE**					
	Dental prophylaxis					
01110	Prophylaxis—adult					
01120	Prophylaxis—child					
	Topical fluoride treatment (office procedure)					
01201	Topical application of fluoride (including prophylaxis)—child					
01203	Topical application of fluoride (excluding prophylaxis)—child					
01204	Topical application of fluoride (excluding prophylaxis)—adult					
01205	Topical application of fluoride (including prophylaxis)—adult					
	Other preventive services					
01351	Sealant—per tooth					
	Space maintenance (passive appliances)					
01510	Space maintainer—fixed—unilateral					
01515	Space maintainer—fixed—bilateral					
01520	Space maintainer—removable—unilateral					
01525	Space maintainer—removable—bilateral					
01550	Recementation of space maintainer					
02000-02999	**III. RESTORATIVE**					
	Amalgam restorations (including polishing)					
02110	Amalgam—one surface, primary					
02120	Amalgam—two surfaces, primary					
02130	Amalgam—three surfaces, primary					
02131	Amalgam—four or more surfaces, primary					

Code	Procedure	Number of Procedures	Value of Procedure	Total Value	% of Total Value	% of Total Procedures
02140	Amalgam—one surface, permanent					
02150	Amalgam—two surfaces, permanent					
02160	Amalgam—three surfaces, permanent					
02161	Amalgam—four or more surfaces, permanent					
	Resin restorations					
02330	Resin—one surface, anterior					
02331	Resin—two surfaces, anterior					
02332	Resin—three surfaces, anterior					
02335	Resin—four or more surfaces or involving incisal angle (anterior)					
02336	Composite resin crown—anterior—primary					
02380	Resin—one surface, posterior—primary					
02381	Resin—two surfaces, posterior—primary					
02382	Resin—three or more surfaces, posterior—primary					
02385	Resin—one surface, posterior—permanent					
02386	Resin—two surfaces, posterior—permanent					
02387	Resin—three or more surfaces, posterior—permanent					
	Inlay restorations					
02510	Inlay—metallic—one surface					
02520	Inlay—metallic—two surfaces					
02530	Inlay—metallic—three surfaces					
02540	Onlay—metallic—per tooth (in addition to inlay)					
02610	Inlay—porcelain/ceramic—one surface					
02620	Inlay—porcelain/ceramic—two surfaces					
02630	Inlay—porcelain/ceramic—three surfaces					
02640	Onlay—porcelain/ceramic—per tooth (in addition to inlay)					
02650	Inlay—composite/resin—one surface (laboratory processed)					

Code	Procedure	Number of Procedures	Value of Procedure	Total Value	% of Total Value	% of Total Procedures
02651	Inlay—composite/resin—two surfaces (laboratory processed)					
02652	Inlay—composite/resin—three surfaces (laboratory processed)					
02660	Onlay—composite/resin—per tooth (in addition to inlay—laboratory processed)					
	Crowns—single restoration only					
02710	Crown—resin (laboratory)					
02720	Crown—resin with high noble metal					
02721	Crown—resin with predominantly base metal					
02722	Crown—resin with noble metal					
02740	Crown—porcelain/ceramic substrate					
02750	Crown—porcelain fused to high noble metal					
02751	Crown—porcelain fused to predominantly base metal					
02752	Crown—porcelain fused to noble metal					
02790	Crown—full cast high noble metal					
02791	Crown—full cast predominantly base metal					
02792	Crown—full cast noble metal					
02810	Crown—¾ cast metallic					
	Other restorative services					
02910	Recement inlay					
02920	Recement crown					
02930	Prefabricated stainless steel crown—primary tooth					
02932	Prefabricated resin crown					
02940	Sedative filling					
02950	Core buildup, including any pins					
02951	Pin retention—per tooth, in addition to restoration					
02952	Cast post and core in addition to crown					
02954	Prefabricated post and core in addition to crown					

Code	Procedure	Number of Procedures	Value of Procedure	Total Value	% of Total Value	% of Total Procedures
02970	Temporary crown (fractured tooth)					
02980	Crown repair, by report					
03000-03999	**IV. ENDODONTICS**					
	Pulp capping					
03110	Pulp cap—direct (excluding final restoration)					
	Pulpotomy					
03220	Therapeutic pulpotomy (excluding final restoration)					
	Root canal therapy (including treatment plan, clinical procedures and followup care)					
03310	Anterior (excluding final restoration)					
03320	Bicuspid (excluding final restoration)					
03330	Molar (excluding final restoration)					
	Periapical services					
03410	Apicoectomy/periradicular surgery—anterior					
03421	Apicoectomy/periradicular surgery—bicuspid (first root)					
03425	Apicoectomy/periradicular surgery—molar (first root)					
03426	Apicoectomy/periradicular surgery—(each additional root)					
03450	Root amputation—per root					
03470	Intentional replantation (including necessary splinting)					
04000-04999	**V. PERIODONTICS**					
	Surgical services (including usual postoperative services)					
04210	Gingivectomy or gingivoplasty—per quadrant					
04211	Gingivectomy or gingivoplasty—per tooth					
04220	Gingival curettage, surgical, per quadrant, by report					
04240	Gingival flap procedure, including root planing—per quadrant					
04249	Crown lengthening—hard and soft tissue, by report					

Code	Procedure	Number of Procedures	Value of Procedure	Total Value	% of Total Value	% of Total Procedures
04250	Mucogingival surgery—per quadrant					
04260	Osseous surgery (including flap entry and closure)—per quadrant					
04261	Bone replacement graft—single site (including flap entry and closure)					
04262	Bone replacement graft—multiple sites (including flap entry and closure)					
04268	Guided tissue regeneration (includes the surgery and reentry)					
04270	Pedicle soft tissue graft					
04271	Free soft tissue graft procedure (including donor site)					
	Active periodontal services					
04341	Periodontal scaling and root planing—per quadrant					
04345	Periodontal scaling performed in the presence of gingival inflammation					
	Other periodontal services					
04910	Periodontal maintenance procedures (following active therapy)					
05000-05999	**VI. PROSTHODONTICS (REMOVABLE)**					
	Complete dentures (including routine postdelivery care)					
05110	Complete upper					
05120	Complete lower					
05130	Immediate upper					
05140	Immediate lower					
	Partial dentures (including routine postdelivery care)					
05211	Upper partial—resin base (including any conventional clasps, rests and teeth)					
05212	Lower partial—resin base (including any conventional clasps, rests and teeth)					

Code	Procedure	Number of Procedures	Value of Procedure	Total Value	% of Total Value	% of Total Procedures
05213	Upper partial—cast metal (including any conventional clasps, rests and teeth)					
05214	Lower partial—cast metal (including any conventional clasps, rests and teeth)					
05281	Removable unilateral partial denture—one piece cast metal (including any conventional clasps, rests and teeth)					
05410	Adjust complete denture—upper					
05411	Adjust complete denture—lower					
05421	Adjust partial denture—upper					
05422	Adjust partial denture—lower					
	Repairs to complete dentures					
05510	Repair broken complete denture base					
05520	Replace missing or broken teeth (complete dentures)—each tooth					
	Repairs to partial dentures					
05610	Repair resin saddle or base					
05620	Repair cast framework					
05630	Repair or replace broken clasp					
05640	Replace broken teeth—per tooth					
05650	Add tooth to existing partial denture					
05660	Add clasp to existing partial denture					
	Denture rebase procedures					
05710	Rebase complete upper denture					
05711	Rebase complete lower denture					
05720	Rebase upper partial denture					
05721	Rebase lower partial denture					
	Denture reline procedures					
05730	Reline complete upper denture (chairside)					
05731	Reline complete lower denture (chairside)					

Code	Procedure	Number of Procedures	Value of Procedure	Total Value	% of Total Value	% of Total Procedures
05740	Reline upper partial denture (chairside)					
05741	Reline lower partial denture (chairside)					
05750	Reline complete upper denture (laboratory)					
05751	Reline complete lower denture (laboratory)					
05760	Reline upper partial denture (laboratory)					
05761	Reline lower partial denture (laboratory)					
	Other removable prosthetic services					
05850	Tissue conditioning, upper—per denture unit					
05851	Tissue conditioning, lower—per denture unit					
06200-06999	**IX. PROSTHODONTICS FIXED (each abutment and each pontic constitute a unit in a bridge)**					
	Bridge pontics					
06210	Pontic—cast high noble metal					
06211	Pontic—cast predominantly base metal					
06212	Pontic—cast noble metal					
06240	Pontic—porcelain fused to high noble metal					
06241	Pontic—porcelain fused to predominantly base metal					
06242	Pontic—porcelain fused to noble metal					
06250	Pontic—resin with high noble metal					
06251	Pontic—resin with predominantly base metal					
06252	Pontic—resin with noble metal					
	Retainers					
06520	Inlay—metallic—two surfaces					
06530	Inlay—metallic—three or more surfaces					
06540	Onlay—metallic—per tooth (in addition to inlay)					
06545	Retainer—cast metal for acid-etched fixed prosthesis					
	Bridge retainers—crowns					
06720	Crown—resin with high noble metal					

Code	Procedure	Number of Procedures	Value of Procedure	Total Value	% of Total Value	% of Total Procedures
06721	Crown—resin with predominantly base metal					
06722	Crown—resin with noble metal					
06750	Crown—porcelain fused to high noble metal					
06751	Crown—porcelain fused to predominantly base metal					
06752	Crown—porcelain fused to noble metal					
06780	Crown—¾ cast high noble metal					
06790	Crown—full cast high noble metal					
06791	Crown—full cast predominantly base metal					
06792	Crown—full cast noble metal					
	Other fixed prosthetic services					
06930	Recement bridge					
06970	Cast post and core in addition to bridge retainer					
06971	Cast post as part of bridge retainer					
06972	Prefabricated post and core in addition to bridge retainer					
06973	Core buildup for retainer, including any pins					
06980	Bridge repair, by report					
07000-07999	**ORAL SURGERY**					
	Extractions (includes local anesthesia and routine postoperative care)					
07110	Single tooth					
07120	Each additional tooth					
07130	Root removal—exposed roots					
	Surgical extractions (includes local anesthesia and routine postoperative care)					
07210	Surgical removal of erupted tooth . . .					
07220	Removal of impacted tooth—soft tissue					
07230	Removal of impacted tooth—partially bony					
07240	Removal of impacted tooth—completely bony					

Code	Procedure	Number of Procedures	Value of Procedure	Total Value	% of Total Value	% of Total Procedures
07250	Surgical removal of residual tooth roots (cutting procedure)					
	Other surgical procedures					
07270	Tooth reimplantation and/or stabilization of accidentally evulsed . . .					
07271	Tooth implantation					
07280	Surgical exposure of impacted or unerupted tooth for orthodontic reasons					
07281	Surgical exposure of impacted or unerupted tooth to aid eruption					
	Alveoplasty—surgical preparation of ridge for dentures					
07310	Alveoplasty in conjunction with extractions—per quadrant					
07320	Alveoplasty not in conjunction with extractions—per quadrant					
	Vestibuloplasty					
07340	Vestibuloplasty—ridge extension (secondary epithelialization)					
07350	Vestibuloplasty—ridge extension (including . . .)					
	Removal of tumors, cysts and neoplasms					
07430	Excision of benign tumor—lesion diameter up to 1.25 cm					
07440	Excision of malignant tumor—lesion diameter up to 1.25 cm					
07450	Removal of odontogenic cyst or tumor—lesion diameter up to 1.25 cm					
07460	Removal of nonodontogenic cyst or tumor—lesion diameter up to 1.25 cm					
	Excision of bone tissue					
07470	Removal of exostosis—maxilla or mandible					
	Surgical incision					
07510	Incision and drainage of abscess—intraoral soft tissue					

Code	Procedure	Number of Procedures	Value of Procedure	Total Value	% of Total Value	% of Total Procedures
07520	Incision and drainage of abscess—extraoral soft tissue					
07530	Removal of foreign body, skin or subcutaneous areolar tissue					
07910	Suture of recent small wounds up to 5 cm					
	Complicated suturing (reconstruction requiring delicate handling . . .)					
07911	Complicated suture—up to 5 cm					
08000-08999	**XI. ORTHODONTICS**					
	Minor treatment for tooth guidance					
08110	Removable appliance therapy					
08120	Fixed appliance therapy					
	Minor treatment to control harmful habits					
08210	Removable appliance therapy					
08220	Fixed appliance therapy					
	Interceptive orthodontic treatment					
08360	Removable appliance therapy					
08370	Fixed appliance therapy					
	Comprehensive orthodontic treatment—transitional dentition					
08460	Class I malocclusion					
08470	Class II malocclusion					
08480	Class III malocclusion					
	Comprehensive orthodontic treatment—permanent dentition					
08560	Class I malocclusion					
08570	Class II malocclusion					
08580	Class III malocclusion					

Code	Procedure	Number of Procedures	Value of Procedure	Total Value	% of Total Value	% of Total Procedures
	Other orthodontic devices					
08650	Treatment for the atypical or extended skeletal case					
08750	Post-treatment stabilization					
08999	Unspecified orthodontic procedure, by report					
09000-09999	**XII. ADJUNCTIVE GENERAL SERVICES**					
	Unclassified treatment					
09110	Palliative (emergency) treatment of dental pain—minor procedures					
	Anesthesia					
09210	Local anesthesia not in conjunction with operative or surgical procedures					
09212	Trigeminal division block anesthesia					
	Professional consultation					
09310	Consultation					
	Drugs					
09610	Therapeutic drug injects					
09630	Other drugs and/or medicaments, by report					
	Miscellaneous services					
09910	Application of desensitizing medicaments					
09940	Occlusal guards, by report					
09941	Fabrication of athletic mouthguards					
09951	Occlusal adjustment—limited					
09952	Occlusal adjustment—complete					
	Grand Totals				100.0%	100.0%

See Appendix E for complete listing of American Dental Association "Code on Dental Procedures and Nomenclature."
"Code on Dental Procedures and Nomenclature" ©American Dental Association.

Exhibit 14-D

Detail of Treatment—Annual (by Patient and by Office)
Office of IMA Dentist, D.D.S.

Social Security #	Last Name	First Name	Relationship	Date of Service	ADA Code	ADA Procedure	Copayment
000-00-0000	Adams	Ann	Spouse	12/17/92	0110	Initial examination	$ 0
				12/17/92	0272	Bitewing X-rays	0
				12/17/92	1110	Prophylaxis—adult	0
				1/ 4/93	2110	Amalgam—one surface	0
				1/ 4/93	2120	Amalgam—two surfaces	0
				1/ 4/93	2130	Amalgam—three surfaces	0
				6/ 2/93	0120	Periodic examination	0
				6/ 2/93	1110	Prophylaxis—adult	0
				7/14/93	4341	Scaling and root planing	20
000-00-0000	Adams	Ira	Dependent	12/17/92	0110	Initial examination	0
				12/17/92	0272	Bitewing X-rays	0
				12/17/92	1120	Prophylaxis—child	0
				12/17/92	1201	Fluoride treatment	0
				6/ 2/93	0120	Periodic examination	0
				6/ 2/93	1120	Prophylaxis—child	0
000-00-0000	Adams	John	Employee	12/17/92	0110	Initial examination	0
				12/17/92	0272	Bitewing X-rays	0
				12/17/92	1110	Prophylaxis—adult	0
				1/ 3/93	3310	Root canal—anterior	30
				1/19/93	2750	Crown—porc high noble	80
				2/16/93	5214	Lower partial denture	100
				6/ 2/93	0120	Periodic examination	0
				6/ 2/93	1110	Prophylaxis—adult	0

15 Quality Assessment/Assurance

Why Quality Assurance?

In a perfect world, the state board of dental examiners would monitor the quality of dentistry within its jurisdiction on an ongoing basis. Unfortunately, monitoring is usually by exception. Once a dentist takes the examination for a license, the dentist is rarely required to take the same examination again. Unless an insurance company or patient files a complaint against a dentist with the state board of dental examiners or the dental society's peer review committee, it is highly unlikely that the dentist's competence (or incompetence) will ever be challenged.

The local dental society's peer review committee should handle isolated quality problems. The committee may be found in the white pages of the telephone directory or by contacting the American Dental Association (see Appendix A). If the problem is serious or recurrent, the state board of dental examiners should be contacted. The reason for this is simple. If the state board is effective, and most are, a dentist providing poor quality services (or committing other transgressions) can have his or her license placed in jeopardy, which is no small matter. This is also the least cumbersome and least expensive approach from the complainant's perspective. The shortcoming, however, may be time. It seems to take forever before the board takes any action on a complaint.

Having reviewed many dental offices throughout the United States, the author believes that, overall, there is no serious problem with the quality of dental care provided by American dentists. Most dentists are honest, capable and dedicated. The problem for a purchaser is that a small percentage of dentists can, and do, cause serious problems. It is the author's observation that many of these substandard offices are attracted to dental HMO plans and, if the plan or administrator does not have an effective quality assessment/assurance program, the participants may be playing Russian roulette with their dental health—and their pocketbooks. Therefore, it is essential for the purchaser to have a basic understanding of quality assessment and quality assurance when purchasing a dental HMO plan.

Background

The purchaser and the participant want assurance that the quality of the program and care are acceptable. Quality assessment is the vehicle to provide that assurance. Both should be ongoing and require the use of experienced auditors.

When *quality* is mentioned in connection with a dental program, it usually refers to how well the services were performed by the dentist, i.e., technical quality. *Quality* encompasses much more than that, as we shall see.

A little history may be in order. After years of relative obscurity, this country's principal gurus of quality, W. Edward Deming and J. M. Juran, are being recognized. They received international recognition (principally from Japan) long before this country realized the importance of what they were saying. However, during the past decade *quality* has become a widespread obsession in American companies.

Ironically, American health care professionals have a long history of being proactive in addressing issues related to quality in health care. *Quality* is not a new concept to them. In the 1860s, state dental boards were established to examine dentists and grant licenses; i.e., dentists had to demonstrate a level of competence in order to receive a license to practice. Later, in the early 1900s, Ernest Amroy Codman proposed a method for monitoring "end results." In 1917, the American College of Surgeons published *Minimum Standard of Care*. Then in 1933 Lee and Jones offered a concept of quality that included the assessment of the "process of care."

Organized dentistry has long been involved in issues related to quality, and in 1982 the American Dental Association (ADA) established the Office of Quality Assurance, which now has a full-time director for quality assurance. However, the dental profession's historic interest in quality has not yet resulted in eliminating the need for independent quality assessment and assurance programs.

Purchasers of health care, having had to address quality problems within their own institutions, are now looking for assurances that the same high standards of quality demanded by and of them are applied to the health care they purchase. Purchasers principally seek two things when buying health care: cost management and quality assurance. The purchaser no longer passively accepts a doctor's or vendor's assurances that "trust me, you are getting quality care." That time has passed.

Concurrent with actions taken to manage health care costs is an increasing concern about the quality of health care provided. The key question is: "How much money can you wring out of the health care system before the quality of care provided is adversely affected?" The concern that controlling cost may have a negative impact on the quality of health care is a valid one. However, it is the author's opinion that paying top dollar has never been the primary indicator of quality dental care or a quality program.

To some, the demands made by cost management and quality assurance appear to be in conflict. However, many purchasers have successfully met the challenge of reducing cost while improving quality and now have the same expectations from the providers of health care. Purchasers have a fiduciary responsibility for cost management and quality assurance because they are picking up a major portion of the tab for the beneficiaries.

Demanding quality assurance and cost management is one thing; obtaining it may be another.

Total quality management (TQM), zero defects, continuous quality improvement (CQI), statistical quality control (SQC) and *strategic quality management (SQM)* are among the buzzwords bandied about today in the quest for quality.

From this milieu of terms, approaches, theories and just plain hyperbole, how can one sort out a practical approach to assuring that quality care is received in a dental HMO plan?

Rather than err on the side of becoming too technical and describing in detail a quality assessment/assurance protocol, the author has chosen to sweep aside the impractical, theoretical and highly technical and describe several approaches to quality assessment and quality assurance that can be understood by almost any purchaser and be used to "evaluate the evaluators." This is necessary because, for a credible assessment of quality, the purchaser must usually rely on consultants and auditors.

The core question on quality becomes, "Is the level of quality in our dental HMO plan acceptable?" In this chapter several views and key areas are outlined that may assist the purchaser in the review and evaluation of quality assessment/assurance programs—and the reports from their consultants and auditors.

The Basics of Quality in Dental HMOs

It is important to keep in mind that quality encompasses more than "Is that a good filling or crown?" Quality must be viewed in a much broader context that includes:

- Cost
- Use
- Professional care
- Environment
- Preventive orientation
- Dental health status of participants
- Participant satisfaction.

The author has identified these as the essential areas the purchaser should examine when considering any quality assessment/assurance program. If any of these are missing, the plan is flawed and may be unacceptable. If any one of these areas is deemed unacceptable in a quality assessment review, the dental plan is not acceptable unless the problem is corrected. If the purchaser has a reputable consultant and these areas receive a passing mark, there is a high degree of probability the purchaser has an acceptable dental HMO plan.

Cost

Premium dollars spent over and above "fair value" are dollars that could be used for other purposes. Few purchasers have the luxury of not caring whether they are paying more than fair value for a product. In many HMO plans, the purchaser has no idea of the plan's true value. If the premium appears reasonable, then many times that is good enough for the purchaser. Chapter 17 will assist in assessing the value of your dental plan.

However, paying too little can also impact negatively on a dental HMO plan. If the dentist is at risk and is underpaid, there is an inducement to reduce that risk by providing too few or poor quality services (i.e., rationing care).

Use of the Program

It matters little if the services provided in a dental plan are of exceptional quality if they are provided to only a few participants. A minimum of 50% of those eligible should use a program on an annual basis. If less than 50% of eligible individuals are using the program, something is wrong. Either the program has problems, such as not offering dual choice, or the program has access restraints, such as too few offices, poor office locations or other barriers to care (see Chapter 11).

Professional Care

The quality of care provided must meet professional standards. This is best determined by an audit (see Chapter 16). Both the quality of individual services and the overall mix of services (see Chapter 8) must be reviewed. Providing high-quality dentures is of little consequence if filling decayed teeth could have prevented the need for dentures. By the same token, services of poor quality are unacceptable.

A quality assurance program for dental offices should consist of:

- Development of professional standards
- Measuring practice against those standards (quality assessment)
- Feedback to the dentists with explicit expectations for corrections
- Reevaluation on a periodic basis.

Environment of Plan and Office

Clean and attractive offices with pleasant personnel where participants feel comfortable and welcome are important components of a quality dental plan.

Office audits should address this in their review. Participant surveys (see Appendix H) are very helpful in determining the participant's view.

Preventive Orientation

As discussed in the Overview and Chapter 2, dental diseases are largely preventable. A good program recognizes the importance of emphasizing a strong preventive program by encouraging participants to use the program, having participants' dental needs taken care of on a timely basis, teaching participants to maintain good oral hygiene and having an active recall system so participants visit the dentist on a regular basis. These points should be addressed in an office audit.

Dental Health Status

If all the aforementioned criteria are more than adequately met but the participants do not have good dental health, then the program is not acceptable. However, the better the rating of the preceding elements, the more likely that the dental health status will be good. The mission of any dental plan must be good dental health for participants. No other outcome is acceptable. An audit of utilization data from the plan administrator and dental office records are the two best sources for determining dental health status of participants.

Participant Satisfaction

Participant satisfaction is an integral component of quality. It is similar to "dental health status" in that if all the other criteria are acceptable but the participants are not satisfied, something vital is missing and the program is not acceptable. Dissatisfied participants will eventually stop using the program. Dissatisfaction by participants is best determined by participant surveys (see Appendix H). The surveys may reveal underlying problems that may have been overlooked by a well thought out and planned quality assurance program.

An acceptable dental program will meet all of the above standards. Everyone—the purchaser, the participant and the dentist—can be a winner. If any one of these three is shortchanged, the program will be a failure.

Structure, Process and Outcome

Moving from the pragmatic to a more objective approach to quality assessment, the most widely used approach to quality assessment—structure, process and outcome—cannot be overlooked. This approach is based upon the studies and writings of one of health care's most respected and prolific writers on quality in health care, Avedis Donabedian, M.D., M.P.H. Essentially, Dr. Donabedian divides quality assessment into three components: structure, process and outcome.

The following, a simplified outline of Donabedian's three major components, should be included in the quality assessment of dental HMO plans.

Structure

Structure consists essentially of buildings, equipment, people, cost, management, patient records, education, licensing, training, cleanliness, sterilization, patient management and other items not included under *process* and *outcome*.

Process

Process is, in essence, "what the dentist does" and how well it is done, i.e., diagnosis, treatment planning and treatment. Process also includes how well the patients maintain good oral hygiene.

Outcome

Outcome is the end result in terms of dental health and value. Many quality assessment programs are based primarily on outcomes, i.e., the improvement in the dental health of the covered group as a consequence of coverage by the dental plan. The author agrees with those who view this as the most critical component.

No matter how well structured a quality assurance program is or how great the process, if the outcome is not improved dental health for the participants, the program is not acceptable. Acceptable outcomes may vary by group, depending upon the group's needs and other variables but, at a minimum, the outcome should be better dental health for the participants. This includes:

- 50% or more of eligibles visited the dentist.
- There is an absence or active treatment of tooth decay, gum disease, infections and tumors.
- Missing critical teeth have been replaced or are in the process of being replaced.
- 70% of participants viewed the program as acceptable.
- The dental services provided met professional standards.

Quality Checklist

In an attempt to assist the readers, the author has developed a quality assurance checklist that can be used to review dental HMO plans' quality assurance programs:

1. Precontract quality audit (office evaluation and patient record audit) was performed on dental office with acceptable results.
2. Audit was performed at the end of the first year of participation.
3. Audits subsequent to the precontract audit were performed by an independent auditor experienced in quality audits, or reviewed and approved by an independent auditor.
4. Independent audit substantiates that the value of the services provided is not less than 80% of the premium paid.
5. At least 50% of eligible participants use the program on an annual basis, with offices conveniently located and no dentist-induced barriers.

6. Independent audit substantiates that needed services were provided and that the dental services provided were necessary, appropriate and of acceptable quality.
7. Participants are treated with respect and feel welcome, with 70% finding the program acceptable or excellent.
8. Patients are recalled on a regular basis, oral hygiene instruction is given and treatment is rendered on a timely basis.
9. 65% of those using the program are "on maintenance," free of any dental diseases or conditions or are under active treatment with tooth decay and gum (periodontal) disease treated or in process of treatment.
10. There is existing protocol for correcting problems in dental offices or removing such offices from the network.

What to Do

Compare your current or anticipated dental HMO plan's quality assessment/assurance procedures with the information in this chapter. Ask to see copies of audits and utilization reports. Have the reports reviewed by an experienced consultant. If no reports are available, retain a consultant to perform a comprehensive review (see Sections I and II).

If you do not know what to do or who to turn to for help or if you simply wish to learn more about quality assessment/assurance, you may wish to contact one or more of the following (addresses and phone numbers can be found in Appendix A):

- American Academy of Dental Group Practice
- American Association for Ambulatory Health Care
- American Board of Quality Assurance and Utilization Review Physicians
- American Dental Association.

16 Audits

Despite the other attractive aspects of a dental plan, the most important and overriding consideration in evaluating a dental plan is its performance; the plan must be audited. There is simply no rational excuse for not doing so. Auditing is not an option; it is a necessity. It is the only way to ascertain that the plan is performing as stated; auditing is an ongoing and integral part of the purchaser's oversight. Dental HMO plans are not an exception. They may be subject to more abuse than fee-for-service dental plans.

There is no substitute for an audit. To be valid, an audit must be performed, or verified, by an independent auditor.

Audits generally fall into two categories: auditing the administrator and auditing the dentist(s).

There is a major difference in emphasis between auditing a dental HMO plan and auditing a fee-for-service dental plan. In dental HMO plans the dentist is at risk; serious problems of undertreatment or creative ways to do as little as possible are more likely to occur in the dental office. The temptation in a dental office may change from overtreatment in fee for service, to undertreatment in HMO plans in which the dentist is usually paid the same amount irrespective of the number or type of services provided—or not provided.

In fee-for-service plans the administrator is at risk if the plan is insured; the purchaser is at risk if the plan is self-funded. Payments are based upon claims submitted by the dentist after being screened, priced and paid by the administrator. Payment is claims driven. Payment levels, and review of proposed services prior to payment, play an important role in managing the cost of the plan. There are usually certain requirements for the dentist, such as submitting X-rays to support the dentist's diagnosis and proposed treatment. In fee-for-service plans, it is highly unlikely that the dentist will undertreat or underreport. The dentist's incentive may be to overtreat or overreport. If no service is provided, no payment is received and, the more services provided, the more income generated for the dentist. As a consequence, the emphasis for audit in fee-for-service dental plans should be on the plan administrator's claims adjudication and utilization review.

Auditing the Administrator

The audit of the HMO plan administrator is usually performed by an auditor retained by the purchaser. Chapters 8, 11, 14 and 17 provide baseline information to assist in assuring that the audit addresses key issues. It is not possible to do a reliable audit of a dental HMO plan without visiting the dental office. Unlike fee-for-service plans, where the dentist usually submits X-rays and other data to the administrator to verify that services were necessary, appropriate and provided, the only thing usually submitted in an HMO plan is a report on what was performed. And many times even this information is not provided to the administrator by the dentist. What is being provided or not provided in an HMO plan is not monitored with the same intensity or timeliness as in fee-for-service plans. Some plans collect no data at all from the dental offices. As a consequence, problems may be building that are not apparent until the reported data are validated by an audit of the dental office.

Administrative cost is a very important consideration. It is important to know the amount of dollars going to the dentists and the amount retained by the administrator to cover overhead and profits. This is one area frequently overlooked by auditors. They tend to look at the reported value of services and compare that with the premium to arrive at an estimate of administrative cost. What is often overlooked is that the administrator may be keeping a far greater portion of the premium than is apparent. The audit must determine the total percentage of dollars going to the dentists and to the administrator. If the administrator is not passing through enough of the premium dollars to the dentists providing the services, the dentists may be more likely to undertreat or not treat the plan participants.

Administrators do have one recurring problem with dentists in dental HMO plans—a small number, 10-15%, do not report the service they have provided. The patients may be treated appropriately, but the dentists feel it is a burden to report the services to the plan administrator. Although services can be verified by an office audit, the dentists should be required to report item-specific detail of procedures performed on some type of claim or encounter form. The paperwork requirement should not be burdensome to the office as this just adds an additional cost. In addition, the plan administrator can design inducements for the dentists to submit all treatment data, such as performance bonuses and guarantees against antiselection. Problems of underreporting occur more frequently when special forms or systems are required for a small percentage of patients.

Reviewing the training and effectiveness of the administrator's staff is standard auditing practice. It is important that the administrator has staff members who fully understand dental HMOs and can communicate effectively with the dental office.

There are key differences between fee-for-service plans and HMO plans. Fee-for-service plans are *claims driven;* i.e., the dentist must submit a claim to be paid, and claims processing is a major function and expense. All activities revolve around payment, or nonpayment, of claims. All this activity occurs in-house at the administrator's facility.

In dental HMOs there are no claims, which is a major change in doing business. All the administrator does, in-house, is maintain eligibility, receive data, develop reports and handle participant concerns. There is no sense of urgency relative to entering data or producing data, as there is in fee-for-service plans where the turnaround time for claims processing is a critical measurement. The critical element in dental HMOs that is often overlooked by administrators, especially those with long experience in fee-for-service plans, is the importance of maintaining a good relationship with the dental office.

One of the mistakes most frequently made by administrators in dental HMOs is running the HMO as though it were a fee-for-service plan. This alienates the dentists and does not make for a successful dental plan.

In summary, auditing the administrator includes, at a minimum, auditing:

- Validity of the data and reports
- Value of services provided
- Quality assurance protocols, procedures and dental office compliance
- Administrative cost (overhead plus profit)
- Cost effectiveness
- Staff training and effectiveness—technical/analytical staff, professional relations staff, customer service, problem identification and solving capabilities
- Administrative and monitoring capabilities—computer hardware, computer software.

Auditing the Dentist(s)

The plan administrator should audit all dental offices prior to admitting them as participating offices in the dental HMO network. The audit should include an extensive review of office practices and procedures as well as a record review to determine the quality of the care being provided by the dental office. The plan administrator should have these audits performed by either an independent or a staff auditor experienced in conducting such audits. The auditor should be either a dentist or a dental hygienist. Any office that does not measure up should either be rejected or reevaluated when the identified problems have been corrected. If the plan administrator does not have this audit procedure in place, the plan is unacceptable, and the purchaser should look elsewhere.

Because the administrator has an inherent conflict of interest in obtaining favorable audits, the purchaser should use an independent consultant to review the purchaser's audits to ascertain their validity. If the purchaser is not satisfied or serious questions arise about the validity of the audits, the purchaser must reserve the right to call in an independent auditor to verify the administrator's audit reports. A common problem with administrators' audits is that they are confined to the facilities and do not review the dental records for the quality of care being provided in the office.

Auditing dental offices in dental HMOs plans is easier than in fee-for-service plans because there are far fewer dentists providing services. The audit generally encompasses three areas: assuring that the dental care meets accepted standards of dental practice; identifying any barriers to care; and verifying the validity of data being submitted to the administrator (after the first year).

These baseline audits are absolutely essential. Copies of these audits should be available for review by the purchaser or consultant. However, there are quite a few dental HMO plans that do not perform audits prior to, or after, signing up a dental office to participate in the plan. Many times, the only contact with the dental office is a letter containing an invitation and agreement to participate. Such plans should be avoided.

After the first year of participation, all offices providing significant volumes of services—for example, over $25,000—should be audited. Frequency of subsequent audits may be based upon the levels of annual gross payment to the dental office for services provided or findings in the first audit. These dollar levels may be used to establish cost-effective priorities and frequencies for future dental office audits. For example, offices with less than $25,000 in annual payments may be audited on a random basis; offices with at least $25,000 in annual payments may be audited every two to four years if practice patterns are normal and there are no unusual patient complaints; and offices receiving over $50,000 should be audited at least every two or three years.

Offices that have correctable quality problems may have to be audited on a more frequent basis.

Additional reasons for more frequent audits include utilization data that suggest unusual practice patterns or participant complaints that suggest all is not well at a particular office. If there are no unusual reporting patterns or patient complaints, a modified audit may suffice. The author does not subscribe to the practice of auditing every office, every year, as recommended by some. If an office has been audited and no problems found, it is an unnecessary expense to audit that office annually. Offices can be monitored by reviewing the utilization data, monitoring patient complaints and doing random checks—for example, sending a letter to a participant asking him or her to verify the date of treatment and the services provided. Because dental treatment or lack of treatment leaves an audit trail, it is relatively easy to do audits covering multiple years.

The author has a major problem with dental offices or administrators that do not report data. Dental offices that do not report data should not be permitted to be providers of dental care in the plan. Administrators of dental plans that do not provide data should not be allowed to stay in business. If data are not reported, it is impossible to do an effective audit. It is the author's observation that when data are not reported there is usually a specific reason (frequently the dental office is shortchanging the plan participants). The administrator does not want the purchaser to know the vast margin of profit in undertreating the dental needs of the participants.

In summary, auditing the dentist(s) includes, at a minimum, auditing the:

- Quality of care
- Compliance with accepted standards of dental care
- Barriers to care
- Reporting
- Validity of data
- Increasing value of services through fragmentation, also called *unbundling* or *a la carting* or using high fees to overvalue services
- Not reporting services.

17 Value Checker

What is the value of the services provided under a dental HMO plan? What is a fair premium? These are essential questions to answer if one is to determine if value is being received in a dental HMO plan.

The two methods described in this chapter will assist the reader in determining a reasonable value for services provided in a dental HMO plan, as well as a reasonable premium. The two methods are a *time-unit* method and a *fee-for-service* method. With good data, appropriate coding, average mix of services and a mature group with no unusual exceptions, both methods should provide an estimated value of plus or minus 10%. However, there are many variables, and it is important to keep in mind that the values obtained are estimates and not exact values. A difference of 20% may have a rational explanation. Having said that, if your calculation is within 10% of total procedure value or premium, you probably are getting value.

The time-unit method is usually, on average, 4-6% less than the fee-for-service method. Part of the reason for this is that some dentists report a higher fee to insurance companies, or when responding to a survey, than they "usually" charge private noninsured patients. As a consequence of this, fee schedules based upon dentist "reported charges" are often artificially high.

Another reason for a difference between the time-unit method and the fee-for-service method may be in the mix of services. The time-unit method is designed to allow the dentist a uniform hourly rate irrespective of the services being performed. It allows a greater value than a fee-for-service dental plan for low-profit basic services such as examinations, amalgam fillings and scaling and root planing. Conversely, the time-unit method reduces the allowance—and profit—for higher cost services such as dentures, root canals and fixed bridges. A greater number of the higher profit services will result in a significantly higher value when using the fee-for-service method.

For the reasons stated above, the *value checker* is not to be used as a substitute for an experienced consultant who can identify, and adjust for, any variables not taken into consideration in the value checker. Other variables may be services covered, payment levels, coding variations, upgrading of value, demographic variations and falsification of data.

Both methods use 56 procedures. These 56 procedures have been selected by identifying, in a variety of plans, procedures that represent approximately 93% of the value of services provided. Hundreds of services were reported, but routinely these 56 procedures represented over 93% of the total value of the plans reviewed.

This method for determining value was first presented in a paper by Richard E. Ullman in 1979, in *Transactions* 31, the Society of Actuaries journal. Mr. Ullman conducted a study of dental group contracts involving 250,000 persons covered by Blue Cross and Blue Shield of Greater New York. The study excluded orthodontics. Mr. Ullman stated in his paper: "Of the 273 procedures, we selected for the study 44 procedures that represented 91.1% of dental claims cost."

The larger the group purchasing a dental HMO plan, generally the greater the discount that can be negotiated. An even greater discount may be expected if the dental services are provided by a *closed panel,* that is, a dental plan where the patients must go to a specific office or offices. Many times for large groups, a dental office is established specifically to serve closed panel dental HMO plans. If the services are provided by a network of dentists in private practice, dentist "busyness" becomes a factor. If the dentists are busy and have no empty chair time, it is less likely they will participate in dental HMO plans. However, if dentists have empty chair time, it may be to their advantage to participate (see Chapter 19 for the dentist's perspective). In 1990 the average dental office had expenses of 61% of gross revenues.[1] If the dental office overhead is $90 an hour, generating an income of $90 eliminates that loss. Filling empty time generates income and reduces overhead. New patients are also a source for referral of additional new patients. One happy patient will generally refer two new patients. Another advantage to a dental office with a large number of dental HMO patients (assuming the capitation payment is adequate) is that there are far fewer collection problems; the check comes every month. The participating dentists also have the advantage of having their practices marketed to the beneficiaries. Collection of copayments and deductibles from patients may still be a problem for the dentists because beneficiaries "think everything is covered."

When comparing the premiums paid for dental plans, it is necessary to add any patient copayments and deductibles to arrive at the total paid for care.

Time-Unit Method

The time-unit method is designed to remove significant variations in determining the value of dental procedures. Generally, in a fee-for-service dental plan, crowns, dentures and other high-priced procedures have a higher profit margin than examinations, teeth cleaning and basic fillings. The time-unit method provides a more equitable determination of value because the value is determined on a time basis, not on a procedure basis. Ideally, the value for the time spent should be the same regardless of which procedure is performed. If value is determined or a dentist reimbursed on a time-unit basis, diagnostic, preventive and other basic services are valued, or reimbursed, on a time basis at the same hourly rate as higher valued services such as crowns, dentures and root canals plus laboratory costs.

The time unit is especially applicable if the dental services are provided by salaried dentists, i.e., paid on an hourly basis.

Value Checker Worksheet—1
"Time-Unit Method"

Obtain the annual frequency of each procedure listed on the worksheet from the administrator's utilization reports and place that number in the column "number performed."

The time-unit value is already provided. Each unit represents ten-minute segments of time (six units equal one hour). For example, an examination has a time-unit value of 1.5, which equals 15 minutes.

The unit value is also provided. The unit value is based upon the 1990 national average of dentists' and hygienists' gross annual income[2] (see time-unit value worksheet). Note that there are two sets of values. The procedures with a $29.80 per unit are based upon a dentist's average hourly income of $178.82. The procedures with a per unit value of $7.71 are based upon a hygienist's average hourly pay of $18.50 (increased to $46.25 to allow for overhead expenses). The services valued at $7.71, per ten-minute unit, are generally not performed by a dentist. They are usually performed by a dental auxiliary—either a dental hygienist or a dental assistant—and consequently have a lower hourly value than procedures that must be performed by a dentist.

Then multiply each line as follows:

Number Performed × Time Unit × Unit Value = Value

Total the value column to determine the value of procedures.

Adjustments should then be made.

Add 7%. To adjust for the procedures not listed. To do this, divide value of procedures by 0.93.

CPI adjustment. If necessary, the dental component of the Consumer Price Index is used to adjust the value for the time frame for which the value is being determined (see Appendix C). Unit value data is from 1990.

Area adjustment is needed to allow for differing values of dental services in different areas of the country. Obviously a plan located in Manhattan will have a higher unit value than one located in Boise, Idaho. City adjustments are located in Appendix B. If your city is not listed, select the one that most closely mirrors your local economy.

Laboratory costs. The time units do not take into consideration the laboratory cost of making dentures, crowns and other dental services that entail a laboratory cost to the dentist; therefore, it must be calculated. This may be done on the laboratory cost worksheet.

Administrative fee is generally in the range of 10-20% over and above the value of the services. If it is higher than 20%, there must be compelling reasons, for example, many dental offices spread over a wide geographic area. If the plan is a closed panel with very few offices, there may no administrative fee.

Fee-for-Service Method

The fee-for-service method uses "dentist charges" as the basis for determining value. There are a number of sources of dentist fees. The best national data can be obtained from the American Dental Association, and the best regional data is developed by the Health Insurance Association of America (HIAA). However, HIAA data are not readily available.

The best source for dentist fees in a specific geographic area may be a preferred provider organization (PPO) operating in that area. A PPO usually pays dentists on the basis of a fee schedule and has an arrangement with the dentist to accept the schedule as payment in full. This type of schedule(s) will more accurately reflect the value at which dental services may be purchased in that specific market. If the network of dentists is small, it may indicate the fees are too low. If the network is large enough to handle the covered population, the fee schedule is probably a valid method for determining what services can be purchased for in that market. It is recommended that the administrator of the plan be contacted to discuss the plan's experience.

The fee-for-service method is especially applicable if the dental services in the dental HMO network are provided either entirely, or principally, by dentists engaged in regular private practices, i.e., not offices set up specifically to service the dental HMO plan. It is the easiest for the dentist and purchaser to understand, and it approximates what price the services might have been purchased for in that marketplace.

Value Checker Worksheet—2 "Fee-for-Service Method"

Worksheet 2 is to be used when fees are obtainable on a local or regional basis.

Obtain the annual frequency of each procedure listed on the worksheet from the administrator's utilization reports and place that number in the column "Number Performed."

Place the value for each listed procedure obtained from a local or regional fee schedule in the column "Single Procedure Value."

Then multiply each line as follows:

Number Performed × Single Procedure Value = Value

Total the value column to determine the value of procedures.

Adjustments should then be made.

Add 7%. To adjust for the procedures not listed. To do this, divide value of procedure by 0.93.

CPI adjustment. If necessary, the dental component of the Consumer Price Index is used to adjust for the time frame in which the value is being determined (see Appendix C).

Area adjustment is not needed if local fees are used. However, if the fees represent a national database, an adjustment may be necessary. City adjustments are located in Appendix B. If your city is not listed, select the one that most closely mirrors your local economy.

Value Checker Worksheet—3 "Fee-for-Service Method"

Worksheet 3 is very similar to worksheet 2 except it has fees in the column headed "Single Procedure Value" and it is necessary to adjust the national value for the geographic area being calculated. The fees listed are the 50th percentile of fees obtained from the American Dental Association.

The 1990 Survey of Dental Fees. At the 50th percentile, half of the dentists charged more for a procedure and the other half charged less. A dental HMO plan should not be valued using fees above the 50th percentile. As a rule of thumb, one may expect a discount of 10% below this level for medium or large size groups.

See Exhibits 17-A, 17-B, 17-C and 17-D for examples of value checker work-sheets and the time-unit value calculation for worksheet 1.

Endnotes

1. *The 1991 Survey of Dental Practice* by the American Dental Association.
2. Ibid.

Exhibit 17-A

Value Checker Worksheet—1 "Time-Unit Method"

(56 procedures should represent approximately 93% of plan value)

Code	Procedure	Number Performed		Time Unit		Unit Value*		Value
DIAGNOSTIC								
00110	Initial oral examination	______	×	1.50	×	$29.80	=	______
00120	Periodic oral examination	______	×	0.50	×	29.80	=	______
00130	Emergency oral examination	______	×	0.50	×	29.80	=	______
00210	Intraoral—complete series (including bitewings)	______	×	2.50	×	7.71	=	______
00220	Intraoral—periapical—first film	______	×	0.25	×	7.71	=	______
00230	Intraoral—periapical—each additional film	______	×	0.10	×	7.71	=	______
00270	Bitewings—single film	______	×	0.25	×	7.71	=	______
00272	Bitewings—two films	______	×	0.35	×	7.71	=	______
00274	Bitewings—four films	______	×	0.55	×	7.71	=	______
00330	Panoramic film	______	×	0.75	×	7.71	=	______
PREVENTIVE								
01110	Prophylaxis—adult	______	×	4.00	×	7.71	=	______
01120	Prophylaxis—child	______	×	2.00	×	7.71	=	______
01201	Topical appli. of fluoride (includ. prophylaxis)—child	______	×	2.50	×	7.71	=	______
01203	Topical appli. of fluoride (exclud. prophylaxis)—child	______	×	0.50	×	7.71	=	______
01351	Sealant—per tooth	______	×	0.50	×	29.80	=	______
RESTORATIVE								
02110	Amalgam—one surface, primary	______	×	1.00	×	29.80	=	______
02120	Amalgam—two surfaces, primary	______	×	1.50	×	29.80	=	______
02130	Amalgam—three surfaces, primary	______	×	2.00	×	29.80	=	______
02140	Amalgam—one surface, permanent	______	×	1.50	×	29.80	=	______
02150	Amalgam—two surfaces, permanent	______	×	2.00	×	29.80	=	______
02160	Amalgam—three surfaces, permanent	______	×	2.50	×	29.80	=	______

Code	Procedure	Number Performed		Time Unit		Unit Value*		Value
02161	Amalgam—four or more surfaces, permanent		×	2.50	×	$29.80	=	
02330	Resin—one surface, anterior		×	2.00	×	29.80	=	
02331	Resin—two surfaces, anterior		×	3.00	×	29.80	=	
02332	Resin—three surfaces, anterior		×	3.50	×	29.80	=	
02335	Resin—four or more surfaces or involving incisal angle		×	4.00	×	29.80	=	
02750	Crown—porcelain fused to high noble metal		×	6.00	×	29.80	=	
02751	Crown—porcelain fused to predom. base metal		×	6.00	×	29.80	=	
02752	Crown—porcelain fused to noble metal		×	6.00	×	29.80	=	
02790	Crown—full cast high noble metal		×	6.00	×	29.80	=	
02920	Recement crown		×	0.50	×	29.80	=	
02940	Sedative filling		×	2.00	×	29.80	=	
02950	Core buildup, including any pins		×	3.50	×	29.80	=	
02951	Pin retention—per tooth, in addition to restoration		×	0.50	×	29.80	=	
ENDODONTICS								
03220	Therapeutic pulpotomy (excluding final restoration)		×	1.00	×	29.80	=	
03310	Anterior (excluding final restoration)		×	5.00	×	29.80	=	
03320	Bicuspid (excluding final restoration)		×	6.00	×	29.80	=	
03330	Molar (excluding final restoration)		×	10.00	×	29.80	=	
PERIODONTICS								
04220	Gingival curettage, surgical, per quadrant, by report		×	2.50	×	29.80	=	
04260	Osseous surg. (inc. flap entry and close)—per quad.		×	5.00	×	29.80	=	
04341	Periodontal scaling and root planing—per quadrant		×	5.00	×	7.71	=	
04910	Periodontal maintenance procedures		×	5.00	×	7.71	=	
PROSTHODONTICS, REMOVABLE								
05110	Complete upper		×	8.00	×	29.80	=	
05213	Upper part'l—cast metal (inc. clasps, rests and teeth)		×	3.00	×	29.80	=	
05214	Lower part'l—cast metal (inc. clasps, rests and teeth)		×	3.00	×	29.80	=	
PROSTHODONTICS, FIXED								
06240	Pontic—porcelain fused to high noble metal		×	0.50	×	29.80	=	
06242	Pontic—porcelain fused to noble metal		×	0.50	×	29.80	=	

Code	Procedure	Number Performed		Time Unit		Unit Value*		Value
06750	Crown—porcelain fused to high noble metal	______	×	6.00	×	$29.80	=	______
06752	Crown—porcelain fused to noble metal	______	×	6.00	×	29.80	=	______
06790	Crown—full cast high noble metal	______	×	6.00	×	29.80	=	______
06792	Crown—full cast noble metal	______	×	6.00	×	29.80	=	______
ORAL SURGERY								
07110	Single tooth	______	×	1.00	×	29.80	=	______
07120	Each additional tooth	______	×	1.00	×	29.80	=	______
07210	Surgical removal of erupted tooth	______	×	1.50	×	29.80	=	______
07240	Removal of impacted tooth—completely bony	______	×	4.00	×	29.80	=	______
ADJUNCTIVE GENERAL SERVICES								
09110	Palliative (emergency) treatment of dental pain	______	×	1.00	×	29.80	=	______
ORTHODONTICS								______
LABORATORY COST—see LABORATORY SERVICES WORKSHEET.								______
				Value of Procedures				______

ADJUSTMENTS

Add 7% for procedures not listed (divide **Value of Procedures** by .93). ______

Area—Multiply amount in previous line by "Area Adjustment Factor" (see Appendix B). ______

+ **CPI**—Add appropriate increase for Dental Component (see Appendix C). + ______

+ **Administrative Fee**—Add 10% to 20%—less if closed panel. + ______

Total Value = [ ]

INSTRUCTIONS

Place number of services performed annually in column **Number Performed**.
Multiply **Number Performed** × **Time Unit** × **Single Procedure Value**.
Obtain total value of orthodontic services and add to line **Orthodontics**.
Add **Value** column for **Value of Procedures**.
For **Total Value** add adjustments to **Value of Procedures**.

***Unit Value** is for year 1990—based on data from American Dental Association *1991 Survey of Dental Practice*.
Code on Dental Procedures and Nomenclature ©American Dental Association.
Time-Unit Values courtesy John R. Amsterdam, D.M.D., M.B.A., Radnor, PA.
Value Checker ©Don Mayes & Associates.

Value Checker Worksheet—1
Laboratory Services Worksheet for Time-Unit Method

Code	Procedure	Number Performed		Single Procedure Value*		Value
RESTORATIVE						
02750	Crown—porcelain fused to high noble metal	______	×	$425	=	______
02751	Crown—porcelain fused to predom. base metal	______	×	395	=	______
02752	Crown—porcelain fused to noble metal	______	×	410	=	______
02790	Crown—full cast high noble metal	______	×	415	=	______
PROSTHODONTICS, REMOVABLE						
05110	Complete upper	______	×	500	=	______
05213	Upper part'l—cast metal (inc. clasps, rests and teeth)	______	×	565	=	______
05214	Lower part'l—cast metal (inc. clasps, rests and teeth)	______	×	564	=	______
PROSTHODONTICS, FIXED						
06240	Pontic—porcelain fused to high noble metal	______	×	425	=	______
06242	Pontic—procelain fused to noble metal	______	×	[410]	=	______
06750	Crown—porcelain fused to high noble metal	______	×	425	=	______
06752	Crown—porcelain fused to noble metal	______	×	[410]	=	______
06790	Crown—full cast high noble metal	______	×	410	=	______
06792	Crown—full cast noble metal	______	×	[410]	=	______
	Total Value of Laboratory Procedures					[ ]
	Divide Total Value by 3.5 = Laboratory Cost					[ ]

[ ] Indicates estimated value in **Single Procedure Value** column—no ADA value available.

INSTRUCTIONS

Place number of services performed annually in column **Number Performed**.
Multiply **Number Performed** by **Single Procedure Value**.
Add **Value** column for **Total Value of Laboratory Procedures**.
Divide **Total Value of Laboratory Procedures** by 3.5 for **Laboratory Cost**.

***Single Procedure Values** ©American Dental Association, *The 1990 Survey of Dental Fees.*

Exhibit 17-B

Time-Unit Value Calculation for Worksheet—1
Independent Dentists Primary Practice Gross Income for the Year 1990

DENTISTS:

Primary practice income (1) page 41	$291,010
Chair time (2) page 8	1,627.4
Ten-minute unit cost =	**$ 29.80**

CALCULATION:

$$\frac{\$291{,}010}{1{,}627.4} = \frac{\$178.82/\text{hour}}{6} = \$29.80/\text{ten-minute unit}$$

HYGIENISTS:

1990 mean hourly rate (3)	$18.50
Overhead adjustment (× 2.5)	$46.25
Ten-minute unit cost =	**$ 7.71**

American Dental Association *1991 Survey of Dental Practice* (1990 data).

Exhibit 17-C

Value Checker Worksheet—2 "Fee-for-Service Method"

(56 procedures should represent approximately 93% of plan value)

Code	Procedure	Number Performed		Single Procedure Value		Value
DIAGNOSTIC						
00110	Initial oral examination	______	×	______	=	______
00120	Periodic oral examination	______	×	______	=	______
00130	Emergency oral examination	______	×	______	=	______
00210	Intraoral—complete series (including bitewings)	______	×	______	=	______
00220	Intraoral—periapical—first film	______	×	______	=	______
00230	Intraoral—periapical—each additional film	______	×	______	=	______
00270	Bitewings—single film	______	×	______	=	______
00272	Bitewings—two films	______	×	______	=	______
00274	Bitewings—four films	______	×	______	=	______
00330	Panoramic film	______	×	______	=	______
PREVENTIVE						
01110	Prophylaxis—adult	______	×	______	=	______
01120	Prophylaxis—child	______	×	______	=	______
01201	Topical appli. of fluoride (includ. prophylaxis)—child	______	×	______	=	______
01203	Topical appli. of fluoride (exclud. prophylaxis)—child	______	×	______	=	______
01351	Sealant—per tooth	______	×	______	=	______
RESTORATIVE						
02110	Amalgam—one surface, primary	______	×	______	=	______
02120	Amalgam—two surfaces, primary	______	×	______	=	______
02130	Amalgam—three surfaces, primary	______	×	______	=	______
02140	Amalgam—one surface, permanent	______	×	______	=	______
02150	Amalgam—two surfaces, permanent	______	×	______	=	______
02160	Amalgam—three surfaces, permanent	______	×	______	=	______

Code	Procedure	Number Performed		Single Procedure Value		Value
02161	Amalgam—four or more surfaces, permanent		×		=	
02330	Resin—one surface, anterior		×		=	
02331	Resin—two surfaces, anterior		×		=	
02332	Resin—three surfaces, anterior		×		=	
02335	Resin—four or more surfaces or involving incisal angle		×		=	
02750	Crown—porcelain fused to high noble metal		×		=	
02751	Crown—porcelain fused to predom. base metal		×		=	
02752	Crown—porcelain fused to noble metal		×		=	
02790	Crown—full cast high noble metal		×		=	
02920	Recement crown		×		=	
02940	Sedative filling		×		=	
02950	Core buildup, including any pins		×		=	
02951	Pin retention—per tooth, in addition to restoration		×		=	
ENDODONTICS						
03220	Therapeutic pulpotomy (excluding final restoration)		×		=	
03310	Anterior (excluding final restoration)		×		=	
03320	Bicuspid (excluding final restoration)		×		=	
03330	Molar (excluding final restoration)		×		=	
PERIODONTICS						
04220	Gingival curettage, surgical, per quadrant, by report		×		=	
04260	Osseous surg. (inc. flap entry and close)—per quad.		×		=	
04341	Periodontal scaling and root planing—per quadrant		×		=	
04910	Periodontal maintenance procedures		×		=	
PROSTHODONTICS, REMOVABLE						
05110	Complete upper		×		=	
05213	Upper part'l—cast metal (inc. clasps, rests and teeth)		×		=	
05214	Lower part'l—cast metal (inc. clasps, rests and teeth)		×		=	
PROSTHODONTICS, FIXED						
06240	Pontic—porcelain fused to high noble metal		×		=	
06242	Pontic—porcelain fused to noble metal		×		=	

Code	Procedure	Number Performed		Single Procedure Value		Value
06750	Crown—porcelain fused to high noble metal	____	×	____	=	____
06752	Crown—porcelain fused to noble metal	____	×	____	=	____
06790	Crown—full cast high noble metal	____	×	____	=	____
06792	Crown—full cast noble metal	____	×	____	=	____
ORAL SURGERY						
07110	Single tooth	____	×	____	=	____
07120	Each additional tooth	____	×	____	=	____
07210	Surgical removal of erupted tooth	____	×	____	=	____
07240	Removal of impacted tooth—completely bony	____	×	____	=	____
ADJUNCTIVE GENERAL SERVICES						
09110	Palliative (emergency) treatment of dental pain	____	×	____	=	____
ORTHODONTICS						____
				Value of Procedures		____

ADJUSTMENTS

Add 7% for procedures not listed (divide **Value of Procedures** by .93).		____
Area—Multiply amount in previous line by *Area Adjustment Factor* (see Appendix B).		____
+ **CPI**—Add appropriate increase for Dental Component (see Appendix C).	+	____
+ **Administrative Fee**—Add 10% to 20%—less if closed panel.	+	____
Total Value	=	☐

INSTRUCTIONS

Place number of services performed annually in column **Number Performed**.
Place value of procedure in column **Single Procedure Value**.
Multiply **Number Performed** by **Single Procedure Value**.
Obtain value of orthodontic services and add in line **Orthodontics**.
Add **Value** column for **Value of Procedures**.
For **Total Value** add adjustments to **Value of Procedures**.

Exhibit 17-D

Value Checker Worksheet—3 "Fee-for-Service Method"

(56 procedures should represent approximately 93% of plan value)

Code	Procedure	Number Performed		Single Procedure Value*		Value
DIAGNOSTIC						
00110	Initial oral examination	______	×	$18	=	______
00120	Periodic oral examination	______	×	14	=	______
00130	Emergency oral examination	______	×	19	=	______
00210	Intraoral—complete series (including bitewings)	______	×	45	=	______
00220	Intraoral—periapical—first film	______	×	8	=	______
00230	Intraoral—periapical—each additional film	______	×	6	=	______
00270	Bitewings—single film	______	×	10	=	______
00272	Bitewings—two films	______	×	14	=	______
00274	Bitewings—four films	______	×	20	=	______
00330	Panoramic film	______	×	39	=	______
PREVENTIVE						
01110	Prophylaxis—adult	______	×	30	=	______
01120	Prophylaxis—child	______	×	22	=	______
01201	Topical appli. of fluoride (includ. prophylaxis)—child	______	×	28	=	______
01203	Topical appli. of fluoride (exclud. prophylaxis)—child	______	×	13	=	______
01351	Sealant—per tooth	______	×	15	=	______
RESTORATIVE						
02110	Amalgam—one surface, primary	______	×	30	=	______
02120	Amalgam—two surfaces, primary	______	×	41	=	______
02130	Amalgam—three surfaces, primary	______	×	50	=	______
02140	Amalgam—one surface, permanent	______	×	34	=	______
02150	Amalgam—two surfaces, permanent	______	×	45	=	______
02160	Amalgam—three surfaces, permanent	______	×	56	=	______

Code	Procedure	Number Performed		Single Procedure Value*		Value
02161	Amalgam—four or more surfaces, permanent	______	×	$ 67	=	______
02330	Resin—one surface, anterior	______	×	40	=	______
02331	Resin—two surfaces, anterior	______	×	54	=	______
02332	Resin—three surfaces, anterior	______	×	65	=	______
02335	Resin—four or more surfaces or involving incisal angle	______	×	80	=	______
02750	Crown—porcelain fused to high noble metal	______	×	425	=	______
02751	Crown—porcelain fused to predom. base metal	______	×	395	=	______
02752	Crown—porcelain fused to noble metal	______	×	410	=	______
02790	Crown—full cast high noble metal	______	×	415	=	______
02920	Recement crown	______	×	28	=	______
02940	Sedative filling	______	×	30	=	______
02950	Core buildup, including any pins	______	×	77	=	______
02951	Pin retention—per tooth, in addition to restoration	______	×	21	=	______
ENDODONTICS						
03220	Therapeutic pulpotomy (excluding final restoration)	______	×	50	=	______
03310	Anterior (excluding final restoration)	______	×	210	=	______
03320	Bicuspid (excluding final restoration)	______	×	265	=	______
03330	Molar (excluding final restoration)	______	×	350	=	______
PERIODONTICS						
04220	Gingival curettage, surgical, per quadrant, by report	______	×	75	=	______
04260	Osseous surg. (inc. flap entry and close)—per quad.	______	×	325	=	______
04341	Periodontal scaling and root planing—per quadrant	______	×	75	=	______
04910	Periodontal maintenance procedures	______	×	38	=	______
PROSTHODONTICS, REMOVABLE						
05110	Complete upper	______	×	500	=	______
05213	Upper part'l—cast metal (inc. clasps, rests and teeth)	______	×	565	=	______
05214	Lower part'l—cast metal (inc. clasps, rests and teeth)	______	×	564	=	______
PROSTHODONTICS, FIXED						
06240	Pontic—porcelain fused to high noble metal	______	×	425	=	______
06242	Pontic—porcelain fused to noble metal	______	×	410	=	______

Code	Procedure	Number Performed		Single Procedure Value*		Value
06750	Crown—porcelain fused to high noble metal	____	×	$425	=	____
06752	Crown—porcelain fused to noble metal	____	×	[410]	=	____
06790	Crown—full cast high noble metal	____	×	410	=	____
06792	Crown—full cast noble metal	____	×	[410]	=	____
ORAL SURGERY						
07110	Single tooth	____	×	40	=	____
07120	Each additional tooth	____	×	38	=	____
07210	Surgical removal of erupted tooth	____	×	75	=	____
07240	Removal of impacted tooth—completely bony	____	×	169	=	____
ADJUNCTIVE GENERAL SERVICES						
09110	Palliative (emergency) treatment of dental pain	____	×	30	=	____
ORTHODONTICS						____
				Value of Procedures		____

ADJUSTMENTS

Add 7% for procedures not listed (divide **Value of Procedures** by .93). ____

Area—Multiply amount in previous line by *Area Adjustment Factor* (see Appendix B). ____

+ **CPI**—Add appropriate increase for Dental Component (see Appendix C). + ____

+ **Administrative Fee**—Add 10% to 20%—less if closed panel. + ____

Total Value = [ ]

INSTRUCTIONS

Place number of services performed annually in column **Number Performed**.
Multiply **Number Performed** by **Single Procedure Value**.
Obtain value of orthodontic services and add in line **Orthodontics**.
Add **Value** column for **Value of Procedures**.
For **Total Value** add adjustments to **Value of Procedures**.

[ ] Indicates estimated value in **Single Procedure Value** column—no ADA value available.

***Single Procedure Values** ©American Dental Association, *The 1990 Survey of Dental Fees.*
Code on Dental Procedures and Nomenclature ©American Dental Association.
Value Checker ©Don Mayes & Associates.

18 One Company's Experience

In 1987, Hewlett-Packard offered a dental HMO plan on a pilot basis to employees in three locations: Boise, Idaho; Colorado Springs, Colorado; and the San Francisco Bay area. This HMO plan, referred to as Dental Plan II, was offered on a dual choice basis with Hewlett-Packard's regular fee-for-service dental plan.

The pilot project was undertaken because Hewlett-Packard's dental plan costs had been increasing faster than the dental care component of the Consumer Price Index. "I hoped the new program would assure quality, manage costs, provide employee satisfaction, and be fair to the dentists providing the services," said Art Young, Hewlett-Packard's benefits manager for corporate personnel. "We wanted it to work for everyone—dentists, our employees, and Hewlett-Packard."

The author, then employed by U.S. Administrators, was called in by Hewlett-Packard to develop the plan, sign up the panel of dentists, conduct the ongoing quality audits and administer the plan. Mr. Young did not want future increases for the dental HMO to exceed 6% annually.

After three years' experience, Mr. Young has this endorsement for the dental HMO: "It appears to be a good model. We are now reviewing the opportunities to make it more widely available to employees."

Costs of Plan Compared

From 1986 to 1989, Hewlett-Packard's regular dental plan costs increased 27%, while the dental HMO costs decreased 4%. The 1989 cost to the company per employee was $282 for the regular plan and $193 for Dental Plan II.

Other figures for the three years show that the dental HMO:

- Cost Hewlett-Packard less money per employee than the regular dental plan
- Cost the employee less out-of-pocket expenses than the regular plan
- Has had large increases in the number of employees choosing it
- Had more employees visiting the dentist than the regular dental plan
- Has had little dentist dissatisfaction
- Has improved the dental health of the users.

At the same time the dental HMO cost Hewlett-Packard less per employee than the regular plan, and the users of Dental Plan II paid a significantly lower percentage of charges than those using the regular plan, 17% and 47%, respectively.

The data indicate that Dental Plan II has had a favorable impact on the dental health of enrolled Hewlett-Packard employees and dependents: a much greater percentage of charges related to diagnostic and preventive services than the regular plan—35% and 23%, respectively. The author believes that this suggests that a greater number of Dental Plan II patients are reaching "maintenance."

These figures offer further support that Dental Plan II patients have a higher level of maintenance than the regular plan patients: Dental Plan II patients had fewer teeth extracted and replaced with dentures or fixed bridges than regular plan patients, and they also had a higher percentage of endodontic and periodontal services—procedures that help in tooth retention—than the regular plan patients.

While Dental Plan II had a more favorable impact on the dental health of its enrollees than the regular plan had, it cost 32% less than the regular plan in 1989. That percentage does not take into account Dental Plan II's 20% more comprehensive benefits.

The author believes that the data also suggest a change in the behavior of dentists participating in Dental Plan II. Quality audits of dental offices were used as an educational tool for dentists.

Selecting Providers

Crucial to the success of a dental HMO is the selection of dental offices. The author believes two aspects of a dental practice are absolutely vital in choosing preferred providers.

Management Expertise

Dental office management expertise is essential for involvement in a dental HMO. The dentists in Dental Plan II have a financial incentive to get their patients on maintenance and prevent problems from becoming serious and costly to treat. They must have the management knowledge to be able to accomplish this in a timely and cost-effective manner.

Dedication to Quality

Participating dentists must provide quality care. The dentist to be avoided is the one who is good in business but poor in dentistry. Dentists who are both good business managers and dedicated to quality dentistry are the cornerstone to success of a dental HMO.

The author credits Hewlett-Packard's dedication to quality employee benefits and concern about employee satisfaction as the key necessary to the implementation of this creative benefit plan design. (See Figures 18-1 and 18-2.)

Figure 18-1

HEWLETT-PACKARD DENTAL PLANS COMPARISON—ANNUAL INCREASES

	1987	1988	1989
Dental Plan II—costs	0.0%	−5.6%	1.6%
Regular dental plan—costs	8.3	8.5	10.0
CPI—dental	6.8	6.8	6.2
CPI—all items	3.7	4.1	4.8

Figure 18-2

COMPARISON
HEWLETT-PACKARD
REGULAR DENTAL PLAN AND DENTAL PLAN II

<table>
<tr><th rowspan="2">Types of Benefits</th><th colspan="2">Deductible</th><th colspan="2">Plan Pays</th></tr>
<tr><th>Regular Dental Plan</th><th>Dental Plan II</th><th>Regular Dental Plan</th><th>Dental Plan II</th></tr>
<tr><td>Diagnostic services
Teeth cleaning
Fluoride treatment
Plaque control program*</td><td rowspan="4">$50 per individual ($150 per family) during calendar year</td><td>No deductible</td><td>80%</td><td>100%</td></tr>
<tr><td>Amalgam fillings
Resin fillings
Simple extractions
Surgical extractions
Nonsurgical periodontics
Mouth prop devices
Drugs dispensed in office
Sealants*
Space maintainers</td><td rowspan="3">$25 per individual ($75 per family) during calendar year</td><td>80%</td><td>100%**</td></tr>
<tr><td>Crowns and caps</td><td>80%</td><td>80%</td></tr>
<tr><td>Surgical periodontics
Prosthodontics
Root canals
Apicoectomy
Crowns part of bridge</td><td>50%</td><td>50%</td></tr>
<tr><td>Annual maximum</td><td></td><td></td><td>$1,500</td><td>$2,500</td></tr>
<tr><th colspan="5">Orthodontics</th></tr>
<tr><td rowspan="2">Orthodontics</td><td rowspan="2">$50/$150</td><td rowspan="2">No deductible</td><td>50%</td><td>$1,075 charge to employee</td></tr>
<tr><td colspan="2">$1,000 lifetime maximum</td></tr>
</table>

*Not covered under the regular dental plan.
**Oral surgery for impacted teeth covered at 50%.

19 The Dentist's Perspective

The following paper was written for dentists by the author and his son (a practicing dentist).

Dental HMO plans are the most rapidly growing segment of dental benefits. Millions of dollars are being spent in their development and promotion.

Many companies offering HMO plans are reporting substantial growth. The National Association of Prepaid Dental Plans (another term for dental HMO plans) reported in December of 1992 that dental HMO plans rose approximately 25% in 1991 to 10.4 million enrollees, and they project enrollment to be at approximately 13.5 million lives by the end of 1993.

Dental HMO plans, also called *prepaid dental plans, dental HMOs* or *dental maintenance organizations (DMOs)*, use a different method of reimbursement than typical fee-for-service reimbursement plans. In a dental HMO, the dental office is paid a fixed amount, per enrolled individual (or family), on a periodic basis, usually monthly, for specific services, except for any deductibles, copayments or services not covered. The dentist is "at risk" for covered services.

Whether or not to participate in a dental HMO plan is a very important decision that can have a significant financial impact, either positively or negatively, on your practice.

The following question and response format has been developed to assist you in deciding whether your office should become involved with a dental HMO plan.

Questions to Ask Yourself

What is your practice philosophy? There are many ways to treat a correctly diagnosed condition. What are you comfortable doing? Is the only "acceptable" dentistry the most costly?

Either explicit or implicit, every office has a practice philosophy. If you have strong feelings about being independent and think insurance is an imposition, then you probably should not participate in an HMO. If you consider services such as removable prosthetics, amalgam and composite restorations as unacceptable services, a dental HMO may not be to your liking—especially if inlays, crowns, gold foils and crown and bridge services are not covered or are optional services. However, even if this is the case, new dental HMO patients may add significant revenues to your practice by providing noncovered services on a fee-for-service basis.

It is important to recognize that almost all dental benefit plans are designed primarily to cover affordable, basic and needed services. That does not preclude, however, patients electing and paying for more expensive, optional, "better" services.

If your practice is prevention oriented, a well-designed dental HMO plan could be a natural addition. You are paid to keep people well.

What is the practice direction? Are the number of patients increasing, stable or decreasing? Is the practice new? Are you planning on adding an associate?

Take an honest look at your practice—where it is and in what direction it is going. Evaluate the practice you currently have, the one you want and the one you can realistically expect to have in the future.

If your practice has room to grow, a dental HMO can be a valuable source of new patients—both HMO and fee-for-service patients come to you via referral from your capitation patients. A well-managed HMO practice should realize two new fee-for-service referrals for every satisfied HMO patient.

What type of practice do you have?

A rural practice is far less likely to get significant patient volume by participating in an HMO program. In an urban setting, dental HMOs can be a valuable source of new patients. A group practice can more easily handle a greater number of new patients than a solo practice under comparable circumstances.

How busy is your practice?

An empty chair cost $50 to $100 an hour. If you become part of a dental HMO plan, income for empty chair time goes directly to the bottom line. For a dental HMO to be financially attractive, you should be able to accept at least 500 new patients. This may sound like a lot of new patients but, spread over a one-year period, it should be no problem for a well-managed practice.

What is your business ability?

Dental HMOs must be actively managed. It is not something you can dabble in. It cannot be administered passively. You must understand and apply basic business principles. If you are unsure of your managerial ability, it may be advisable to enroll in college level business courses. It is your practice and deserves your undivided attention.

Are there specialists in the practice?

Practices that include specialists are able to provide a broader array of services and do not have to refer as many patients out of the office. When you are at risk, the greater number of specialist referrals, the greater the possibility of losing money.

What is your facility like? Is it accessible? Is it clean and attractive?

The office should be attractive and conveniently located for participants. There should be three operatories (dental chairs and equipment) or room for expansion.

What quality control mechanisms are in place?

In addition to providing services of acceptable quality, dental and medical histories should be dated and updated. Caries and periodontal pockets over 3 mm should be consistently charted. X-rays should be of good quality, mounted and dated. Oral hygiene instruction should be provided, and oral hygiene status recorded, dated and the provider identified.

What is your opinion of the plan operator? What experience has it had? What is its reputation in the industry? Among dentists? Is it financially sound?

Look for a plan operator with whom you feel comfortable. Just because a company is big does not mean that it has a good plan, nor is a plan bad simply because it is small. Make some phone calls. Get the answers before you sign up, not after.

Questions to Ask the Plan Operator

Who is responsible for the plan?

If the operator's marketing department directs the activities of the dental HMO plan, watch out. They may keep changing the ground rules, permitting enrollees to drop out at any time or selling to small groups.

Someone who understands the problems of the dental office, as well as the needs of the subscribers, should control the plan policies.

Who is your contact? A dentist?

Except for administrative matters, the dental office should be able to deal with a dentist familiar with dental HMOs. You should also have access to the person in charge of the plan. If a problem arises, you must be able to reach the decision maker.

Is management advice provided?

The plan operator should supply advice related to management problems that may arise. Don't expect the operator to manage your office for you, but you should be able to discuss problems with a knowledgeable dentist.

What is the length of the contract? Are you allowed to participate in other dental HMO plans?

You should be able to leave the dental HMO arrangement on 60 days' notice after the first year. Do not get involved in a plan unless you believe it will be a long-term arrangement. A "divorce" can be messy. Patients may become suspicious concerning why you dropped out and will leave your practice.

Do not sign a contract that does not permit participation in other plans or penalizes you for doing so. Something better may come along. You should be able to take advantage of it.

What is the group size?

There is a big difference between a group of 1,000 and 100 groups of ten. Smaller groups drop coverage more frequently. A small group may have its needs taken care of and then drop the plan. This can be costly to the dental office.

What is the turnover of the group?

A high annual employee turnover results in people having necessary dental work done and then dropping out. This can be very costly to the dental practice.

Has the group had dental coverage previously?

If it has, then the members should be in reasonably good dental health. If not, there will probably be a large backlog of needed treatment.

What has been the group's previous dental experience? If covered by dental insurance, what was the cost per person per month?

It is important to know what services were provided as a predictor of what will be needed. A high percentage of diagnostic and preventive services suggests a group on maintenance. A high incidence of extractions, endodontics and prosthetics may indicate a significant backlog of need.

What are the demographics of the group? What number live within or surrounding the practice ZIP code area? What is the socioeconomic status of the group?

The closer to your office, the greater the enrollment. White collar employees are higher users than blue collar employees; women are greater consumers of dental care than men; young people seek more services than older people; educated persons seek more care than uneducated ones.

How many patients can be expected?

There should be a minimum of 100 to 200. If not, you are taking the risk of getting a few patients with extensive treatment needs and less chance of recouping your losses.

Can the practice limit the number of dental HMO patients?

If there is limited open chair time, you should be able to limit the number of patients to 500. If the practice cannot accept at least 200 people, it may not be worthwhile for the plan operator to have your practice included.

How many dental offices are going to be involved and where are they located?

If there are too many dental offices for the number of employees involved, it may not be worth your effort. You are less likely to get a sufficient number of patients. However, it is reasonable to expect offices to be located in a manner that provides patients with a choice.

Is it a closed panel or dual choice?

Philosophically, dual choice is preferred; however, a closed panel does provide for a "captive" patient group. One problem with a closed panel is that if another office is opened nearby, you could lose a number of patients. This may also happen in a dual choice plan if the patients feel they are not being treated properly.

Will enrollment in the dental HMO be primary or secondary?

In *primary* enrollment, every subscriber is assigned to the dental HMO unless a request is made for fee-for-service coverage. In *secondary,* the reverse occurs. In primary, even the nonusers are immediately enrolled. In secondary, only the users are initially enrolled. You should expect a higher capitation rate if the program uses secondary enrollment.

Can family members enroll in different offices?

If this is the case, be careful. The dental office near the workplace will be visited by the employees who probably have the greatest need, while the dental office in the suburbs will be used by the children who have fewer needs.

What protection do I have against patients dropping out?

The plan should commit enrolled patients to at least one year with automatic reenrollment in your office unless they opt out of the dental HMO plan. Exceptions to the one-year guarantee would include job changes, moves and other similar changes.

What protection do I have against financial loss?

The plan should guarantee that you will receive not less than 70% of your fee-for-service equivalent.

How will I be paid? Is it per family, per person or other?

It is best to be paid on a per person basis, because there is a tendency for families to join more so than singles.

What is the basis of the capitation rate?

It should be based on actual group experience. The best indicator of the future is past experience.

When does the office begin receiving payments?

It should be the date the program starts, not the date the patient first sees the dentist.

Have benefits been increased over previous programs?

A comparison of previous and presently offered coverage should be available. The value of any increase should be assessed.

What percentage of total plan costs are administration and profit?

If these figures are not disclosed to you, don't get involved. Some plan administrators are taking as much as 30-50%.

Who is paying the premium? The employer or the employee?

The higher the employee contribution, the greater the use by those enrolled.

What reports are available?

In addition to the enrollment report, a report should be supplied regularly that includes services provided by category, value of the services, capitation payments and other information that will enable you to monitor and manage the program.

What are the limitations and exclusions?

They should include:

- An alternate treatment clause
- Oral surgery limited to extractions and preparation of the mouth for dentures
- Exclusion for cosmetic dentistry
- Exclusion for replacement of teeth missing before employment
- No responsibility for previous treatment plans
- Exclusion for treatment of TMJ
- Exclusion for splinting, full-mouth rehabilitation and altering vertical dimension
- Right to charge for broken appointments.

DENTAL HMO DON'TS

Don't be a passive observer. You may have only one opportunity to participate in a successful dental HMO program.

Don't turn down an opportunity to discuss the program with those offering it. If you elect not to participate, you will be an informed competitor. If your practice is largely dependent upon dental insurance, you had better be interested.

Don't be arrogant with those offering an opportunity to participate in a dental HMO plan. Even if you decide not to participate this time, you may change your mind next year.

Don't pay to participate. If payment is necessary, it is an indication that the program may be insufficiently funded or not well managed.

Don't think dental HMOs are a fad. They are here to stay. They will probably level off at about 20-25% of dental coverage.

Don't think dental HMOs are going to eliminate fee-for-service dental coverage. They won't. Fee for service will simply be a smaller percent of coverage. Fee-for-service dental coverage will be around a long time.

Don't think dental HMOs will not affect your practice. They will, whether or not you participate, either by adding to or subtracting from your practice. The only unknown is the extent to which this will occur.

Don't delude yourself that you have a ''special'' doctor-patient relationship with all of your patients, and that they won't leave you to look for lower prices. Some won't, but many will. They are as concerned about cost as you are.

Don't get caught up in the attempts to thwart or boycott dental HMOs. In the first place, these efforts won't work. In the second place, boycotts and other activities may be illegal. Finally, and more important, those involved won't pay your bills if your practice suffers because you failed to get involved with dental HMOs when the opportunity came.

Don't displace your fee-for-service patients with dental HMO patients. If you are that busy, you are better off not participating in dental HMOs.

Don't assume you are losing money if your capitation payments and co-payments are less than you would have received on a fee-for-service basis. Any money received for empty chair time is profit.

Don't abdicate your management role in dental HMOs. If you commit to do it, make it work. It requires effort and the ability to manage.

If you are seriously interested in becoming involved in dental HMOs, you should consider all offers as potential opportunities. You may only receive one such opportunity, and you have nothing to lose by talking. At the very least, you should want to learn about what the competition is doing.

Talk to dental offices that are successfully involved in dental HMOs; offices out of your area will be more candid.

Ask questions, of yourself and the plan operator—and get answers.

Don't consider dental HMOs if you—

- Have no empty chair time and no room for expansion
- Want to be politically involved in organized dentistry
- Have a philosophical problem with dental HMOs
- Have few patients with dental insurance and little chance of getting any
- Feel uncomfortable with the plan operator
- Refer out most oral surgery, periodontics and endodontics
- Do not have a business manager and/or much interest in the business aspects of your practice
- Do not want your office scrutinized relative to quality
- Feel that you may have to compromise your professional standards.

Sources of Information

A

American Dental Association

There are several sources of information at the American Dental Association that may be valuable to the purchaser of dental plans or plan administrators.

American Dental Association
211 East Chicago Avenue
Chicago, IL 60611
Phone (312) 440-2500

Bureau of Economic and Behavioral Research. This ADA bureau is a virtual gold mine of information on almost all aspects of the practice of dentistry. Write to the bureau and request its 1993 Publication Price List.

The following are recommended publications.

Survey of Dental Practice. This survey is conducted annually and a number of reports are generated from the survey, including:

- *Income from the Private Practice of Dentistry*
- *Employment of Dental Practice Personnel*
- *Dentists in Non-Solo and Solo Practice*
- *Patients of Dentists in Private Practice*
- *General Characteristics of Dentists*
- Annual Expenses of Operating a Dental Practice
- Dental Fees Charged by General Practitioners and Selected Specialists
- *Survey of Dental Services Rendered*

Manpower.

- *State and County Level Demographic Reports*

- *Changes in the Dental Manpower Pool: The Recent Experience by State*
- *Distribution of Dentists in the U.S. by Region and State*

Reprints. The reprints available are updated frequently. At press time a series of 1991 Trends articles from the *Journal of the American Dental Association* were available and include:

- "Key Dental Facts"
- "Measuring Dental Fees"
- "Dental Fees and Inflation"
- "Excess Capacity in Dentistry or a Shortage?"
- "Is the Solo Practice Doomed?"
- "Spending for Dental Care Since 1980"

Bureau of Library Services. There are a number of excellent services available from the Bureau of Library Services. Write or call for the booklet entitled *Books and Package Libraries for Dentists.* This booklet contains a rather lengthy list of currently available books, journals and package libraries. Books and journals are not available to nonmembers of the ADA. However, if you contact your dentist, and he or she is an ADA member, the dentist will have access to the library and will be able to obtain the information for you.

Package libraries are available to nonmembers. The cost is $35 each, plus shipping cost. In addition, the reader who is looking for specific information may call the library and be directed to likely sources of that information.

Package libraries that may be of interest are:

- Capitation Dentistry
- Dental Clinics
- Fees, Dental
- Group Practice
- Health Care Delivery
- Health Planning
- Independent Practice Associations
- Insurance, Dental
- Legislation, Dental
- Marketing of Health Services
- Mass Screening
- Motivation of Patients
- National Health Insurance, U.S.
- Partnership, Associates
- Peer Review
- Periodontal Diseases: Diagnosis, Occurrence, Prevention
- Practice Management: Appointment Control, Recall Systems
- Preferred Provider Organizations
- Preventive Dentistry
- Productivity
- Quality of Dental Care

- Records
- Utilization
- Work Simplification.

Council on Dental Care Programs. This ADA council is also an excellent source of information. The council has a direct line for purchaser information: (312) 440-2746. The author has found the council staff ready, willing and able to answer a vast array of queries on dental benefits and recommends purchasers avail themselves of this service. Recommended publications are:

- *American Dental Association CDT-1 Current Dental Terminology,* First Edition 1990-1995. This publication lists all recognized Codes on Dental Procedures and Nomenclature as well as their descriptions. There is also a glossary of dental benefit terms and a list of common dental terms. Additional information includes an explanation of the tooth numbering system, human jaw and teeth, and the dental claim form.
- *Designing Your Dental Benefits Plan*
- Brochures entitled "A Guide for Employers—Selecting a Dental Benefits Plan" and "Offering a Dental Benefits Plan—Economic and Design Considerations for Plan Sponsors."

Office of Quality Assurance (OQA). The ADA established this office in 1982, and it serves as a clearing house for literature and information on quality. The OQA is a valuable source of information on quality and has a number of publications available at no cost. It has also developed a publication entitled *U.S. Directory of Quality Assurance and Assessment Programs,* which is available for a modest charge.

Direct phone (312) 440-2858.

American Academy of Dental Group Practice. The American Academy of Dental Group Practice has been at the forefront of establishing quality standards for dental offices. It has an office accreditation program that is quite exhaustive. If a dental office has been accredited by the academy, it is a mark of distinction that almost assures that quality care is being provided. The academy has now turned over the process of accreditation to the American Association for Ambulatory Health Care. Both have available for sale a book the author highly recommends entitled, *Accreditation Handbook for Ambulatory Health Care.*

American Academy of Dental Group Practice
5110 North 40th Street, Suite 250
Phoenix, AZ 85018
Phone (602) 381-1185

Accreditation Association for Ambulatory Health Care. As mentioned under the American Academy of Dental Group Practice, the association has made available a book the author highly recommends entitled *Accreditation Handbook for Ambulatory Health Care.*

Accreditation Association for Ambulatory Health Care
9933 Lawler Avenue
Skokie, IL 60077
Phone (708) 676-9610

American Board of Quality Assurance and Utilization Review Physicians (ABQAURP). Established in 1977, ABQAURP is a nonprofit certification board that has certified over 4,000 physicians and 2,500 other health care professionals in the United States who are involved in quality and utilization review activities. The board conducts certifying examinations approximately four times annually. Beginning in 1993 the examination will be administered by the National Board of Medical Examiners. ABQAURP is a good source for names of professionals who passed a certifying examination on quality assurance and utilization review. The author highly recommends its course that covers a core body of knowledge for those involved, or interested, in quality and utilization review activities.

American Board of Quality Assurance
and Utilization Review Physicians
890 West Kennedy Blvd., Suite 260
Tampa, FL 33609
Phone (813) 286-4411
Fax (813) 286-4387

Dental School Departments of Community Dentistry, Dental Public Health, Delivery, etc. An often overlooked source of information is dental schools. Many have departments devoted specifically to the financing and delivery of dental care. An inquiry to your local dental society will enable you to locate the nearest dental school.

American Journal of Medical Quality. This publication is the official journal of the American College of Medical Quality and is a good source of articles on quality and utilization issues in health care.

David J. Jones, M.D., Editor
Quality Assurance and Utilization Review
Penn State University at Harrisburg
Capitol College (39)
Middletown, PA 17057
Phone (717) 948-6227

Area Adjustment Factors

B

Atlanta	1.06	Minneapolis	1.00
Boise	0.89	Nashville	0.89
Boston	1.24	New Orleans	0.91
Charlotte (NC)	0.92	New York City	1.44
Chicago	1.07	Oklahoma City	0.90
Cleveland	0.96	Omaha	0.82
Dallas	1.08	Philadelphia	1.11
Denver	1.07	Phoenix	1.01
Des Moines	0.86	Pittsburgh (PA)	0.94
Detroit	1.04	Portland (ME)	0.94
Harrisburg (PA)	0.88	Portland (OR)	1.04
Houston	1.10	Richmond	0.97
Indianapolis	0.86	Salt Lake City	0.84
Jacksonville	0.99	San Diego	1.21
Las Vegas	0.99	San Francisco	1.35
Little Rock	0.85	Seattle	1.27
Los Angeles	1.33	St. Louis	1.01
Madison	0.90	Tucson	0.97
Memphis	0.89	Washington, DC	1.25
Miami	1.23	Total U.S.	1.00

The above list illustrates the relative average fee levels vs. the national average for a standard mix of dental services covered by dental programs in the fee-for-service environment. These are estimates for 1992 based upon Milliman & Robertson's continuing research on dental insurance costs as included in Milliman & Robertson's "1993 Dental Cost Guidelines." These guidelines are a detailed step-by-step approach for evaluating the cost of various dental programs by geographic location. However, the relativities do not reflect differences in the utilization and mix of services by geographic location that may be affected by fluoridation, differences in practice patterns, availability of services or other reasons. These factors can only be considered as a starting point for estimating dental fee differences for different parts of the country.

Milliman & Robertson, Inc. is a firm of actuaries and consultants serving the insurance and employee benefits industry with more than 25 offices nationwide and as part of the Woodrow Milliman group has locations in over 20 different countries.

Consumer Price Index

C

AVERAGE ANNUAL INCREASE FROM PREVIOUS YEAR 1981-1992

Year	Dental Services	All Items	Medical Care	Physician Services	Hospital Room	All Services
1981	**9.6**	10.4	10.8	11.0	14.8	13.1
1982	**7.7**	6.1	11.6	9.4	15.7	9.0
1983	**6.7**	3.2	8.7	7.7	11.3	3.5
1984	**8.1**	4.3	6.2	7.0	8.3	5.2
1985	**6.3**	3.6	6.2	5.8	5.9	5.1
1986	**5.6**	1.9	7.5	7.2	6.0	5.0
1987	**6.8**	3.7	6.6	7.3	7.2	4.1
1988	**6.8**	4.1	6.5	7.2	9.3	4.6
1989	**6.2**	4.8	7.7	7.4	10.3	4.9
1990	**6.7**	5.4	9.1	7.1	10.9	5.5
1991	**7.5**	4.2	8.7	6.0	9.4	5.1
1992*	**5.8**	2.9	6.6	6.3	8.9	3.6

*Estimated.
Source: U.S. Department of Labor.

Fast Facts

D

AMERICAN DENTAL ASSOCIATION

138,092 dentists in active private practice—full or part time in 1991[3]
$34.0 billion spent for dental services[2]
5.1% of total amount spent for all health care[2]
91.6% of professionally active dentists are private practitioners[3]
15.6% of professionally active dentists are 60 years old or older[1]
55.3% of private practitioners are under 45 years of age[1]
71.6% of dentists graduated since 1965[1]

1. American Dental Association, 1991 *Survey of Dental Practice.*
2. "National Health Expenditures 1990," *Health Care Financing Review*, Fall 1991.
3. American Dental Association, *1991 Distribution of Dentists in the US by Region and State.*

1985—AMERICAN DENTAL ASSOCIATION

(Last Available Report) for the Year 198?

Dental benefits

73.3%	UCR/R&C
14.5%	Table of allowances
7.7%	UCR/table of allowance combination
3.2%	Capitation (dental HMOs)—1985 (Author's estimate is 11% in 1992)
0.5%	Direct reimbursement

95% of dental benefits are fee for service

Service benefit plans = 23.3% of dental benefits

1990
HOW DENTISTS PRACTICE[1]

68.4%	Work with no other dentists
20.2%	Work with one other dentist
11.4%	Work with two or more dentists

1. American Dental Association, 1991 *Survey of Dental Practice*

SOURCE OF INCOME[1]
INDEPENDENT DENTISTS
GENERAL PRACTITIONERS' PRIMARY PRACTICE
MEAN GROSS INCOME RECEIVED FROM

United States		Middle Atlantic Region
44.2%	Direct patient payment	49.9%
50.6%	Private dental insurance	47.3%
4.4%	Government programs	2.4%
0.9%	Other sources	0.6%
59.5%	No payment from government programs	
1.5%	No payment from private dental plans	

1. American Dental Association, 1991 *Survey of Dental Practice*

CHANGES IN HOW DENTISTS PRACTICE[1]

	1983	1984	1985	1986	1987	1988	1989	1990	'83 thru '90 Change
Work alone	74%	72%	67%	70%	69%	66%	67%	68%	−8%
Work with one other dentist	17	18	19	17	20	21	20	20	+18
Work with two or more dentists	9	10	14	13	11	13	13	11	+22
Employed dentists (includes independent contractors)	5.5	5.6	6.9	6.9	7.3	10.6	9.4	8.5	+55

1. American Dental Association, 1991 *Survey of Dental Practice*

1990
PRIMARY PRIVATE PRACTICE MEAN NET INCOME[1]

$ 88,530	Independent general practitioners
$142,910	Independent specialists mean

1. American Dental Association, 1991 *Survey of Dental Practice*

INDEPENDENT DENTISTS' MEAN GROSS INCOME FROM PRIMARY PRACTICE[1]
—PER DENTIST—

$273,700	General practitioners
$399,470	Specialists
$291,010	All independent dentists

1. American Dental Association, 1991 *Survey of Dental Practice*

EXPENSES[1]

61.5%	Independent general practitioners' expenses
56.8%	Independent specialists' expenses

1. American Dental Association, 1991 *Survey of Dental Practice*

HOURS PER YEAR TREATING PATIENTS, ALL DENTISTS[1]
(Primary Practice)

1,627.4

HOURS PER YEAR IN THE OFFICE
(Primary Practice)

1,810.6

1. American Dental Association, 1991 *Survey of Dental Practice*

OWNERSHIP OF PRACTICE[1]

91.5% of dentists own their practices

1. American Dental Association, 1991 *Survey of Dental Practice*

COMPUTERS[1]

48% of dentists have in-office computers

11% of dentists use computers for electronic claims processing

1. "Journal of The American Dental Association," Vol. 123, February 1992, *Computers in Dentistry on the Rise*

STATUS OF 1989 DENTAL GRADUATES IN 1990[1]

70%	In active private practice
6%	In armed services
4%	Looking for openings

1. American Dental Association, Summary of 1990 *Survey of Dental Graduates*

1989 DENTAL GRADUATES IN PRIVATE PRACTICE IN 1990[1]

31%	Own practice
36%	Are associates
20%	Are independent contractors
13%	Are employees

1. American Dental Association, Summary of 1990 *Survey of Dental Graduates*

1989 GRADUATES IN 1990[1]

	Female	Male
Distribution	28%	72%
In active private practice	68	71
Full-time private practice	51	61
Part-time private practice	13	7
Looking for openings	6	3
Percentage of associates	41	35
Percentage of independent contractors	22	19
Percentage of employees	16	12

1. American Dental Association, Summary of 1990 *Survey of Dental Graduates*

COMPARISON OF MEDICAL AND DENTAL SPECIALTIES IN PRIMARY CARE

Physicians per AMA on 12/2/92—As of 1/1/90			
Total physicians	615,421		
Recognized medical specialties	**23**		
Total in **primary** care			
Internal medicine		98,349	**16.0%**
Pediatrics		40,893	**6.6**
Family practice		47,639	**7.7**
General practice		22,841	**3.7**
OB/GYN		33,697	**5.5**
Total in **primary** care		243,419	**39.5%**
Dentists in private practice—Active private practitioners, 1991[1]			
General practice		112,564	**81.5%**
Recognized dental specialties	**8**		
Endodontists		2,566	**1.9**
Pediatric dentists		2,948	**2.1**
Periodontists		3,810	**2.8**
Prosthodontists		2,323	**1.7**
Oral surgeons		5,188	**3.7**
Orthodontists		8,342	**6.0**
Oral pathologists		107	**0.1**
Public health dentists		244	**0.2**
Totals		138,092	**100.0%**

1. American Dental Association, *1991 Distribution of Dentists in the US by Region and State*

COMPARISON AVERAGE ANNUAL NET INCOME OF SELECTED PROFESSIONALS 1986

Physicians	**$119,500**
Family practice	80,300
Internal medicine	109,400
Surgery	162,400
OB/GYN	135,900
Veterinarians	**51,064**
Dentists	**74,870**
General practice	66,790
Specialties	96,900

BEGINNING SALARIES OF COLLEGE GRADUATES BY MAJOR 1989

Accounting	$25,290
Business	22,274
Marketing	22,523
Mathematics	26,789
Computer Science	28,557

Source: September 1991, *Dental Practice Outlook*

1990 Code on Dental Procedures and Nomenclature

E

American Dental Association

Code	
00100-00999	**I. Diagnostic**
	Clinical oral examinations
00110	Initial oral examination
00120	Periodic oral examination
00130	Emergency oral examination
	Radiographs
00210	Intraoral—complete series (including bitewings)
00220	Intraoral—periapical—first film
00230	Intraoral—periapical—each additional film
00240	Intraoral—occlusal film
00250	Extraoral—first film
00260	Extraoral—each additional film
00270	Bitewings—single film
00272	Bitewings—two films
00274	Bitewings—four films
00290	Posterior—anterior or lateral skull and facial bone survey film
00310	Sialography
00320	Temporomandibular joint arthrogram, including injection
00321	Other temporomandibular joint films, by report
00322	Tomographic survey
00330	Panoramic film
00340	Cephalometric film
	Tests and laboratory examinations
00415	Bacteriologic studies for determination of pathologic agents
00425	Caries susceptibility tests
00460	Pulp vitality tests
00470	Diagnostic casts

Code	
00471	Diagnostic photographs
00501	Histopathologic examinations
00502	Other oral pathology procedures, by report
00999	Unspecified diagnostic procedure, by report
01000-01999	**II. Preventive**
	Dental prophylaxis
01110	Prophylaxis—adult
01120	Prophylaxis—child
	Topical fluoride treatment (office procedure)
01201	Topical application of fluoride (including prophylaxis)—child
01203	Topical application of fluoride (excluding prophylaxis)—child
01204	Topical application of fluoride (excluding prophylaxis)—adult
01205	Topical application of fluoride (including prophylaxis)—adult
	Other preventive services
01310	Nutritional counseling for the control of dental disease
01330	Oral hygiene instruction
01351	Sealant—per tooth
	Space maintenance (passive appliances)
01510	Space maintainer—fixed—unilateral
01515	Space maintainer—fixed—bilateral
01520	Space maintainer—removable—unilateral
01525	Space maintainer—removable—bilateral
01550	Recementation of space maintainer
02000-02999	**III. Restorative**
	Amalgam restorations (including polishing)
02110	Amalgam—one surface, primary
02120	Amalgam—two surfaces, primary
02130	Amalgam—three surfaces, primary
02131	Amalgam—four or more surfaces, primary
02140	Amalgam—one surface, permanent
02150	Amalgam—two surfaces, permanent
02160	Amalgam—three surfaces, permanent
02161	Amalgam—four or more surfaces, permanent
	Silicate restorations
02210	Silicate cement—per restoration
	Resin restorations
02330	Resin—one surface, anterior
02331	Resin—two surfaces, anterior
02332	Resin—three surfaces, anterior
02335	Resin—four or more surfaces or involving incisal angle (anterior)
02336	Composite resin crown—anterior—primary
02380	Resin—one surface, posterior—primary
02381	Resin—two surfaces, posterior—primary
02382	Resin—three or more surfaces, posterior—primary
02385	Resin—one surface, posterior—permanent

Code	
02386	Resin—two surfaces, posterior—permanent
02387	Resin—three or more surfaces, posterior—permanent
	Gold foil restorations
02410	Gold foil—one surface
02420	Gold foil—two surfaces
02430	Gold foil—three surfaces
	Inlay restorations
02510	Inlay—metallic—one surface
02520	Inlay—metallic—two surfaces
02530	Inlay—metallic—three surfaces
02540	Onlay—metallic—per tooth (in addition to inlay)
02610	Inlay—porcelain/ceramic—one surface
02620	Inlay—porcelain/ceramic—two surfaces
02630	Inlay—porcelain/ceramic—three surfaces
02640	Onlay—porcelain/ceramic—per tooth (in addition to inlay)
02650	Inlay—composite/resin—one surface (laboratory processed)
02651	Inlay—composite/resin—two surfaces (laboratory processed)
02652	Inlay—composite/resin—three surfaces (laboratory processed)
02660	Onlay—composite/resin—per tooth (in addition to inlay—laboratory processed)
	Crowns—single restoration only
02710	Crown—resin (laboratory)
02720	Crown—resin with high noble metal
02721	Crown—resin with predominantly base metal
02722	Crown—resin with noble metal
02740	Crown—porcelain/ceramic substrate
02750	Crown—porcelain fused to high noble metal
02751	Crown—porcelain fused to predominantly base metal
02752	Crown—porcelain fused to noble metal
02790	Crown—full cast high noble metal
02791	Crown—full cast predominantly base metal
02792	Crown—full cast noble metal
02810	Crown—¾ cast metallic
	Other restorative services
02910	Recement inlay
02920	Recement crown
02930	Prefabricated stainless steel crown—primary tooth
02931	Prefabricated stainless steel crown—permanent tooth
02932	Prefabricated resin crown
02933	Prefabricated stainless steel crown with resin window
02940	Sedative filling
02950	Core buildup, including any pins
02951	Pin retention—per tooth, in addition to restoration
02952	Cast post and core in addition to crown
02954	Prefabricated post and core in addition to crown
02960	Labial veneer (laminate)—chairside
02961	Labial veneer (resin laminate)—laboratory

Code	
02962	Labial veneer (porcelain laminate)—laboratory
02970	Temporary crown (fractured tooth)
02980	Crown repair, by report
02999	Unspecified restorative procedure, by report
03000-03999	**IV. Endodontics**
	Pulp capping
03110	Pulp cap—direct (excluding final restoration)
03120	Pulp cap—indirect (excluding final restoration)
	Pulpotomy
03220	Therapeutic pulpotomy (excluding final restoration)
	Root canal therapy (including treatment plan, clinical procedures and followup care)
03310	Anterior (excluding final restoration)
03320	Bicuspid (excluding final restoration)
03330	Molar (excluding final restoration)
03346	Retreatment—anterior, by report
03347	Retreatment—bicuspid, by report
03348	Retreatment—molar, by report
03351	Apexification/recalcification—initial visit (apical closure/calcific repair of perforations, root resorption, etc.)
03352	Apexification/recalcification—interim medication replacement (apical closure/calcific repair of perforations, root resorption, etc.)
03353	Apexification/recalcification—final visit (includes completed root canal therapy—apical closure/calcific repair of perforations, root resorption, etc.)
	Periapical services
03410	Apicoectomy/periradicular surgery—anterior
03421	Apicoectomy/periradicular surgery—bicuspid (first root)
03425	Apicoectomy/periradicular surgery—molar (first root)
03426	Apicoectomy/periradicular surgery (each additional root)
03430	Retrograde filling—per root
03450	Root amputation—per root
03460	Endodontic endosseous implant
03470	Intentional replantation (including necessary splinting)
	Other endodontic procedures
03910	Surgical procedure for isolation of tooth with rubber dam
03920	Hemisection (including any root removal), not including root canal therapy
03950	Canal preparation and fitting of preformed dowel or post
03960	Bleaching of discolored tooth
03999	Unspecified endodontic procedure, by report
04000-04999	**V. Periodontics**
	Surgical services (including usual postoperative services)
04210	Gingivectomy or gingivoplasty—per quadrant
04211	Gingivectomy or gingivoplasty—per tooth
04220	Gingival curettage, surgical, per quadrant, by report
04240	Gingival flap procedure, including root planing—per quadrant
04249	Crown lengthening—hard and soft tissue, by report

Code	
04250	Mucogingival surgery—per quadrant
04260	Osseous surgery (including flap entry and closure)—per quadrant
04261	Bone replacement graft—single site (including flap entry and closure)
04262	Bone replacement graft—multiple sites (including flap entry and closure)
04268	Guided tissue regeneration (includes the surgery and reentry)
04270	Pedicle soft tissue graft procedure
04271	Free soft tissue graft procedure (including donor site)
	Adjunctive periodontal services
04320	Provisional splinting—intracoronal
04321	Provisional splinting—extracoronal
04341	Periodontal scaling and root planing—per quadrant
04345	Periodontal scaling performed in the presence of gingival inflammation
	Other periodontal services
04910	Periodontal maintenance procedures (following active therapy)
04920	Unscheduled dressing change (by someone other than treating dentist)
04999	Unspecified periodontal procedure, by report
05000-05899	**VI. Prosthodontics (removable)**
	Complete dentures (including routine postdelivery care)
05110	Complete upper
05120	Complete lower
05130	Immediate upper
05140	Immediate lower
	Partial dentures (including routine postdelivery care)
05211	Upper partial—resin base (including any conventional clasps, rests and teeth)
05212	Lower partial—resin base (including any conventional clasps, rests and teeth)
05213	Upper partial—cast metal base with resin saddles (including any conventional clasps, rests and teeth)
05214	Lower partial—cast metal base with resin saddles (including any conventional clasps, rests and teeth)
05281	Removable unilateral partial denture—one piece cast metal (including clasps and pontics)
	Adjustments to removable prostheses
05410	Adjust complete denture—upper
05411	Adjust complete denture—lower
05421	Adjust partial denture—upper
05422	Adjust partial denture—lower
	Repairs to complete dentures
05510	Repair broken complete denture base
05520	Replace missing or broken teeth—complete denture (each tooth)
	Repairs to partial dentures
05610	Repair resin saddle or base
05620	Repair cast framework
05630	Repair or replace broken clasp
05640	Replace broken teeth—per tooth
05650	Add tooth to existing partial denture
05660	Add clasp to existing partial denture

Code	
	Denture rebase procedures
05710	Rebase complete upper denture
05711	Rebase complete lower denture
05720	Rebase upper partial denture
05721	Rebase lower partial denture
	Denture reline procedures
05730	Reline complete upper denture (chairside)
05731	Reline complete lower denture (chairside)
05740	Reline upper partial denture (chairside)
05741	Reline lower partial denture (chairside)
05750	Reline complete upper denture (laboratory)
05751	Reline complete lower denture (laboratory)
05760	Reline upper partial denture (laboratory)
05761	Reline lower partial denture (laboratory)
	Other removable prosthetic services
05810	Interim complete denture (upper)
05811	Interim complete denture (lower)
05820	Interim partial denture (upper)
05821	Interim partial denture (lower)
05850	Tissue conditioning, upper—per denture unit
05851	Tissue conditioning, lower—per denture unit
05860	Overdenture—complete, by report
05861	Overdenture—partial, by report
05862	Precision attachment, by report
05899	Unspecified removable prosthodontic procedure, by report
05900-05999	**VII. Maxillofacial prosthetics**
05911	Facial moulage (sectional)
05912	Facial moulage (complete)
05913	Nasal prosthesis
05914	Auricular prosthesis
05915	Orbital prosthesis
05916	Ocular prosthesis
05919	Facial prosthesis
05922	Nasal septal prosthesis
05923	Ocular prosthesis, interim
05924	Cranial prosthesis
05925	Facial augmentation implant prosthesis
05926	Nasal prosthesis, replacement
05927	Auricular prosthesis, replacement
05928	Orbital prosthesis, replacement
05929	Facial prosthesis, replacement
05931	Obturator prosthesis, surgical
05932	Obturator prosthesis, definitive
05933	Obturator prosthesis, modification
05934	Mandibular resection prosthesis with guide flange

Code	
05935	Mandibular resection prosthesis without guide flange
05936	Obturator prosthesis, interim
05937	Trismus appliance (not for TMD treatment)
05951	Feeding aid
05952	Speech aid prosthesis, pediatric
05953	Speech aid prosthesis, adult
05954	Palatal augmentation prosthesis
05955	Palatal lift prosthesis, definitive
05958	Palatal lift prosthesis, interim
05959	Palatal lift prosthesis, modification
05960	Speech aid prosthesis, modification
05982	Surgical stent
05983	Radiation carrier
05984	Radiation shield
05985	Radiation cone locator
05986	Fluoride gel carrier
05987	Commissure splint
05988	Surgical splint
05999	Unspecified maxillofacial prosthesis, by report
06000-06199	**VIII. Implant services**
06030	Endosseous implant (in the bone)
06040	Subperiosteal implant
06050	Transosseous implant
06055	Implant connecting bar
06080	Implant maintenance procedures, including: removal of prosthesis, cleansing of prosthesis and abutments, reinsertion of prosthesis
06090	Repair implant, by report
06100	Implant removal, by report
06199	Unspecified implant procedure, by report
06200-06999	**IX. Prosthodontics, fixed (each abutment and each pontic constitute a unit in a bridge)**
	Bridge pontics
06210	Pontic—cast high noble metal
06211	Pontic—cast predominantly base metal
06212	Pontic—cast noble metal
06240	Pontic—porcelain fused to high noble metal
06241	Pontic—porcelain fused to predominantly base metal
06242	Pontic—porcelain fused to noble metal
06250	Pontic—resin with high noble metal
06251	Pontic—resin with predominantly base metal
06252	Pontic—resin with noble metal
	Retainers
06520	Inlay—metallic—two surfaces
06530	Inlay—metallic—three or more surfaces
06540	Onlay—metallic—per tooth (in addition to inlay)
06545	Retainer—cast metal for acid-etched fixed prosthesis

Code	
	Bridge retainers—crowns
06720	Crown—resin with high noble metal
06721	Crown—resin with predominantly base metal
06722	Crown—resin with noble metal
06750	Crown—porcelain fused to high noble metal
06751	Crown—porcelain fused to predominantly base metal
06752	Crown—porcelain fused to noble metal
06780	Crown—¾ cast high noble metal
06790	Crown—full cast high noble metal
06791	Crown—full cast predominantly base metal
06792	Crown—full cast noble metal
	Other fixed prosthetic services
06930	Recement bridge
06940	Stress breaker
06950	Precision attachment
06970	Cast post and core in addition to bridge retainer
06971	Cast post as part of bridge retainer
06972	Prefabricated post and core in addition to bridge retainer
06973	Core buildup for retainer, including any pins
06975	Coping—metal
06980	Bridge repair, by report
06999	Unspecified fixed prosthodontic procedure, by report
07000-07999	**X. Oral surgery**
	Extractions—includes local anesthesia and routine postoperative care
07110	Single tooth
07120	Each additional tooth
07130	Root removal—exposed roots
	Surgical extractions—includes local anesthesia and routine postoperative care
07210	Surgical removal of erupted tooth requiring elevation of mucoperiosteal flap and removal of bone and/or section of tooth
07220	Removal of impacted tooth—soft tissue
07230	Removal of impacted tooth—partially bony
07240	Removal of impacted tooth—completely bony
07241	Removal of impacted tooth—completely bony, with unusual surgical complications
07250	Surgical removal of residual tooth roots (cutting procedure)
	Other surgical procedures
07260	Oral antral fistula closure
07270	Tooth reimplantation and/or stabilization of accidentally evulsed or displaced tooth and/or alveolus
07271	Tooth implantation
07272	Tooth transplantation
07280	Surgical exposure of impacted or unerupted tooth for orthodontic reasons (including orthodontic attachments)
07281	Surgical exposure of impacted or unerupted tooth to aid eruption
07285	Biopsy of oral tissue—hard
07286	Biopsy of oral tissue—soft

Code	
07290	Surgical repositioning of teeth
07291	Transseptal fiberotomy
	Alveoplasty—surgical preparation of ridge for dentures
07310	Alveoplasty in conjunction with extractions—per quadrant
07320	Alveoplasty not in conjunction with extractions—per quadrant
	Vestibuloplasty
07340	Vestibuloplasty—ridge extension (secondary epithelialization)
07350	Vestibuloplasty—ridge extension (including soft tissue grafts, muscle reattachments, revision of soft tissue attachment, and management of hypertrophied and hyperplastic tissue)
	Surgical excision of reactive inflammatory lesions (scar tissue or localized congenital lesions)
07410	Radical excision—lesion diameter up to 1.25 cm
07420	Radical excision—lesion diameter greater than 1.25 cm
	Removal of tumors, cysts and neoplasms
07430	Excision of benign tumor—lesion diameter up to 1.25 cm
07431	Excision of benign tumor—lesion diameter greater than 1.25 cm
07440	Excision of malignant tumor—lesion diameter up to 1.25 cm
07441	Excision of malignant tumor—lesion diameter greater than 1.25 cm
07450	Removal of odontogenic cyst or tumor—lesion diameter up to 1.25 cm
07451	Removal of odontogenic cyst or tumor—lesion diameter greater than 1.25 cm
07460	Removal of nonodontogenic cyst or tumor—lesion diameter up to 1.25 cm
07461	Removal of nonodontogenic cyst or tumor—lesion diameter greater than 1.25 cm
07465	Destruction of lesion(s) by physical or chemical method, by report
	Excision of bone tissue
07470	Removal of exostosis—maxilla or mandible
07480	Partial ostectomy (guttering or saucerization)
07490	Radical resection of mandible with bone graft
	Surgical incision
07510	Incision and drainage of abscess—intraoral soft tissue
07520	Incision and drainage of abscess—extraoral soft tissue
07530	Removal of foreign body, skin or subcutaneous areolar tissue
07540	Removal of reaction-producing foreign bodies—musculoskeletal system
07550	Sequestrectomy for osteomyelitis
07560	Maxillary sinusotomy for removal of tooth fragment or foreign body
	Treatment of fracture—simple
07610	Maxilla—open reduction (teeth immobilized if present)
07620	Maxilla—closed reduction (teeth immobilized if present)
07630	Mandible—open reduction (teeth immobilized if present)
07640	Mandible—closed reduction (teeth immobilized if present)
07650	Malar and/or zygomatic arch—open reduction
07660	Malar and/or zygomatic arch—closed reduction
07670	Alveolus—stabilization of teeth, open reduction splinting
07680	Facial bones—complicated reduction with fixation and multiple surgical approaches
	Treatment of fractures—compound
07710	Maxilla—open reduction

Code	
07720	Maxilla—closed reduction
07730	Mandible—open reduction
07740	Mandible—closed reduction
07750	Malar and/or zygomatic arch—open reduction
07760	Malar and/or zygomatic arch—closed reduction
07770	Alveolus—stabilization of teeth, open reduction splinting
07780	Facial bones—complicated reduction with fixation and multiple surgical approaches
	Reduction of dislocation and management of other temporomandibular joint dysfunctions
07810	Open reduction of dislocation
07820	Closed reduction of dislocation
07830	Manipulation under anesthesia
07840	Condylectomy
07850	Surgical discectomy; with/without implant
07852	Disc repair
07854	Synovectomy
07856	Myotomy
07858	Joint reconstruction
07860	Arthrotomy
07865	Arthroplasty
07870	Arthrocentesis
07872	Arthroscopy—diagnosis, with or without biopsy
07873	Arthroscopy—surgical: lavage and lysis of adhesions
07874	Arthroscopy—surgical: disc repositioning and stabilization
07875	Arthroscopy—surgical: synovectomy
07876	Arthroscopy—surgical: discectomy
07877	Arthroscopy—surgical: debridement
07880	Occlusal orthotic device, by report
07899	Unspecified TMD therapy, by report
	Repair of traumatic wounds
07910	Suture of recent small wounds up to 5 cm
	Complicated suturing (reconstruction requiring delicate handling of tissues and wide undermining for meticulous closure)
07911	Complicated suture—up to 5 cm
07912	Complicated suture—greater than 5 cm
	Other repair procedures
07920	Skin grafts (identify defect covered, location and type of graft)
07940	Osteoplasty—for orthognathic deformities
07941	Osteotomy—ramus, closed
07942	Osteotomy—ramus, open
07943	Osteotomy—ramus, open with bone graft
07944	Osteotomy—segmented or subapical—per sextant or quadrant
07945	Osteotomy—body of mandible
07946	LeFort I (maxilla—total)
07947	LeFort I (maxilla—segmented)

Code	
07948	LeFort II or LeFort III (osteoplasty of facial bone for midface hypoplasia or retrusion)—without bone graft
07949	LeFort II or LeFort III—with bone graft
07950	Osseous, osteoperiosteal, periosteal or cartilage graft of the mandible—autogenous or nonautogenous
07955	Repair of maxillofacial soft and hard tissue defects
07960	Frenulectomy (frenectomy or frenotomy)—separate procedure
07970	Excision of hyperplastic tissue—per arch
07971	Excision of pericoronal gingiva
07980	Sialolithotomy
07981	Excision of salivary gland
07982	Sialodochoplasty
07983	Closure of salivary fistula
07990	Emergency tracheotomy
07991	Coronoidectomy
07993	Implant—facial bones (homologous, heterologous or alloplastic)
07994	Implant—other than facial bones
07999	Unspecified oral surgery procedure, by report
08000-08999	**XI. Orthodontics**
	Minor treatment for tooth guidance
08110	Removable appliance therapy
08120	Fixed appliance therapy
	Minor treatment to control harmful habits
08210	Removable appliance therapy
08220	Fixed appliance therapy
	Interceptive orthodontic treatment
08360	Removable appliance therapy
08370	Fixed appliance therapy
	Comprehensive orthodontic treatment—transitional dentition
08460	Class I malocclusion
08470	Class II malocclusion
08480	Class III malocclusion
	Comprehensive orthodontic treatment—permanent dentition
08560	Class I malocclusion
08570	Class II malocclusion
08580	Class III malocclusion
	Other orthodontic devices
08650	Treatment for the atypical or extended skeletal case
08750	Posttreatment stabilization
08999	Unspecified orthodontic procedure, by report
09000-09999	**XII. Adjunctive general services**
	Unclassified treatment
09110	Palliative (emergency) treatment of dental pain—minor procedures
	Anesthesia
09210	Local anesthesia not in conjunction with operative or surgical procedures

Code	
09211	Regional block anesthesia
09212	Trigeminal division block anesthesia
09215	Local anesthesia
09220	General anesthesia—first 30 minutes
09221	General anesthesia—each additional 15 minutes
09230	Analgesia
09240	Intravenous sedation
	Professional consultation
09310	Consultation (diagnostic service provided by dentist or physician other than practitioner providing treatment)
	Professional visits
09410	House call
09420	Hospital call
09430	Office visit for observation (during regularly scheduled hours)—no other services performed
09440	Office visit—after regularly scheduled hours
	Drugs
09610	Therapeutic drug injection, by report
09630	Other drugs and/or medicaments, by report
	Miscellaneous services
09910	Application of desensitizing medicaments
09920	Behavior management, by report
09930	Treatment of complication (postsurgical)—unusual circumstances, by report
09940	Occlusal guards, by report
09941	Fabrication of athletic mouthguards
09950	Occlusion analysis—mounted case
09951	Occlusal adjustment—limited
09952	Occlusal adjustment—complete
09999	Unspecified adjunctive procedure, by report

F

Glossary of Dental Benefits Terms

American Dental Association

A

Administrative Costs: Overhead expenses incurred in the operation of a dental benefits program, exclusive of costs of dental services provided.

Administrative Services Only (ASO): An arrangement under which a third party, for a fee, processes claims and handles paperwork for a self-funded group. This frequently includes all insurance company services (actuarial services, underwriting, benefit description, etc.) except assumption of risk.

Administrator: One who manages or directs a dental benefits program on behalf of the program's sponsor. (See *Third Party Administrator, Dental Benefits Organization.*)

Adverse Selection: A statistical condition within a group when there is a greater demand for dental services and/or more services necessary than the average expected for that group.

Allowable Charge: The maximum dollar amount on which benefit payment is based for each dental procedure.

Alternate Benefit: A provision in a dental plan contract that allows the third party payer to determine the benefit based on an alternative procedure that is generally less expensive than the one provided or proposed.

Alternative Benefit Plan: A plan, other than a traditional (fee-for-service, freedom-of-choice) indemnity or service corporation plan, for reimbursing a participating dentist for providing treatment to an enrolled patient population.

Alternative Delivery System: An arrangement for the provision of dental services in other than the traditional (e.g., licensed dentist providing treatment in a fee-for-service dental office) way.

Assignment of Benefits: A procedure whereby a beneficiary/patient authorizes the administrator of the program to forward payment for a covered procedure directly to the treating dentist.

Attending Dentist's Statement: Also known as *dental claim form*. A form used to report dental procedures to a third party payer, the claim form was developed by the American Dental Association.

Audit: An examination of records or accounts to check their accuracy. A post-treatment record review or clinical examination to verify information reported on claims.

B

Bad Faith Insurance Practices: The failure to deal with a beneficiary of a dental benefits plan fairly and in good faith; or an activity that impairs the right of the beneficiary to receive the appropriate benefits of a dental benefits plan or to receive them in a timely manner. Some examples of bad faith insurance practices include: evaluating claims based on standards that are significantly at variance with the standards of the community; failure to properly investigate a claim for benefits; and unreasonably and purposely delaying and/or withholding payment of a claim.

Balance Billing: Billing a patient for the difference between the dentist's actual charge and the amount reimbursed under the patient's dental benefits plan.

Beneficiary: A person who receives benefits under a dental benefit contract. (See also *Covered Person, Insured, Member, Subscriber.*)

Benefit: (1) The amount payable by a third party toward the cost of various covered dental services. (2) The dental service or procedure covered by the plan.

Benefit Booklet: A booklet or pamphlet provided to the subscriber that contains a general explanation of the benefits and related provisions of the dental benefits program. Also known as a *summary plan description.*

Benefit Plan Summary: The description or synopsis of employee benefits required by ERISA to be distributed to the employees.

Birthday Rule: Coordination-of-benefits regulation stipulating that the primary payer of benefits for dependent children is determined by the parents' birth dates. Regardless of which parent is older, the dental benefits program of the parent whose birth date falls first in a calendar year is considered primary. (Does not apply to self-funded programs.)

C

Cafeteria Plan: Employee benefits plan in which employees select their medical insurance coverage and other nontaxable fringe benefits from a list of options provided by the employer. Cafeteria plan participants may receive additional, taxable cash compensation if they select less expensive benefits.

Capitation: A capitation dental benefit program is one in which a dentist or dentists contract with the program's sponsor or administrator to provide all or most of the dental services covered under the program to subscribers in return for payment on a per capita basis.

Carrier: See *Third Party.*

Case Management: The monitoring and coordination of treatment rendered to patients with specific diagnoses or requiring high-cost or extensive services.

Certificate Holder: (1) The person, usually the employee, who represents the family unit covered by the dental benefits program; other family members are referred to as *dependents.* (2) Generally refers to a subscriber of a traditional indemnity program. (3) In reference to the program for dependents of active duty military personnel, the certificate holder is called the *sponsor.* (See *Subscriber.*)

Claim: (1) A request for payment under a dental benefits plan. (2) A statement listing services rendered, the dates of services and itemization of costs. Includes a statement signed by the beneficiary and treating dentist that services have been rendered. The completed form serves as the basis for payment of benefits.

Claim Form: The form used to file for benefits under a dental benefits program; includes sections for the patient and the dentist to complete.

Claimant: Person who files a claim for benefits. May be the patient or the certificate holder.

Claims Payment Fraud: The intentional manipulation or alteration of facts submitted by a treating dentist resulting in a lower payment to the beneficiary and/or the treating dentist than would have been paid if the manipulation had not occurred.

Claims Reporting Fraud: The intentional misrepresentation of material facts concerning treatment provided and/or charges made, in that this misrepresentation would cause a higher payment.

Closed Panel: A closed panel dental benefits plan exists when patients eligible to receive benefits can receive them only if services are provided by dentists who have signed an agreement with the benefits plan to provide treatment to eligible patients. As a result of the dentist reimbursement methods characteristic of a closed panel plan, only a small percentage of practicing dentists in a given geographical area are typically contracted by the plan to provide dental services.

Coinsurance: A provision of a dental benefits program by which the beneficiary shares in the cost of covered services, generally on a percentage basis. The percentage of a covered dental expense that a beneficiary must pay (after the deductible is paid). A typical coinsurance arrangement is one in which the third party pays 80% of the allowed benefit of the covered dental service and the beneficiary pays the remainder of the charged fee. Percentages vary and may apply to table-of-allowance plans; usual, customary and reasonable plans; and direct reimbursement programs.

Consolidated Omnibus Budget Reconciliation Act (COBRA): Legislation relative to mandated benefits for all types of employee benefits plans. The most significant aspects within this context are the requirements for continued coverage for 18 months (30 months for dependents in the event of the employee's death) for employees and/or their dependents who would otherwise lose coverage.

Contract: A legally enforceable agreement between two or more individuals or entities that confers rights and duties on the parties. Common types of contracts include: (1) contracts between a dental benefits organization and an individual dentist to provide dental treatment to members of an alternative benefits plan. These contracts define the dentist's duties both to beneficiaries of the dental benefits plan and to the dental benefits organization and usually define the manner in which the dentist will be reimbursed. (2) Contracts between a dental benefits organization and a group plan sponsor. These contracts typically describe the benefits of the group plan and the rates to be charged for those benefits.

Contract Dentist: A practitioner who contractually agrees to provide services under special terms, conditions and financial reimbursement arrangements.

Contract Fee Schedule Plan: A dental benefits plan in which participating dentists agree to accept a list of specific fees as the total fees for dental treatment provided.

Contract Practice: Dental practice in which an employer or third party administrator contracts directly with a dentist or group of dentists to provide dental services for beneficiaries of a plan. (See *Closed Panel*.)

Contract Term: The period of time, usually 12 months, for which a contract is written.

Contributory Program: A dental benefits program in which the enrollee shares in the monthly premium of the program with the program sponsor (usually the employer). Generally done through payroll deduction.

Coordination of Benefits (COB): A method of integrating benefits payable under more than one plan. Benefits from all sources should not exceed 100% of the total charges.

Copayment: Beneficiary's share of the dentist fee after the benefits plan has paid.

Corporate Dentistry: Company-owned and -operated dental care facility that provides services to employees and sometimes dependents.

Cost Containment: Features of a dental benefits program or of the administration of the program designed to reduce or eliminate certain charges to the plan.

Cost Sharing: The share of health expenses that a beneficiary must pay, including the deductibles, copayments, coinsurance and charges over the amount reimbursed by the dental benefits plan.

Coverage: Benefits available to an individual covered under a dental benefits plan.

Covered Charges: Charges for services rendered or supplies furnished by a dentist that qualify as covered services and are paid for in whole or in part by the dental benefits program. May be subject to deductibles, copayments, coinsurance, annual or lifetime maximums, or table of allowances, as specified by the terms of the contract.

Covered Person: An individual who is eligible for benefits under a dental benefits program.

Covered Services: Services for which payment is provided under the terms of the dental benefits contract.

Current Dental Terminology (CDT): A listing of descriptive terms and identifying codes developed by the American Dental Association (ADA) for reporting dental services and procedures to dental benefits plans.

Current Procedural Terminology (CPT): A listing of descriptive terms and identifying codes developed by the American Medical Association (AMA) for reporting practitioner services and procedures to medical plans and Medicare.

Customary Fee: The fee level determined by the administrator of a dental benefits plan from actual submitted fees for a specific dental procedure to establish the maximum benefit payable under a given plan for that specific procedure. (See also *Usual Fee* and *Reasonable Fee*.)

D

Deductible: The amount of dental expense for which the beneficiary is responsible before a third party will assume any liability for payment of benefits. Deductible may be an annual or one-time charge and may vary in amount from program to program. (See *Family Deductible*.)

Dental Benefits Organization: Any organization offering a dental benefits plan. Also known as *dental plan organization*.

Dental Benefits Plan: Entitles covered individuals to specified dental services in return for a fixed, periodic payment made in advance of treatment. Such plans often include the use of deductibles, coinsurance and/or maximums to control the cost of the program to the purchaser.

Dental Benefits Program: The specific dental benefits plan being offered to enrollees by the sponsor.

Dental Insurance: A plan that financially assists in the expense of treatment and care of dental disease and accidents to teeth.

Dental Prepayment: A method of financing the cost of dental services in advance of their receipt.

Dental Service Corporation: A legally constituted, not-for-profit organization that negotiates and administers contracts for dental care. Delta Dental Plans and Blue Cross and Blue Shield Plans are such plans.

Dependents: Generally spouse and children of covered individual, as defined by terms of the dental benefit contract.

Direct Billing: A process whereby the dentist bills a patient directly for his or her fees.

Direct Reimbursement: A self-funded program in which the individual is reimbursed based on a percentage of dollars spent for dental care provided and that allows beneficiaries to seek treatment from the dentist of their choice.

Downcoding: A practice of third party payers in which the benefits code has been changed to a less complex and/or lower cost procedure than was reported.

DRGs (Diagnosis-Related Groups): A system of classifying hospital patients on the basis of diagnosis, consisting of distinct groupings. A DRG assignment to a case is based on the patient's (1) principal diagnosis, (2) treatment procedures performed, (3) age, (4) gender and (5) discharge status.

Dual Choice Program: A benefits package from which an eligible individual can choose to enroll in either an alternative dental benefits program or a traditional dental benefits program.

E

Eligibility Date: The date an individual and/or dependents become eligible for benefits under a dental benefits contract. Often referred to as *effective date.*

Eligible Person: See *Beneficiary.*

Employee Retirement Income Security Act (ERISA): A federal act, passed in 1974, that established new standards and reporting/disclosure requirements for employer-funded pension and health benefit programs. To date, self-funded health benefit plans operating under ERISA have been held to be exempt from state insurance laws. This exemption is currently under review.

Enrollee: Individual covered by a benefit plan. (See *Beneficiary.*)

Exclusions: Dental services not covered under a dental benefits program.

Exclusive Provider Organization (EPO): A dental benefits plan that provides benefits only if care is rendered by institutional and professional providers with whom the plan contracts (with some exceptions for emergency and out-of-area services).

Expiration Date: (1) The date on which the dental benefits contract expires; (2) The date an individual ceases to be eligible for benefits.

Explanation of Benefits: A written statement, from a third party payer, to a beneficiary after a claim has been reported, indicating the benefit/charges covered or not covered by the dental benefits plan.

Extension of Benefits: Extension of eligibility for benefits for covered services, usually designed to ensure completion of treatment commenced prior to the expiration date. Duration is generally expressed in terms of days.

F

Family Deductible: A deductible that is satisfied by combined expenses of all covered family members. For example, a program with a $25 deductible may limit its application to a maximum of three deductibles, or $75 for the family, regardless of the number of family members. (See *Deductible.*)

Fee for Service: A method of paying practitioners on a service-by-service rather than a salaried or capitated basis.

Fee Schedule: A list of the charges established or agreed to by a dentist for specific dental services.

Flexible Benefits: A benefit program in which an employee has a choice of credits or dollars for distribution among various benefit options, e.g., health and disability insurance, dental benefits, child care or pension benefits. (See *Cafeteria Plans, Flexible Spending Account.*)

Flexible Spending Account: Employee reimbursement account primarily funded with employee-designated salary reductions. Funds are reimbursed to employee for health care (medical and/or dental), dependent care and/or legal expenses, and are considered a nontaxable benefit.

Franchise Dentistry: Refers to a system for marketing a dental practice, usually under a trade name, where permitted by state laws. In return for a financial investment or other consideration, participating dentists may also receive the benefits of media advertising, a national referral system and financial and management consultation.

Freedom of Choice: A provision in a dental benefits program that permits the insured to choose any licensed dentist to provide his or her dental care and receive full benefits under the program.

G

Gatekeeper System: A managed care concept used by some alternative benefits plans, in which enrollees elect a primary care dentist, usually a general practitioner or pediatric dentist, who is responsible for providing nonspecialty care and managing referrals, as appropriate, for specialty and ancillary services.

H

Health Maintenance Organization (HMO): A legal entity that accepts responsibility and financial risk for providing specified services to a defined population during a defined period of time at a fixed price. An organized system of health care delivery that provides comprehensive care to enrollees through designated providers. Enrollees are generally assessed a monthly payment for health care services and may be required to remain in the program for a specified amount of time.

Hold Harmless Clause: A contract provision in which one party to the contract promises to be responsible for liability incurred by the other party. Hold harmless clauses frequently appear in the following contexts: (1) Contracts between dental benefits organizations and an individual dentist often contain a promise by the dentist to reimburse the dental benefits organization for any liability the organization incurs because of dental treatment provided to beneficiaries of the organization's dental benefits plan. This may include a promise to pay the dental benefits organization's attorney fees and related costs. (2) Contracts between dental benefits organizations and a group plan sponsor may include a promise by the dental benefits organization to assume responsibility for disputes between a beneficiary of the group plan and an individual dentist when the dentist's charge exceeds the amount the organization pays for the service on behalf of the beneficiary. If the dentist takes action against the patient to recover the difference between the amount billed by the dentist and the amount paid by the organization, the dental benefits organization will take over the defense of the claim and will pay any judgments and court costs.

I

Incentive Program: A dental benefits program that pays an increasing share of the treatment cost, provided that the covered individual utilizes the benefits of the program during each incentive period (usually a year) and receives the treatment prescribed. For example, a 70-30% copayment program in the first year of coverage may become an 80-20% program in the second year if the subscriber visits the dentist in the first year as stipulated in the program. Most frequently, there is a corresponding percentage reduction in the program's copayment level if the covered individual fails to visit the dentist in a given year (but never below the initial copayment level).

Indemnification Schedule: See *Table of Allowances*.

Indemnity Plan: A dental plan where a third party payer provides payment of an amount for specific services, regardless of the actual charges made by the provider. Payment may be made either to enrollees or, by assignment, directly to dentists. Schedule of allowances, table of allowances or reasonable and customary plans are examples of indemnity plans.

Individual Practice Association (IPA): A legal entity organized and operated on behalf of individual participating dentists for the primary purpose of collectively entering into contracts to provide dental services to enrolled populations. Dentists may practice in their own offices and may provide care to patients not covered by the contract as well as IPA patients.

Insured: Person covered by the program. (See *Beneficiary.*)

Insurer: An organization that bears the financial risk for the cost of defined categories or services for a defined group of beneficiaries. (See *Third Party.*)

International Classification of Diseases (ICD): Diagnostic codes designed for the classification of morbidity and mortality information for statistical purposes, and for the indexing of hospital records by disease and operations, for data storage and retrieval.

L

Least Expensive Alternative Treatment (LEAT): A limitation in a dental benefits plan that will only allow benefits for the least expensive treatment. Also referred to as *least expensive professionally acceptable alternative treatment (LEPAAT)*.

Liability: An obligation for a specified amount or action.

Limitations: Restrictive conditions stated in a dental benefits contract, such as age, length of time covered and waiting periods, which affect an individual's or group's coverage. The contract may also exclude certain benefits or services, or it may limit the extent or conditions under which certain services are provided. (See *Exclusions.*)

M

Managed Care: Refers to a cost-containment system that directs the utilization of health benefits by: (1) restricting the type, level and frequency of treatment; (2) limiting the access to care; and (3) controlling the level of reimbursement for services.

Maximum Allowance: The maximum dollar amount a dental program will pay toward the cost of a dental service as specified in the program's contract provisions, e.g., UCR, table of allowances.

Maximum Benefit: The maximum dollar amount a program will pay toward the cost of dental care incurred by an individual or family in a specified period, usually a calendar year.

Maximum Fee Schedule: A compensation arrangement in which a participating dentist agrees to accept a prescribed sum as the total fee for one or more covered services.

Medicaid: A federal assistance program established as Title XIX under the Social Security Amendments of 1965 that provides payment for medical care for certain low-income individuals and families. The program is funded jointly by the state and federal governments and administered by states.

Medically Necessary Care: The reasonable and appropriate diagnosis, treatment and followup care (including supplies, appliances and devices) as determined and prescribed by qualified, appropriate health care providers in treating any condition, illness, disease, injury or birth developmental malformations. Care is medically necessary for the purpose of: controlling or eliminating infection, pain and disease; and restoring facial configuration or function necessary for speech, swallowing or chewing.

Medicare: A federal insurance program enacted in 1965 as Title XVIII of the Social Security Amendments that provides certain inpatient hospital services and physician services for all persons age 65 and older and eligible disabled individuals. The program is administered by the Health Care Financing Administration.

Member: An individual enrolled in a dental benefits program. (See *Beneficiary*.)

N

Necessary Treatment: A necessary dental procedure or service as determined by a dentist, to either establish or maintain a patient's oral health. Such determinations are based on the professional diagnostic judgment of the dentist and the standards of care that prevail in the professional community.

Noncontributory Program: A method of payment for group coverage in which all of the monthly premium for the program is paid by the sponsor.

Nonduplication of Benefits: This may apply if a subscriber is eligible for benefits under more than one plan. A dental benefits contract provision relieving the third party payer of liability for cost of services if the services are covered under another program. Distinct from a coordination-of-benefits provision, because reimbursement would be limited to the greater level allowed by the two plans, rather than a total of 100% of the charges. Also referred to as *benefit-less-benefit* or *carve-out*.

Nonparticipating Dentist: Any dentist who does not have a contractual agreement with a dental benefits organization to render dental care to members of a dental benefits program.

Not-for-Profit Third Parties: Service corporations or dental benefit organizations established under not-for-profit state statutes for the purpose of providing health care coverage, e.g., Delta Dental Plans, Blue Cross and Blue Shield Plans.

O

Open Enrollment: The annual period in which employees can select from a choice of benefits programs.

Open Panel: A dental benefit plan characterized by three features: (1) Any licensed dentist may elect to participate. (2) The beneficiary may receive dental treatment from among all licensed dentists, with the corresponding benefits being payable to either the beneficiary or the dentist. (3) The dentist may accept or refuse any beneficiary.

Overbilling: Nondisclosure of waiver of patient copayment.

Overcoding: Reporting a more complex and/or higher cost procedure than was actually performed.

P

Participating Dentist: Any dentist who has a contractual agreement with a dental benefits organization to render care to eligible persons.

Payer: In health care, generally refers to entities, other than the patient, that finance or reimburse the cost of health services. In most cases, refers to insurance carriers, other third party payers and/or health plan sponsors (employers or unions).

Peer Review: (1) A retrospective consideration or an examination by one or more individuals of equal standing or rank. (2) A process established to provide for review by licensed dentists of: the care provided by a dentist for a single patient; disputes regarding fees; cases submitted by carriers, initiated by patients or dentists; quality of care and appropriateness of treatment.

Peer Review Organization (PRO): An organization established by an amendment of the Tax Equity and Fiscal Responsibility Act of 1982 (TEFRA), to provide for the review of medical services furnished primarily in a hospital setting and/or in conjunction with care provided under the Medicare and Medicaid programs. In addition to their review and monitoring functions, these entities can invoke sanctions, penalties or other corrective actions for noncompliance in organization standards.

Percentile: The number in a frequency distribution below which a certain percentage of fees will fall. For example, the 90th percentile is the number that divides the distribution of fees into the lower 90% and the upper 10%, or that fee level at which 90% of dentists charge that amount or less, and 10% charge more.

Post-Treatment Review: See *Audit*.

Pre-Authorization: Statement by a third party payer indicating that proposed treatment will be covered under the terms of the dental benefits contract. (See also *Precertification, Predetermination*.)

Precertification: Confirmation by a third party payer of a patient's eligibility for coverage under a dental benefits program. (See also *Pre-Authorization, Predetermination*.)

Predetermination: An administrative procedure that may require the dentist to submit a treatment plan to the third party before treatment is begun. The third party usually returns the treatment plan indicating one or more of the following: patient's eligibility, guarantee of eligibility period, covered services, benefit amounts payable, application of appropriate deductibles, copayment and/or maximum limitation. Under some programs, predetermination by the third party is required when covered charges are expected to exceed a certain amount, such as $200. Also known as *pre-authorization, precertification, pretreatment review, prior authorization*.

Preexisting Condition: Oral health condition of an enrollee that existed before his or her enrollment in a dental program.

Preferred Provider Organization (PPO): A formal agreement between a purchaser of a dental benefits program and a defined group of dentists for the delivery of dental services to a specific patient population, as an adjunct to a traditional plan, using discounted fees for cost savings.

Prefiling of Fees: The submission of a participating dentist's usual fees to a service corporation for the purpose of establishing, in advance, that dentist's usual fees and the customary ranges of fees in a geographic area to determine benefits under a usual, customary and reasonable dental benefits program.

Premium: The amount charged by a dental benefits organization for coverage of a level of benefits for a specified time.

Prepaid Dental Plan: A method of financing the cost of dental care for a defined population, in advance of receipt of services.

Prepaid Group Practice: See *Closed Panel.*

Pretreatment Estimate: See *Predetermination.*

Prevailing Fee: Term used by some dental benefits organizations to refer to the fee most commonly charged for a dental service in a given area.

Preventive Dentistry: Refers to the procedures in dental practice and health programs that prevent the occurrence of oral diseases.

Prior Authorization: See *Predetermination.*

Proof of Loss: Verification of services rendered (expenses incurred) by the submission of claim forms, radiographs, study models and/or other diagnostic material.

Prospective Review: Prior assessment by a payer or payer's agent that proposed services are appropriate for a particular patient, and/or the patient and the category of service are covered by a benefit plan. (See *Pre-Authorization, Precertification, Predetermination, Second Opinion Program.*)

Purchaser: Program sponsor, often employer or union, that contracts with the dental benefits organization to provide dental benefits to an enrolled population.

Q

Quality Assessment: The measure of the quality of care provided in a particular setting.

Quality Assurance: The assessment or measurement of the quality of care and the implementation of any necessary changes to either maintain or improve the quality of care rendered.

R

Reasonable and Customary (R&C) Plan: A dental benefits plan that determines benefits based only on reasonable and customary fee criteria. (See *Usual Fee, Customary Fee* and *Reasonable Fee.*)

Reasonable Fee: The fee charged by a dentist for a specific dental procedure that has been modified by the nature and severity of the condition being treated and by any medical or dental complications or unusual circumstances, and therefore may differ from the dentist's "usual" fee or the benefit administrator's "customary" fee.

Reimbursement: Payment made by a third party to a beneficiary or to a dentist on behalf of the beneficiary, toward repayment of expenses incurred for a service covered by the contractual arrangement.

Reinsurance: Insurance for third party payers to spread their risk for losses (claims paid) over a specified dollar amount.

Relative Value System: Coded listing of professional services with unit values to indicate relative complexity as measured by time, skill and overhead costs. Third party payers typically assign a dollar value per unit to calculate provider reimbursement.

Retail Store Dentistry: Refers to dental services offered within a retail, department or drug store operation. Typically, space is leased from the store by a separate administrative group that, in turn, subleases to a dentist or dental group providing the actual dental services. The dental operation generally maintains the same hours of operation as the store and appointments often are not necessary. Considered to be a type of practice, not a dental benefits plan model.

Retrospective Review: A post-treatment assessment of services on a case-by-case or aggregate basis after the services have been performed.

Risk Pool: A portion of provider fees or capitation payments withheld as financial reserves to cover unanticipated utilization of services in an alternative benefits plan.

S

Schedule of Allowances: See *Table of Allowances.*

Schedule of Benefits: A listing of the services for which payment will be made by a third party payer, without specification of the amount to be paid.

Second Opinion Program: An opinion about the appropriateness of a proposed treatment provided by a practitioner other than the one making the original recommendation; some benefits plans require such opinions for selected services.

Self-Funding: The method of providing employee benefits, in which the sponsor does not purchase conventional insurance, but rather elects to pay for the claims directly, generally through the services of a TPA. Self-funded programs often have stop-loss insurance in place to cover abnormal risks.

Self-Insurance: Setting aside of funds by an individual or organization to meet anticipated dental care expenses or its dental care claims and accumulation of a fund to absorb fluctuations in the amount of expenses or claims. The funds set aside or accumulated are used to provide dental benefits directly instead of purchasing coverage from an insurance carrier.

Statistically Based Utilization Review: A system that examines the distribution of treatment procedures based on claims information; in order to be reasonably reliable, the application of such claims analyses of specific dentists should include data on type of practice, dentist's experience, socioeconomic characteristics and geographic location.

Stop-Loss: A general term referring to that category of coverage that provides insurance protection (reinsurance) to an employer for a self-funded plan.

Subscriber: The person, usually the employee, who represents the family unit in relation to the dental benefits program. This term is most commonly used by service corporation plans. Also known as *certificate holder, enrollee.*

Summary Plan Description: See *Benefit Plan Summary.*

Surcharge: A stated dollar amount paid to the dentist by the beneficiary, in addition to other reimbursement received by third party payer(s).

T

Table of Allowances: A list of covered services with an assigned dollar amount that represents the total obligation of the plan with respect to payment for such service, but does not necessarily represent the dentist's full fee for that service. Also known as *schedule of allowances, indemnity schedule.*

Tax Equity and Fiscal Responsibility Act of 1982 (TEFRA): Legislation (Public Law 97-248) affecting health maintenance organizations and the Medicare and Medicaid programs. Provides regulations for the development of HMO risk contracting with the Medicare program and, through amendment, establishes new provisions for the foundation and operation of peer review organizations.

Termination Date: See *Expiration Date.*

Third Party: The party to a dental benefits contract that may collect premiums, assume financial risk, pay claims and/or provide other administrative services. Also known as *administrative agent, carrier, insurer, underwriter.*

Third Party Administrator (TPA): Claims payer that assumes responsibility for administering health benefit plans without assuming any financial risk. Some commercial insurance carriers and Blue Cross and Blue Shield plans also have TPA operations to accommodate self-funded employers seeking administrative services only (ASO) contracts.

Third Party Payer: An organization other than the patient (first party) or health care provider (second party) involved in the financing of personal health services.

U

Unbundling of Procedures: The separating of a dental procedure into component parts with each part having a charge so that the cumulative charge of the components is greater than the total charge to patients who are not beneficiaries of a dental benefits plan for the same procedure.

Upcode: Using a procedure code that reflects a higher intensity service than would normally be used for the services delivered.

Usual, Customary and Reasonable (UCR) Plans: A dental benefits plan that determines benefits based on usual, customary and reasonable fee criteria. (See *Usual Fee, Customary Fee* and *Reasonable Fee.*)

Usual Fee: The fee that an individual dentist most frequently charges for a given dental service. (See also *Customary Fee* and *Reasonable Fee.*)

Utilization: (1) The extent to which the members of a covered group use a program over a stated period of time; specifically measured as a percentage determined by dividing the number of covered individuals who submitted one or more claims by the total number of covered individuals. (2) An expression of the number and types of services used by the members of a covered group over a specified period of time.

Utilization Management: A set of techniques used by or on behalf of purchasers of health care benefits to manage the cost of health care prior to its provision by influencing patient care decision making through case-by-case assessments of the appropriateness of care based on accepted dental practices.

Utilization Review, Statistically Based: A system that examines the distribution of treatment procedures based on claims information; in order to be reasonably reliable, the application of such claims analyses of specific dentists should include data on type of practice, dentist's experience, socioeconomic characteristics and geographic location.

W

Waiting Period: The period between employment or enrollment in a dental program and the date when a covered person becomes eligible for benefits.

Common Dental Terms

G

American Dental Association

This section contains brief descriptions of some of the terms included in the CDT-1 and is intended to assist those without formal training in dentistry. In several instances, descriptions developed by dental specialty organizations have been included. None of the following descriptions should be construed as official definitions of the American Dental Association.

A

Abutment—a tooth or implant used to support a prosthesis.

Acid Etching—use of a chemical substance to prepare the enamel surface to provide retention for bonding.

Alloplastic—refers to synthetic material often used for tissue augmentation.

Alveolar—referring to the bone to which a tooth is attached.

Alveoplasty—surgical procedure for recontouring alveolar structures, usually in preparation for a prosthesis.

Amalgam—an alloy used in dental restorations; always includes mercury.

Anterior—refers to the teeth in the forward part of the mouth—incisors and canines.

Apex—the tip or end of the root end of the tooth.

Apicoectomy—amputation of the root of a tooth.

Avulsion—separation of tooth from its socket due to trauma (see *Evulsion*).

B

Benign—not malignant.

Biopsy—process of removing tissue for determination of existence of pathology.

Bitewing—interproximal view radiograph of the radiograph coronal portion of the tooth.

Bridge—fixed bridge is a prosthetic replacement of one or more missing teeth usually cemented to the abutment teeth adjacent to the space; removable bridge (partial denture) is a prosthetic replacement of one or more missing teeth on a framework that can be removed by the patient.

Bruxism—involuntary clenching or grinding of the teeth.

Buccal—pertaining to or around the cheek.

C

Calculus—hard deposit of mineralized plaque that is attached to crowns and/or roots of teeth.

Canal—a relatively narrow tabular passage or channel; space inside the root portion of a tooth containing pulp tissue.

Caries—correct technical term for decay.

Cast—see *Diagnostic Cast* or *Study Model*.

Cavity—lesion or hole in tooth caused by caries.

Cement Base—material used under a filling to replace tooth structure lost by the decay process.

Cementum—hard connective tissue covering the tooth root.

Cephalometric—a radiographic head film used to study the radiograph growth of the skull and head.

Chemical Curettage—use of a caustic agent to facilitate subgingival and root curettage (see *Curettage*).

Closed Reduction—closing the space between the fractured bone without cutting through soft tissue or surrounding bone.

Compound Fracture—break in bone so that the broken parts protrude through the soft tissue.

Coping—a thin covering of the coronal portion of the tooth usually without anatomic conformity. It can be used as a definitive restoration or as part of a transfer procedure.

Crown—part of the tooth that is covered with enamel and normally projects beyond the gingival margin; artificial replacement is called by same name.

Crown Lengthening—a surgical procedure exposing more tooth for restorative purposes by apically positioning the gingival margin and/or removing supporting bone.

Curettage—scraping or cleaning the walls of a cavity or gingival pocket.

Cusp—pointed or rounded eminence on or near the masticating surface of a tooth.

D

Debridement—removal of foreign matter.

Decay—the lay term for carious lesions in a tooth; decomposition of tooth structure.

Deciduous—to fall off or shed; a name used for the primary teeth.

Dental Prophylaxis—scaling and polishing procedure performed to remove coronal plaque, calculus and stains.

Dentin—that part of the tooth that is beneath enamel and cementum.

Denture—an artificial substitute for natural teeth and adjacent tissues.

Denture Base—that part of a denture that makes contact with soft tissue and retains the artificial teeth.

Diagnostic Cast—plaster or stone model of teeth and adjoining tissues; also referred to as *Study Model*.

Direct Pulp Cap—procedure in which the exposed pulp is covered with a dressing or cement that protects the pulp and promotes healing and repair.

Displaced Tooth—a partial evulsion of a tooth—may be mesial, distal, facial, lingual or incisal.

Distal—toward the back of the dental arch (or away from the midline).

Dry Socket—localized inflammation of the tooth socket following extraction due to infection or loss of blood clot.

E

Edentulous—without teeth.

Enamel—hard calcified tissue covering dentin of the crown of tooth.

Endodontist—a dental specialist who limits his or her practice to treating disease and injuries of the pulp and associated periradicular conditions.

Equilibration—reshaping of the occlusal surfaces of teeth to create harmonious contact relationships between the upper and lower teeth; also known as *occlusal adjustment*.

Evulsion—complete separation of the tooth from its socket due to trauma (see *Avulsion*).

Examination—*Complete Examination:* A dentist thoroughly evaluates the state of health of the patient including a thorough examination of the hard and soft tissues of the oral cavity and contiguous structures. This includes but is not limited to the use of diagnostic information acquired through interpretation of appropriate dental radiographs and may also include pulp vitality tests, trans-illumination, study models and laboratory tests, when indicated.
Limited Examination: A dentist thoroughly evaluates the state of health of the patient and includes an evaluation of the hard and soft tissues of a portion of the oral cavity. Includes but is not limited to the use of diagnostic information acquired through interpretation of selected dental radiographs; may also include diagnostic information acquired through interpretation of other diagnostic tests, as indicated.

Excision—surgical removal of bone or tissue.

Exostosis—overgrowth of normal bone (see *Torus*).

Extracoronal—outside the crown of a tooth.

Exudate—material such as fluid, cells or other debris deposited in or on tissues, usually as a result of inflammation or necrosis.

F

Filling—a lay term used for the restoring of lost tooth structure by using materials such as metal, plastic or cement.

Foramen—natural opening into or through bone fracture—the breaking of a part, especially of a bony structure; breaking of a tooth.

Frenum—muscle fibers covered by a mucous membrane that attaches the cheek, lips and or tongue to associated dental mucosa.

Furcation—the anatomic area of a multirooted tooth where the roots diverge.

G

Gingiva—soft tissues overlying the crowns of unerupted teeth and encircling the necks of those that have erupted, serving as the supporting structure for subadjacent tissues.

Gingivectomy—the excision or removal of gingiva.

Gingivitis—inflammation of gingival tissue.

Gingivoplasty—surgical procedure to reshape gingiva to create a normal, functional form.

Graft—a piece of tissue or alloplastic material placed in contact with tissue to repair a defect or supplement a deficiency.

H

Hemisection—surgical separation of a multirooted tooth so that one root and the overlaying portion of the crown can be surgically removed.

I

Immediate Denture—prosthesis constructed for placement immediately after removal of remaining natural teeth.

Impacted Tooth—an unerupted or partially erupted tooth that is positioned against another tooth, bone or soft tissue so that complete eruption is unlikely.

Implant—material inserted or grafted into tissue.

Implantation, Tooth—placement of an artificial or natural tooth into a socket.

Indirect Pulp Cap—procedure in which the nearly exposed pulp is covered with a protective dressing to protect the pulp from additional injury and to promote healing and repair via formation of secondary dentin.

Intentional Reimplanation—the intentional removal, radicular repair and replacement of a tooth into its own socket.

Interproximal—between the adjoining surfaces of adjacent teeth.

Intracoronal—referring to *within* the crown of a tooth.

Intraoral—inside the mouth.

J

Jaw—a common name for either the maxilla or the mandible.

L

Labial—pertaining to or around the lip.

Lesion—an injury or wound; area of diseased tissue.

Lingual—pertaining to or around the tongue.

M

Maintenance, Periodontal—therapy for preserving the state of health of the periodontium.

Malar—pertaining to the cheek bone.

Malignant—having the properties of dysplasia, invasion and metastasis.

Malocclusion—improper alignment of biting or chewing surfaces of upper and lower teeth.

Mandible—lower jaw.

Maryland Bridge—trade name that has become synonymous with any acid-etched bridge.

Maxilla—the upper jaw.

Mesial—toward the midline of the dental arch.

Metals, Classification of—the noble metal classification system has been adopted as a more precise method of reporting various alloys used in dentistry. The alloys are defined on the basis of the percentage of noble metal content: high noble—gold (Au), palladium (Pd), and/or platinum (Pt) $> 60\%$ (with at least 40% Au); noble—gold (Au), palladium (Pd), and/or platinum (Pt) $> 25\%$; and predominantly base—gold (Au), palladium (Pd), and/or platinum (Pt) $< 25\%$.

Moulage—a cast of the face that may be wax or plaster.

Mucous Membrane—lining to the oral cavity as well as other canals and cavities of the body; also called *mucosa.*

O

Obturator—a disk or plate that closes an opening; a prosthesis that closes an opening in the palate.

Occlusal Radiograph—an intraoral radiograph made with the film being held between the occluded teeth.

Occlusion—any contact between biting or chewing surfaces of upper and lower teeth.

Onlay—a restoration that replaces a cusp or cusps of the tooth.

Open Reduction—providing access to a fracture for purposes of anatomic approximation by cutting tissue or surrounding bone.

Operculectomy—removal of the operculum.

Operculum—the flap of tissue over an unerupted or partially erupted tooth.

Oral—pertaining to the mouth.

Oral and Maxillo-Facial Surgeon—a dental specialist whose practice is limited to the diagnosis, surgical and adjunctive treatment of diseases, injuries, deformities, defects and esthetic aspects of the oral and maxillo-facial regions.

Oral Pathology—the specialty of dentistry and pathology concerned with recognition, diagnosis, investigation and management of diseases of the oral cavity, jaws and adjacent structures.

Orthodontist—a dental specialist whose practice is limited to the interception and treatment of malocclusion of the teeth and their surrounding structures.

Orthognathic—functional relationship of jaws.

Osteoplasty—surgical procedure that modifies the configuration of bone.

Osteotomy—surgical cutting or transsection of bone.

Overdenture—prosthetic device that is supported by retained roots or implants.

P

Palate—the hard and soft tissues forming the roof of the mouth that separate the oral and nasal cavities.

Palliative—action that relieves pain but is not curative.

Panoramic—an extraoral radiograph on which the maxilla and mandible are depicted on a single film.

Partial Denture—usually refers to the prosthetic device that replaces the missing teeth on a framework that can be removed by the patient.

Pediatric Dentist—a dental specialist whose practice is limited to treatment of children from birth through adolescence; formerly known as a *pedodontist.*

Pedodontist—see *Pediatric Dentist.*

Periapical—the area surrounding the end of the tooth root.

Periapical Radiograph—a radiograph made by the intraoral placement of film for disclosing the apices of the teeth.

Pericoronal—around the crown of a tooth.

Periodontal—pertaining to or around the root portion of a tooth.

Periodontist—a dental specialist whose practice is limited to the treatment of diseases of the supporting and surrounding tissues of the teeth.

Periodontitis—inflammation of the supporting or surrounding structure of teeth.

Periradicular—surrounding the entire root of the tooth.

Plaque—a soft sticky substance that accumulates on teeth and is composed largely of derivatives from the saliva bacterial products.

Pontic—the term used for the artificial tooth on a bridge.

Premedication—the use of medications prior to dental procedures.

Primary Dentition—the first set of teeth; also known as *Deciduous.*

Prophylaxis—scaling and polishing procedure performed to remove coronal plaque, calculus and stains.

Prosthesis—artificial replacement of any part of the body; *definitive prosthesis*—a prosthesis to be used over an extended period of time; *interim prosthesis*—a provisional prosthesis designed for use over a limited period of time, after which it is to be replaced by a more definitive restoration.

Prosthodontist—a dental specialist whose practice is limited to the restoration of the natural teeth and/or the replacement of missing teeth with artificial substitutes.

Pulp—the blood vessels and nerve tissue that occupies the pulp cavity of a tooth.

Pulp Cavity—the space within a tooth that contains the pulp.

Pulpectomy—complete removal of diseased pulp tissue from the root canal space.

Pulpotomy—the removal of the coronal portion of the pulp.

Q

Quadrant—one of the four equal sections into which the dental arches can be divided; begins at the midline of the arch and extends distally to the last tooth; usually includes five or more teeth.

R

Radiograph—X-ray.

Rebase—process of refitting a denture by replacing the base material.

Reline—process of resurfacing the tissue side of a denture with a new base material.

Replantation, Tooth—the return of a tooth to its socket.

Retainer—*orthodontic retainer:* appliance to stabilize teeth following orthodontic treatment; *prosthodontic retainer:* a part of a fixed bridge that attaches a pontic to the abutment tooth.

Retrograde Filling—a method of sealing the root canal by preparing and filling it from the root apex.

Root—the anatomic portion of the tooth that is covered by cementum and is normally suspended in the alveolus.

Root Canal—the portion of the pulp cavity inside the root of a tooth.

Root Canal Therapy—treatment of the pulp cavity to eliminate periapical disease and to promote healing and repair of periapical tissues.

Root Planing—a procedure designed to remove microbial flora, bacterial toxins on the root surface or in the pocket, calculus and diseased cementum or dentin.

S

Scaling—removal of plaque, calculus and stain from teeth.

Sextant—one of the six relatively equal sections into which a dental arch can be divided, for example, tooth numbers 1-5; 6-11; 12-16; 17-21; 22-27; 28-32. Sometimes used for recording periodontal charting.

Sialiography—inspection of the salivary ducts and glands by radiograph after the injection of a radiopaque medium.

Splint—a device used to support, protect or immobilize oral structures that have been loosened, replanted, fractured or traumatized. Also refers to devices used in the treatment of temporomandibular joint disorders.

Stomatitis—of the membranes of the mouth.

Study Model—plaster or stone model of teeth and adjoining tissues; also referred to as *Diagnostic Cast.*

Suture—stitch used to repair incision or wound.

T

Temporary Removable Partial Denture—an interim prosthesis designed for use over limited period of time.

Temporomandibular Joint (TMJ)—the connecting hinge mechanism between the mandible (lower jaw) and base of the skull (temporal bone).

Temporomandibular Joint Dysfunction—problems with the jaw joint.

Torus—a bony elevation or protuberance of normal bone.

Transplantation, Tooth—transfer of a tooth from one socket to another, either in the same or a different person.

U

Unerupted—teeth that have not penetrated into the oral cavity.

V

Vestibuloplasty—any of a series of surgical procedures designed to increase relative alveolar ridge height.

Z

Zygomatic bone—quadrangular bone on either side of face that forms the cheek prominence (see *Malar*).

H

Participant Survey

What dental office are you using?

Name ______________________________

Have you used the dental plan this year? ☐ Yes ☐ No

If you did not use the dental plan this year please explain why.

☐ Offices not convenient
☐ Too difficult to get an appointment
☐ Use another dentist
☐ No need for dental care
☐ Other reason
Explain: ______________________________
____

How many times did you use the plan?

☐ Never
☐ Once
☐ More than 2 times—but less than 5 times
☐ More than 5 times

How many days did you have to wait for an appointment?

☐ Less than 7 days
☐ Between 2 and 3 weeks
☐ Between 4 and 6 weeks
☐ More than 6 weeks

How long did you have to wait in the dental office past your scheduled appointment time?

☐ Less than ½ hour
☐ Between ½ and one hour
☐ More than one hour

Did you miss any dental appointments without calling the dental office the day before? ☐ Yes ☐ No

How many appointments did you miss? ______
Were you charged for the broken appointment? ☐ Yes ☐ No
How much? ______

Are the office hours convenient? ☐ Yes ☐ No

What hours would be more convenient? ______

______

Are the dental offices convenient? ☐ Yes ☐ No

How long does it take you to get from your home to the dental office?

☐ Less than ½ hour
☐ Between ½ and one hour
☐ More than one hour

If you had to pay additional for services was the charge explained prior to treatment and given to you in writing? ☐ Yes ☐ No

Were you satisfied with the explanation of treatment and the alternatives? ☐ Yes ☐ No

Has your treatment been completed? ☐ Yes ☐ No

If treatment has not been completed do you have another appointment scheduled? ☐ Yes ☐ No

Were you satisfied with the outcome of the treatment? ☐ Yes ☐ No

Did you use the dental plan for emergency treatment this year? ☐ Yes ☐ No

What was the emergency? ________________________________

____

How long did you have to wait to be seen for emergency treatment?

☐ Same day ☐ 2 days

☐ 1 day ☐ 3 or more days

Explain: ________________________________

____

How do you compare this plan to your previous dental plan?

☐ Better

☐ About same

☐ Not as good

Would you recommend the dental plan to others? ☐ Yes ☐ No

What do you like best about the dental plan?

____

____

____

What do you like least about the dental plan?

____

____

____

On a scale of 1 to 5, with 5 the best rating, how would you rate?

_______ Attitude of dentist

_______ Attitude of staff

_______ Explanation of what was being done

_______ Waiting time for appointments

_______ Waiting time at office

_______ Office location

_______ Quality of dental care given

Please feel free to make any additional comments that will help us evaluate your dental plan.

1990 Survey of Dental Fees— General Practitioner Dental Fees

I

American Dental Association

Code	Procedure	50th Percentile*
DIAGNOSTIC		
	Clinical oral examinations	
00110	Initial oral examination	$18
00120	Periodic oral examination	14
00130	Emergency oral examination	19
	Radiographs	
00210	Intraoral—complete series (including bitewings)	45
00220	Intraoral—periapical—first film	8
00230	Intraoral—periapical—each additional film	6
00272	Bitewings—two films	14
00274	Bitewings—four films	20
00330	Panoramic film	39
	Tests and laboratory examinations	
00470	Diagnostic casts	25
PREVENTIVE		
	Dental prophylaxis	
01110	Prophylaxis—adult	30
01120	Prophylaxis—child	22
	Topical fluoride treatment (office procedure)	
01201	Topical application of fluoride (including prophylaxis)—child	28
01203	Topical application of fluoride (excluding prophylaxis)—child	13
01204	Topical application of fluoride (excluding prophylaxis)—adult	13
01205	Topical application of fluoride (including prophylaxis)—adult	37

Code	Procedure	50th Percentile*
	Other preventive services	
01351	Sealant—per tooth	$ 5
	Space maintenance (passive appliances)	
01510	Space maintainer—fixed—unilateral	95
01515	Space maintainer—fixed—bilateral	150
RESTORATIVE		
	Amalgam restorations (including polishing)	
02110	Amalgam—one surface, primary	30
02120	Amalgam—two surfaces, primary	41
02130	Amalgam—three surfaces, primary	50
02140	Amalgam—one surface, permanent	34
02150	Amalgam—two surfaces, permanent	45
02160	Amalgam—three surfaces, permanent	56
02161	Amalgam—four or more surfaces, permanent	67
	Resin restorations	
02330	Resin—one surface, anterior	40
02331	Resin—two surfaces, anterior	54
02332	Resin—three surfaces, anterior	65
02335	Resin—four or more surfaces or involving incisal angle (anterior)	80
02385	Resin—one surface, posterior—permanent	45
02386	Resin—two surfaces, posterior—permanent	60
02387	Resin—three or more surfaces, posterior—permanent	75
	Inlay restorations	
02510	Inlay—metallic—one surface	250
02520	Inlay—metallic—two surfaces	300
02530	Inlay—metallic—three surfaces	350
02540	Onlay—metallic—per tooth (in addition to inlay)	365
	Crowns—single restoration only	
02720	Crown—resin with high noble metal	415
02740	Crown—porcelain/ceramic substrate	425
02750	Crown—porcelain fused to high noble metal	425
02751	Crown—porcelain fused to predominantly base metal	395
02572	Crown—porcelain fused to noble metal	410
02790	Crown—full cast high noble metal	415
02810	Crown—¾ cast metallic	399
	Other restorative services	
02920	Recement crown	28
02930	Prefabricated stainless steel crown—primary tooth	75
02931	Prefabricated stainless steel crown—permanent tooth	85
02940	Sedative filling	30
02950	Core buildup, including any pins	77
02952	Cast post and core in addition to crown	125
02960	Labial veneer (laminate)—chairside	150
02962	Labial veneer (porcelain laminate)—laboratory	300

Code	Procedure	50th Percentile*
ENDODONTICS		
	Pulp capping	
03110	Pulp cap—direct (excluding final restoration)	$ 20
03120	Pulp cap—indirect (excluding final restoration)	20
	Pulpotomy	
03220	Therapeutic pulpotomy (excluding final restoration)	50
	Root canal therapy (including treatment plan, clinical procedures and followup care)	
03310	Anterior (excluding final restoration)	210
03320	Bicuspid (excluding final restoration)	265
03330	Molar (excluding final restoration)	350
	Periapical services	
03410	Apicoectomy/periradicular surgery—anterior	169
PERIODONTICS		
	Surgical services (including usual postoperative services)	
04210	Gingivectomy or gingivoplasty—per quadrant	175
04211	Gingivectomy or gingivoplasty—per tooth	60
04220	Gingival curettage, surgical, per quadrant, by report	75
04260	Osseous surgery (including flap entry and closure)—per quadrant	325
	Adjunctive periodontal services	
04321	Provisional splinting—extracoronal	100
04341	Periodontal scaling and root planing—per quadrant	75
04345	Periodontal scaling performed in the presence of gingival inflammation	55
PROSTHODONTICS—REMOVABLE		
	Complete dentures (including routine postdelivery care)	
05110	Complete upper	500
05120	Complete lower	500
05130	Immediate upper	550
05140	Immediate lower	550
	Partial dentures (including routine postdelivery care)	
05211	Upper partial—resin base (including any conventional clasps, rests and teeth)	375
05212	Lower partial—resin base (including any conventional clasps, rests and teeth)	375
05213	Upper partial—cast metal (including any conventional clasps, rests and teeth)	565
05214	Lower partial—cast metal (including any conventional clasps, rests and teeth)	564
	Repairs to complete dentures	
05510	Repair broken complete denture base	50
05520	Replace missing or broken teeth (complete dentures)—each tooth	45
	Repairs to partial dentures	
05610	Repair resin saddle or base	50
05620	Repair cast framework	80

Code	Procedure	50th Percentile*
05630	Repair or replace broken clasp	$ 75
05640	Replace broken teeth—per tooth	45
05650	Add tooth to existing partial denture	60
05660	Add clasp to existing partial denture	75
	Denture rebase procedures	
05710	Rebase complete upper denture	165
	Denture reline procedures	
05730	Reline complete upper denture (chairside)	100
05731	Reline complete lower denture (chairside)	100
05750	Reline complete upper denture (laboratory)	150
05751	Reline complete lower denture (laboratory)	150
PROSTHODONTICS—FIXED (each abutment and each pontic constitute a unit in a bridge)		
	Bridge pontics	
06210	Pontic—cast high noble metal	405
06240	Pontic—porcelain fused to high noble metal	425
06241	Pontic—porcelain fused to predominantly base metal	395
	Retainers	
06545	Retainer—cast metal for acid-etched fixed prosthesis	197
	Bridge retainers—crowns	
06720	Crown—resin with high noble metal	423
06750	Crown—porcelain fused to high noble metal	425
06751	Crown—porcelain fused to predominantly base metal	395
06780	Crown—¾ cast high noble metal	400
06790	Crown—full cast high noble metal	410
	Other fixed prosthetic services	
06930	Recement bridge	40
ORAL SURGERY		
	Extractions (includes local anesthesia and routine postoperative care)	
07110	Single tooth	40
07120	Each additional tooth	38
	Surgical extractions (includes local anesthesia and routine postoperative care)	
07210	Surgical removal of erupted tooth . . .	75
07220	Removal of impacted tooth—soft tissue	90
07230	Removal of impacted tooth—partially bony	125
07240	Removal of impacted tooth—completely bony	169
07241	Removal of impacted tooth—completely bony, with unusual surgical complications	198
07250	Surgical removal of residual tooth roots (cutting procedure)	75
	Other surgical procedures	
07281	Surgical exposure of impacted or unerupted tooth to aid eruption	75
	Alveoplasty—surgical preparation of ridge for dentures	
07310	Alveoplasty in conjunction with extractions—per quadrant	75
07320	Alveoplasty not in conjunction with extractions—per quadrant	100
07430	Excision of benign tumor—lesion diameter up to 1.25 cm	86

Code	Procedure	50th Percentile*
	Excision of bone tissue	
07470	Removal of exostosis—maxilla or mandible	$ 150
	Reduction of dislocation and management of other temporomandibular joint dysfunctions	
07880	Occlusal orthotic device, by report	250
	Repair of traumatic wounds	
07910	Suture of recent small wounds up to 5 cm	50
07960	Frenulectomy (frenectomy or frenotomy)—separate procedure	100
07970	Excision of hyperplastic tissue—per arch	100
ORTHODONTICS		
	Minor treatment for tooth guidance	
08110	Removable appliance therapy	250
08120	Fixed appliance therapy	300
	Comprehensive orthodontic treatment—transitional dentition	
08460	Class I malocclusion	2,200
	Comprehensive orthodontic treatment—permanent dentition	
08560	Class I malocclusion	2,397
08570	Class II malocclusion	2,500
ADJUNCTIVE GENERAL SERVICES		
	Unclassified treatment	
09110	Palliative (emergency) treatment of dental pain—minor procedures	30
	Anesthesia	
09211	Regional block anesthesia	0
09230	Analgesia	14
	Miscellaneous services	
09940	Occlusal guards, by report	150
09951	Occlusal adjustment—limited	45
09952	Occlusal adjustment—complete	140

*The 50th percentile is that fee where one-half of the charges are above that fee and one-half are below.

J

National Association of Prepaid Dental Plans Model Act

This act is provided for information only. Publication is not to be construed as an endorsement by the author nor a recommendation for adoption.

National Association of Prepaid Dental Plans

Prepaid Limited Health Service Organization Model Act

Table of Contents

Section 1. Short Title—This act shall be known and may be cited as the "Prepaid Limited Health Service Organization Act of [insert state]."

Section 2. Definitions—As used in this act, unless otherwise defined in this act:

A. "Commissioner (Director, Superintendent)" means the Commissioner (Director, Superintendent) of Insurance.

B. "Enrollee" means an individual, including dependents, who is entitled to limited health services pursuant to a contract with an entity authorized to provide or arrange for such services under this Act.

C. "Evidence of coverage" means the certificate, agreement or contract issued pursuant to Section 9 of this Act setting forth the coverage to which an enrollee is entitled.

D. "Limited health service" means dental care services, vision care services, mental health services, substance abuse services, pharmaceutical services, podiatric care services, and such other services as may be determined by the commissioner to be limited health services. Limited health service shall not include hospital, medical, surgical or emergency services except as such services are provided incident to the limited health services set forth in the preceding sentence.

E. "Net equity" means the excess of total assets over total liabilities, excluding liabilities which have been subordinated in a manner acceptable to the commissioner.

F. "Prepaid limited health service organization" means any corporation, partnership or other entity which, in return for a prepayment, undertakes to provide or arrange for the provision of one or more limited health services to enrollees. Prepaid limited health service organization does not include (1) an entity otherwise authorized pursuant to the laws of this State either to provide any limited health service on a prepayment or other basis or to indemnity for any limited health service; or (2) an entity that meets the requirements of Section 7 of this Act; or (3) a provider or entity when providing or arranging for the provision of limited health services pursuant to a contract with a prepaid limited health service organization or with an entity described in (1) or (2) of this definition.

G. "Provider" means any physician, dentist, health facility, or other person or institution which is duly licensed or otherwise authorized to deliver or furnish limited health care service(s).

H. "Subscriber" means the person whose employment or other status, except for family dependency, is the basis for entitlement to limited health services pursuant to a contract with an entity authorized to provide or arrange for such services under this Act.

I. "Tangible net equity" means net equity reduced by the value assigned to intangible assets including, but not limited to, goodwill; going concern value; organizational expense; starting-up costs; long-term prepayments of deferred charges; nonreturnable deposits; and obligations of officers, directors, owners, or affiliates, except short-term obligations of affiliates for goods or services arising in the normal course of business which are payable on the same terms as equivalent transactions with nonaffiliates and which are not past due.

J. "Uncovered expense" means the cost of health care services that are the obligation of a prepaid limited health organization (1) for which an enrollee may be liable in the event of the insolvency of the organization and (2) for which alternative arrangements acceptable to the commissioner have not been made to cover the costs. Costs incurred by a provider who has agreed in writing not to bill enrollees, except for permissible supplemental charges, shall be considered as covered expense.

Section 3. Certificate of Authority Required—No person, corporation, partnership or other entity may operate a prepaid limited health service organization in this state without obtaining and maintaining a certificate of authority from the commissioner pursuant to this Act.

Section 4. Application for Certificate of Authority—An application for a certificate of authority to operate a prepaid limited health service organization shall be filed with the commissioner on a form prescribed by the organization. Such application shall be verified by an officer or authorized representative of the applicant and shall set forth, or be accompanied by, the following:

A. A copy of the applicant's basic organizational document, such as the articles of incorporation, articles of association, partnership agreement, trust agreement or other applicable documents and all amendment to such documents.

B. A copy of all bylaws, rules and regulations, or similar document, if any, regulating the conduct of the applicant's internal affairs.

C. A list of the names, addresses, official positions and biographical information of the individuals who are responsible for conducting the applicant's affairs, including but not limited to, all members of the board of directors, board of trustees, executive committee, or other governing board or committee, the principal officers; and any person or entity owning or having the right to acquire 10% or more of the voting securities of the applicant, and the partners or members in the case of a partnership or association.

D. A statement generally describing the applicant, its facilities, personnel and the limited health service or services to be offered.

E. A copy of the form of any contract made or to be made between the applicant and any providers regarding the provision of limited health services to enrollees.

F. A copy of the form of any contract made, or to be made between the applicant and any person listed in Paragraph C of this section.

G. A copy of the form of any contract made or to be made between the applicant and any person, corporation, partnership or other entity for the performance on the applicant's behalf of any functions including, but not limited to:
 1. marketing and enrollment;
 2. administration;
 3. investment management; and,
 4. subcontracting for the provision of the limited health service to enrollees.

H. A copy of the form of any contract which is to be issued to employers, unions, trustees, or other organizations or individuals and a copy of any form of evidence of coverage to be issued to subscribers.

I. A copy of the applicant's most recent financial statements audited by independent certified public accountants. If the financial affairs of the applicant's parent company are audited by independent certified public accountants but those of the applicant are not, then a copy of the most recent audited financial statement of the applicant's parent company, certified by an independent certified public accountant, attached to which shall be consolidating financial statements of the applicant, shall satisfy this requirement unless the commissioner determines that additional or more recent financial information is required for the proper administration of this Act.

J. A copy of the applicant's financial plan, including a three-year projection of anticipated operating results, a statement of the sources of working capital, and any other sources of funding and provisions for contingencies.

K. A description of the proposed method of marketing.

L. A statement acknowledging that all lawful process in any legal action or proceeding against the applicant on a cause of action arising in this state is valid if served in accordance with [insert citation to appropriate section of insurance code].

M. A description of the complaint procedures to be established and maintained as required under Section 12 of this Act.

N. A description of the quality assessment and utilization review procedures to be utilized by the applicant.

O. A description of how the applicant will comply with Section 17 of this Act.

P. The fee for issuance of a certificate of authority provided in Section 23 of this Act; and

Q. Such other information as the commissioner may reasonably require to make the determinations required by this Act.

Section 5. Issuance of Certificate of Authority; Denial

A. Following receipt of an application filed pursuant to Section 4, the commissioner shall review such application and notify the applicant of any deficiencies contained therein. The commissioner shall issue a certificate of authority to an applicant provided that the following conditions are met:
   1. The requirements of Section 4 have been fulfilled;
   2. The individuals responsible for conducting the applicant's affairs are competent, trustworthy and possess good reputations, and have had appropriate experience training or education;
   3. The applicant is financially responsible and may reasonably be expected to meet its obligations to enrollees and to prospective enrollees. In making this determination, the commissioner may consider:
      a. the financial soundness of the applicant's arrangements for limited health services
      b. the adequacy of working capital, other sources of funding, and provisions for contingencies;
      c. any agreement for paying the cost of the limited health services or for alternative coverage in the event of insolvency of the prepaid limited health service organization; and
      d. the manner in which the requirements of Section 17 of this Act have been fulfilled;
   4. The agreements with providers for the provision of limited health services contain the provisions required by Section 16 of this Act; and
   5. Any deficiencies identified by the commissioner have been corrected.

B. If the certificate of authority is denied, the commissioner shall notify the applicant and shall specify the reasons for denial in the notice. The prepaid limited health service organization shall have [insert number] days from the date of receipt of the notice to request a hearing before the commissioner pursuant to [insert citation to state's administrative procedures act].

Section 6. Effect on Organizations Operating on Effective Date of This Act—Within [insert number] days after the effective date of this Act, every prepaid limited health service organization operating in this State without a certificate of authority shall summit an application for a certificate of authority to the commissioner. Each such organization may continue to operate during the pendency of its application. In the event an application is denied under this Section, the applicant will then be treated as a prepaid limited health service organization whose certificate of authority has been revoked.

Section 7. Filing Requirements for Authorized Entities

A. Any entity authorized pursuant to the laws of this state to operate a health maintenance organization, an accident and health insurance company, a nonprofit health, hospital or medical service corporation or a fraternal benefit society and which is not otherwise authorized pursuant to the laws of this state to offer limited health services on a per capita or fixed prepayment basis may do so by filing for approval with the commissioner the information requested by Section 4D, E, G, H, J, K, L, and O.

B. If the commissioner disapproves the filing, the procedures set forth in Section 5B of this Act shall be followed.

Section 8. Material Modifications; Addition of Limited Health Services

A. A prepaid limited health service organization shall file with the commissioner prior to use, a notice of any material modification of any matter or document furnished pursuant to Section 4A, B, G, 3 and 4, and H, together with such supporting documents as are necessary to fully explain the change or modification. If the commissioner does not disapprove such filing within [insert number] days of its filing, such filing shall be deemed approved.

B. A prepaid limited health services organization shall file for information purposes only any change to any document furnished pursuant to Section 4, C, D, E, F, G1 and 2, I, J, L, M, N, and O. If the commissioner does not disapprove such filing within [insert number] days of its filing, such filing shall be deemed approved.

C. If a prepaid limited health service organization desires to add one or more limited health services, it shall file a notice with the commissioner and, at the same time, shall submit the information required by Section 4 (if different from that filed with the prepaid limited health service organization's application), and shall demonstrate compliance with Sections 16, 17 and 23. If the commissioner does not disapprove such filing within [insert number] days of its filing, such filing shall be deemed approved.

D. If such filings are disapproved, the commissioner shall notify the prepaid limited health service organization and shall specify the reasons for disapproval in the notice. The prepaid limited health service organization shall have the right to refile any disapproved document on the same basis as set forth in Section 8A and B, or have [insert number] days from the date of receipt of notice to request a hearing before the commissioner pursuant to [insert citation to state's administrative procedures act].

Section 9. Evidence of Coverage

A. Every subscriber shall be issued an evidence of coverage, which shall contain a clear and complete statement of:
   1. the limited health services to which each enrollee is entitled;
   2. any limitation of the services, kinds of services or benefits to be provided, and exclusion, including any deductible, copayment or other charges;
   3. where and in what manner information is available as to where and how services may be obtained; and
   4. the method for resolving complaints.

B. Any amendment to the evidence of coverage may be provided to the subscriber in a separate document.

Section 10. Construction With Other Laws

A. 1. A prepaid limited health service organization organized under the laws of this State shall be deemed to be a domestic insurer for purposes of [insert citation to the state's insurance holding company system regulatory act] unless specifically exempted in writing from one or more of the provisions of such act by the commissioner;
   2. A prepaid limited health service organization shall be subject to [insert citations to pertinent sections of state's unfair insurance trade practices act and penalty provisions governing insurance companies];
   3. No other provision of the insurance code shall apply to a prepaid limited health service organization unless such an organization is specifically mentioned therein.

B. The provision of limited health services by a prepaid limited health service organization or other entity pursuant to this act shall not be deemed to be the practice of medicine or other healing arts.

C. Solicitation to arrange for or provide limited health services in accordance with this Act shall not be construed to violate any provision of law relating to solicitation or advertising by health professionals.

Section 11. Nonduplication of Coverage—Notwithstanding any other law of this State, a prepaid limited health service organization, health maintenance organization, accident and health insurance company, nonprofit health or hospital or medical service corporation or fraternal benefit society may exclude in any contract or policy issued to a group, any coverage that would duplicate the coverage for limited health services (whether in the form of services, supplies or reimbursement), insofar as the coverage for service is provided in accordance with this Act under a contract or policy issued to the same group or to a part of that group by a prepaid limited health service organization, a health maintenance organization, an accident and health insurance company, a nonprofit health or hospital or medical service corporation or a fraternal benefit society.

Section 12. Complaint System—Every prepaid limited health service organization shall establish and maintain a complaint system providing reasonable procedures for resolving written complaints initiated by enrollees and providers. Nothing herein shall be construed to preclude an enrollee or a provider from filing a complaint with the commissioner or as limiting the commissioner's ability to investigate such complaints.

Section 13. Examination of Organization

A. The commissioner may examine the affairs of any prepaid limited health service organization as often as is reasonably necessary to protect the interest of the people of this State, but not less frequently than once every [insert number] years.

B. Every prepaid limited health service organization shall make its relevant books and records available for such examinations and in every way cooperate with the commissioner to facilitate such examinations.

C. The actual expenses of an examination under this section shall be charged to the organization being examined and remitted to the commissioner. Any such payments made shall be deducted from any taxes that may be due pursuant to Section 25 of this Act, or any other fees assessed to the organization except those specified in Section 23.

D. In lieu of such examination, the commissioner may accept the report of an examination made by the commissioner of another state.

Section 14. Investments—The funds of a prepaid limited health service organization shall be invested only in accordance with the guidelines established by the National Association of Insurance Commissions for investments by health maintenance organizations.

Section 15. Agents—No individual may apply, procure, negotiate, or place for others any policy or contract of a prepaid limited health service organization unless that individual holds a license or is otherwise duly authorized to sell accident and health insurance policies, health, hospital or medical service contracts, or health maintenance organization contracts.

Section 16. Contracts With Providers—All contracts with providers or with entities subcontracting for the provision of limited health services to enrollees on a prepayment or other basis shall contain or shall be construed to contain the following terms and conditions:

A. In the event the prepaid limited health service organization fails to pay for limited health services for any reason whatsoever, including but not limited to, insolvency or breach of this contract, the enrollees shall not be liable to the provider for any sums owed the provider under this Contract.

B. No provider, agent, trustee or assignee thereof may maintain an action at law or attempt to collect from the enrollee sums owed to the provider by the prepaid limited health service organization.

C. These provisions do not prohibit collection of uncovered charges consented to by enrollees or collection of copayment from enrollees.

D. These provisions shall survive the termination of this Contract, regardless of the reason giving rise to termination.

E. Termination of this Contract shall not release the provider from completing procedures in progress on enrollees then receiving treatment for a specific condition for a period not to exceed [insert number] days, at the same schedule of copayment or other applicable charge in effect upon the effective date of termination of this Contract.

F. Any amendment to these foregoing provisions of this Contract must be submitted to and be approved by the commissioner prior to becoming effective.

Section 17. Protection Against Insolvency; Deposit

A. 1. Excepted as approved in accordance with Subsection C of this Section, each tangible prepaid limited health service organization shall, at all times, have and maintain tangible net equity equal to the greater of:
   a. $50,000; or
   b. 2% of the organization's annual gross premium income, up to a maximum of:
      i. the required capital and surplus of an accident and health insurer for a limited health service organization providing or arranging for mental health services, substance abuse services, or other limited health services which may involve institutional and/or facility-based care or services;
      ii. $100,000 for all other limited health service organizations;
   2. A prepaid limited health service organization that has uncovered expenses in excess of $50,000 as reported on the most recent annual financial statement filed with the commissioner, shall maintain tangible net equity equal to 25% of the uncovered expenses in excess of $50,000 in addition to the tangible net equity required by Subsection A.1. of this Section.

B. 1. Each prepaid limited health service organization shall deposit with the commissioner or with any organization or trustee acceptable to the commission through which a custodial or controlled account is utilized, cash, securities, or any combination of these or other measures that is acceptable to the commissioner in an amount equal to $25,000 plus 25% of the tangible net equity required in Subsection A of this Section; provided however, that the deposit shall not be required to exceed $100,000;

2. The deposit shall be an admitted asset of the prepaid limited health service organization in the determination of tangible net equity;
3. All income from deposits shall be an asset of the prepaid limited health service organization. A prepaid limited health service organization may withdraw a deposit or any part thereof after making a substitute deposit of equal amount and value. Any securities shall be approved by the commissioner before being substituted;
4. The deposit shall be used to protect the interest of the prepaid limited health service organization's enrollees and to assure continuation of limited health care services to enrollees of a prepaid limited health service organization that is in rehabilitation or conservation. If a limited health service organization is placed in receivership obligation, the deposit shall be an asset subject to provisions of the liquidation act;
5. The commissioner may reduce or eliminate the deposit requirement if the prepaid limited health service organization has made an acceptable deposit with the State or jurisdiction of domicile for the protection of all enrollees, wherever located, and delivers to the commissioner a certificate to such effect, duly authenticated by the appropriate state official holding the deposit.

C. Upon application by a prepaid limited health service organization, the commissioner may waive some or all of the requirements of Subsection A of this Section for any period of time the commissioner shall deem proper upon a finding that either (1) the prepaid limited health service organization has a net equity of at least $5,000,000; or (2) an entity having a net equity of at least $5,000,000 furnishes to the commissioner a written commitment, which is acceptable to the commissioner, to provide for the uncovered expenses of the prepaid limited health service organization.

Section 18. Officers and Employees Fidelity Bond

A. A prepaid limited health service organization shall maintain in force a fidelity bond in its own name on its officers and employees in an amount not less than [insert number] or in any other amount prescribed by the commissioner. Except as otherwise provided by this Subsection, the bond must be issued by an insurance company that is licensed to do business in this state or, if the fidelity bond required by this Subsection is not available from an insurance company that holds a certificate of authority in this State, a fidelity bond procured by a licensed surplus lines agent resident in this State in compliance with [insert citation to insurance code], shall satisfy the requirements of this Subsection.

B. In lieu of the bond specific in Subsection A of this Section, a prepaid limited health service organization may deposit with the [insert appropriate state authority] cash or securities or other investments to the types set forth in Section 14 of this Act. Such a deposit must be maintained in joint custody with the commissioner in the amount and subject to the same conditions required for a bond under this Subsection.

Section 19. Reports

A. Every prepaid limited health service organization shall file with the commissioner annually, on or before April 1, a report verified by an officer(s) covering the preceding calendar year.

B. Such report shall be on forms prescribed by the commissioner and shall include:
   1. A financial statement of the organization, including its balance sheet, income statement and statement of changes in financial position for the preceding year, certified by an independent public accountant or a consolidated audited financial statement of its parent company certified by an independent public accountant, attached to which shall be consolidated financial statements of the prepaid limited health service organization;
   2. The number of subscribers at the beginning of the year, the number of subscribers as of the end of the year, and the number of enrollments terminated during the year; and
   3. Such other information relating to the performance of the organization as is necessary to enable the commissioner to carry out his or her duties under this Act.

C. The commissioner may require more frequent reports containing such information as is necessary to enable the commissioner to carry out his or her duties under this Act.

D. The commissioner may assess a fine of up to $100 per day for each day any required report is late, and the commissioner may suspend the organization's certificate of authority pending the proper filing of the required report by the organization.

Section 20. Suspension of Revocation of Certificate of Authority

A. The commissioner may suspend or revoke the certificate of authority issued to prepaid limited health service organization pursuant to this Act upon determining that any of the following conditions exist:
   1. The prepaid limited health service organization is operating significantly

in contravention of its basic organization document or in a manner contrary to that described in and reasonably inferred from any other information submitted pursuant to Section 4 of this Act, unless amendments to such submissions have been filed and authorized pursuant to Section 8.

2. The prepaid limited health service organization issues an evidence of coverage which does not comply with requirements of Section 9 of this Act;
3. The prepaid limited health service organization is unable to fulfill its obligations to furnish limited health services;
4. The prepaid limited health service organization is not financially responsible and may reasonably be expected not to be able to meet its obligations to enrollees or prospective enrollees;
5. The tangible net equity of the prepaid limited health service organization is less than that reassured by Section 17 or the prepaid limited health service organization has failed to correct any deficiency in its tangible net equity as required by the commissioner;
6. The prepaid limited health service organization has failed to implement in a reasonable manner the complaint system required by Section 12 of this Act;
7. The continued operation of the prepaid limited health service organization would be hazardous to its enrollees;
8. The prepaid limited health service organization has otherwise failed to comply with this Act.

B. If the commissioner has cause to believe that grounds for the suspension or revocation of a certificate of authority exist, he or she shall notify the prepaid limited health service organization in writing specifically stating the grounds for suspension or revocation and fixing a time not more than 60 days thereafter for a hearing on the matter in accordance with the [insert citation to state's administrative procedures act].

C. When the certificate of authority of a prepaid limited health service organization is revoked, such organization shall proceed, immediately following the effective date of the order of revocation, to wind up its affairs, and shall conduct no further business except as may be essential to the orderly conclusion of the affairs of such organization. It shall engage in no further advertising or solicitation whatsoever. The commissioner may, by written order, permit such further operation of the organization as he or she may find to be in the best interest of enrollees, to the end that subscribers will be afforded the greatest practical opportunity to obtain continuing limited health services.

Section 21. Penalties

A. In lieu of any penalty specified elsewhere in this Act, or when no penalty is specifically provided, whenever any prepaid limited health service organization or other person, corporation, partnership or entity subject to this Act has been found, pursuant to [insert citation to the appropriate sections of the state's administrative procedures act] to have violated any provision of this Act, the commissioner may:

1. Issue and cause to be served upon the organization, person, or entity charged with the violation a copy of such findings and an order requiring such organization, person, or entity to cease and desist from engaging in the act or practice which constitutes the violation; and
2. Impose a monetary penalty of not more than $1,000 for each violation, but not to exceed an aggregate penalty of $10,000.

B. A limited health service organization may appeal any action pursuant to Section 20 within [insert number] days from the date of receipt of notice, by requesting a hearing before the commissioner, pursuant to [insert citation to state's administrative procedures act].

Section 22. Rehabilitation, Conservation or Liquidation

A. Any rehabilitation, conservation or liquidation of a prepaid limited health services organization shall be deemed to be the rehabilitation, conservation or liquidation of an insurance company and shall be conducted pursuant to [insert citations to statutory sections governing the rehabilitation, liquidation or conservation of insurance companies].

B. No prepaid limited health service organization shall be subject to the laws and regulations governing insurance insolvency guaranty funds, nor shall any insurance insolvency guaranty fund provide protection to any individuals entitled to receive limited health services from a prepaid limited health service organization.

Section 23. Fees—Every prepaid limited health service organization subject to this Act shall pay to the commissioner the following fees:

A. For filing an application for a certificate of authority or amendment thereto—[insert amount].

B. For filing a material modification or addition of a limited health service pursuant to Section 8.A.—[insert amount].

C. For any informational filing pursuant to Section 8.B., there shall be no fee.

D. For filing each annual report—[insert amount].

E. For filing periodic reports as required by the commissioner—[insert amount].

Section 24. Confidentiality

A. Any information pertaining to the diagnosis, treatment or health of any enrollee obtained from such person or from any provider by any prepaid limited health service organization and any contract with providers submitted pursuant to the requirements of this Act shall be held in confidence and shall not be disclosed to any person except:

1. to the extent that it may be necessary to carry out the purposes of this Act; or
2. upon the express consent of the enrollee or applicant, provider, or prepaid limited health service organization, as appropriate; or
3. pursuant to statute or court order for the production of evidence or the discovery thereof; or
4. in the event of claim or litigation wherein such data or information is relevant.

B. With respect to any information pertaining to the diagnosis, treatment or health of any enrollee or applicant, a prepaid limited health service organization shall be entitled to claim any statutory privileges against disclosure which the provider who furnished such information to the prepaid limited health service organization is entitled to claim.

C. In addition, any information provided to the commissioner that constitutes a trade secret, is privileged information, or is part of a department investigation or examination shall be held in confidence.

Section 25. Taxes—The same tax rate as a percentage of revenue provided for in [insert citation to state's health maintenance organization act] shall be imposed upon each prepaid limited health service organization, and such organization also shall be entitled to the same tax deductions, reductions, abatements and credits that health maintenance organizations are entitled to receive. Any and all fees, except for those specified in Section 23, shall be offset against taxes due by the organization.

Section 26. Severability—If any section, term or provision of this Act shall be adjudged invalid for any reason by a court of competent jurisdiction, such judgment shall not affect, impair, or invalidate any other section, term, or provision of this Act, but the remaining sections, terms and provisions shall be and remain in full force and effect.

Section 27. Regulations—The commissioner may, after notice and hearing, promulgate rules and regulations to carry out the provisions of this Act.

Section 28. Effective Date—The effective date of this Act shall be [insert date].

Index

A

B

C

D

E

F

G

H

I

M

N

O

S

T

U

V